The Politics of
Educational Reform in France
1918-1940

The Politics of Educational Reform in France, 1918-1940

BY JOHN E. TALBOTT

PRINCETON UNIVERSITY PRESS

PRINCETON, NEW JERSEY

1969

For my Mother and Father

Preface

"After bread," Danton once remarked, "instruction is the first need of the people." In the twentieth century, the French revolutionary leader's dictum has taken on new meaning. Technological development and the rapidity of change in industrial society have consigned the barely literate man to an uncertain existence. A democratic nation must therefore not merely ensure that every citizen learns to read and write, but enable each to develop his own abilities to the fullest extent. The demands of expanding economies and the demands of social justice have made the provision of equal educational opportunity an urgent and exceedingly difficult task—one that requires the redesigning of educational systems built over the course of centuries and the reshaping of public educational policy. But there is little agreement about how to do this, no consensus over what "equality of educational opportunity" means. Education has always been an intensely political matter, for to ask who should be educated is to ask who should rule. In the last third of the twentieth century it has become imperative for the leaders of democratic nations to consider how closely public education conforms to their own assumptions about the nature of democracy, not from considerations of justice alone, but because social and political stability demand it.

This book studies an effort to democratize the French educational system. "Democratization" is one of those ill-defined words upon which contemporary historians doubtless place an excessive and slightly irritating reliance. At least we are in honorable company, for the movement toward equality of condition was a major preoccupation of the great Alexis de Tocqueville. Moreover, French educational reformers used the word themselves; I could think of none better. In the following pages I have tried to make clear what they meant by it. However seriously reformers differed over the implications of competitive plans for reform, they agreed that *démocratisation* meant reshaping the structure of the higher reaches of the educational system in order to broaden the social bases of its recruitment. For reasons that will become apparent, secondary education was the locus of their attack on the existing order.

An introductory chapter briefly sets out the historical development of French education, but the real point of departure is the First World War, when the twentieth century truly began. The demands of the long conflict revealed in a most brutal fashion the inadequacies of the prewar institutions of the Third Republic. In a society shaken to its foundations and suddenly confronted with problems foreign to its own immediate past, the assumptions and values upon which the old order had rested were called into question. The educational system helped shape those values. To a number of thoughtful men, it seemed made to meet the needs of a stable world that had vanished forever, and was therefore incapable of responding to the demands of a generation returned from the war. Consequently, they sought to change it. In large part, they failed. But the political failures of men can reveal as much about themselves and their society as can their successes. Greatly maligned and little regretted as the Third Republic has been, it remains the regime Frenchmen accepted for a longer time than any since 1789; it collapsed only as a consequence of the greatest disaster to befall France in modern times. But the Republic acquired and maintained stability at the expense of an extreme reluctance to undertake change, and for this its educational system bore a heavy responsibility. This study might be regarded as an essay on the observation of the distinguished historian and political commentator François Goguel: "The prime reasons that certain traditional values of French culture can slow or block changes in society stems from the educational system. . . . The organization of education constitutes without a doubt a factor of social immobility even more important than the content of instruction."

The interwar years marked the twilight of the Third Republic, but the ideas that shaped the movement for educational reform did not expire along with the regime. If the reformers of the Fifth Republic can justly lay claim to a talent for innovation in many fields, in education they are the direct intellectual heirs of an extraordinary group of young men: veterans of the trenches, they took Danton's injunction seriously.

All advanced industrial societies share certain fundamental characteristics, regardless of how they are governed. All of them have similar educational institutions that perform similar functions. Opportunities for comparison in the study of education are therefore many and obvious. But perhaps there remains some merit in probing the historical experience of a single nation more deeply than a comparative approach would allow; in any event, the reader will not be slow to draw comparisons from his own knowledge and experience. Even generalizations about the French national experience can be a risky business. As Paul Valéry put it: "The essence of France is variety." Nevertheless it is also true, as Matthew Arnold observed: "in some respects France, in that which concerns the historical development of secondary instruction, is a typical country."

THE LARGE number of French institutions, associations and political parties that appear in this book would customarily require a rather extravagant use of italic type. With apologies to purists in such matters, these have been set in roman, which has made the page pleasing to the eye and therefore congenial to the art of the typographer, to whom both writers and readers stand so heavily in debt.

Grants from Stanford University, the Danforth Foundation, The French Government and the University Research Fund of Princeton University enabled me to undertake research in France. The last named also supported the typing of the manuscript. I here record my thanks to all these institutions. In slightly different form parts of Chapter v appeared in the Fall of 1968 number of *French Historical Studies* as "The French Left and the Ideology of Educational Reform, 1919-1939." I am grateful to the editor for permission to include them here. Any scholarly book, however modest in scope, is the work of a kind of community. Responsibility for its contents is the author's alone. I should like all those who helped in the making of this book to be glad of its merits, free of implication in its faults, and assured of my gratitude. I must especially thank Mademoiselle Aline Coutrot, of the Fondation Nationale des Sciences Politiques, who suggested to me the line of inquiry pursued in these pages. There are two people to whom I am grateful beyond my power to express: one is Professor Gordon Wright; the other is my wife.

Princeton
September 1968

Contents

The Politics of
Educational Reform in France
1918-1940

Popular education has sprung out of the ideas and necessities of modern times, and the elementary school for the poor is an institution which has no remote history. With the secondary school it is otherwise. The secondary school has a long history; through a series of changes it goes back, in every European country, to the beginnings of civilised society in that country; from the time when this society had any sort of organisation, a certain sort of school and schooling existed, and between that schooling and the schooling which the children of the richer class of society at this day receive there is an unbroken connection. In no country is this continuity of secondary instruction more visible than in France, notwithstanding her revolutions; and in some respects France, in that which concerns the historical development of secondary instruction, is a typical country.

—MATTHEW ARNOLD, 1882

CHAPTER I. Introduction

> "Pourquoi l'inégalité devant l'instruction . . .
> et quels remèdes?"
> —CHARLES PÉGUY

AS IT stood in 1918, the educational system of the Third Republic had been erected over many years, by different regimes, for different purposes. Under the Old Regime, the Church had had almost exclusive charge of the task of education. But in the eighteenth century the Philosophes argued that education, as a great lever of reform, should be an undertaking of the state in the general interest of the nation. The men of the Great Revolution, from moderates like Talleyrand and Condorcet to radicals Lepeletier de Saint-Fargeau and Saint-Just, had agreed on the great urgency and importance of constructing a national system of education, even if they did not agree on how it should be constructed. But when invasion, civil war and near-bankruptcy threatened to snuff out the Revolution, the task of building an educational system had to be put aside. It fell to Napoleon to undertake what the Revolution had failed to accomplish. Republicans inherited an institution in large part designed to meet the needs of a military dictator.[1]

In 1795 the Convention had placed education under local supervision. But Napoleon had a lively suspicion of local autonomy, and by means of a series of laws and decrees he had education brought increasingly under the control of the cen-

[1] See Antoine Prost, *Histoire de l'enseignement en France, 1800-1967* (Paris, 1968). See also Felix Ponteil, *Histoire de l'enseignement en France; les grandes étapes, 1789-1964* (Paris, 1966), which contains a good bibliography. On the Enlightenment and education, see the remarks in the first chapter of Judith Shklar, *After Utopia. The Decline of Political Faith* (Princeton, 1957). On the work of the Revolution see especially Célestin Hippeau, *L'Instruction publique en France pendant la Révolution*, 2 vols. (Paris, 1881-83); J. Robert Vignery, *The French Revolution and the Schools: Educational Policies of the Mountain, 1792-1794* (Madison, Wisconsin, 1965).

3

tral authority. The most important of these were the laws of May 10, 1806, and March 17, 1808, that established the Imperial University. It must be emphasized that the English word "university" and the French *Université* do not have the same set of meanings. In the United States, "university" connotes an institution of higher education that offers graduate instruction and may support at least one professional school. The Université de Paris is a roughly analogous institution. Yet as an administrative apparatus, no French university possesses the strong centralized authority of most of its American counterparts: the *facultés* of letters, law, medicine, though formally subject to the authority of the university, remain quasi-independent fiefdoms. But the First Empire gave *Université* another meaning. *Université impériale* designated an independent corporation of administrators and teachers under the employ and supervision of the state. This peculiar sense of the word is yet another Napoleonic legacy to contemporary France. *Université* can refer to the entire educational establishment, though it more often includes only secondary and higher education. Thus both secondary-school teachers and university professors are *universitaires*. "University" is used in the more inclusive French sense throughout this book, unless the context clearly indicates another meaning.

At the top of the Napoleonic administrative pyramid stood the Grand Master of the University, whose authority was as extensive as his title was grandiose. Directly under the Grand Master the Conseil de l'Université, composed of professors and administrators, supervised the writing of regulations, drew up the budget, deliberated changes in the curriculum and arbitrated disputes within the University. France was divided into administrative districts called academies, each headed by a rector. An academic council assisted each rector, who also had under his authority two *inspecteurs d'académie*. Directly responsible to the Grand Master were the Inspectors-General, who oversaw the entire educational establishment, but especially concerned themselves with the performance of teachers.[2]

[2] The standard work on the Napoleonic reforms remains Alphonse Aulard, *Napoléon I*er *et le monopole universitaire* (Paris, 1911). See

4

The laws that established the University aimed first of all at the creation of a monopoly of education, in order to combat the competition of the religious schools for students. Though the law laid down that the University was "the corps exclusively charged with instruction and public education in the entire empire," it did not mean that only teachers in the employ of the state would be allowed to teach. Instead, a "legal fiction" declared the personnel of the confessional schools to be incorporated into the University. In addition, the state required each confessional school to pay a yearly fee into the treasury of the University.[3]

The Imperial monopoly of education was never intended to mean that only the state had the right to operate schools. Instead, it was a method of surveillance, both of the religious schools and of the Church that Napoleon regarded as at best an unreliable ally. Nevertheless, the Restoration did not immediately dismantle the monopoly of education. Instead, it sought to turn it to the advantage of the Church. But liberal Catholics like Montalambert remembered that monopoly was a double-edged weapon that could be turned against them, and in the course of the nineteenth century Catholics fought to reestablish freedom of education—at a minimum, that is, the right to open and operate private schools free of the intrusion of the state in all matters but the certification of teachers, the inspection of hygiene and the safeguard of public order. After 1833, only a certificate of competence was required in order to establish a primary school. In 1850, in a panic-stricken reaction against the Revolution of 1848, conservatives passed the Falloux Law, that allowed anyone who possessed a lycée diploma to open a secondary school, dispensed with the need for teaching personnel to possess any diploma whatever, and allowed private religious schools to receive public subsidies. Not until 1875 was freedom of university education made legal, though private universities had for some time operated parallel to the

---

also Jacques Godechot, *Les Institutions de la France sous la Révolution et l'empire* (Paris, 1951), pp. 637ff.

[3] Aulard, *Le Monopole universitaire*, pp. 170-93.

public ones. Nevertheless, to this day the state retains a monopoly of examinations and the conferral of degrees.[4]

The centralized administration survived the Empire; in its main outlines it persisted through the Fourth Republic, despite changes in nomenclature and political regimes. Republicans found the hierarchical lines of authority running from Paris to the provinces quite satisfactory; they saw little reason to change them.

ALONG WITH the administration, secondary education was the great Napoleonic legacy to the educational system of the Third Republic. Regarded as a sort of institutional manifestation of the national genius, the lycée gave articulate Frenchmen greater pride, and at the same time caused greater disagreement among them, than almost any other public institution. The abysmal state of French universities in the nineteenth century was in part both cause and consequence of the attention lavished on secondary education. Indeed, one observer remarked in 1875 that there was no higher education in France. To be sure, no universities existed until 1896. The Revolution had abolished the twenty-two universities of the Old Regime; it gave up the idea of the university as an institution encompassing the whole of human knowledge. In the place of the university, separate institutions—the Ecole polytechnique, the Ecole normale supérieure and other Grandes Ecoles—were founded to provide professional training in specialized subjects.[5] Admitting by rigorous competitive examination the best young minds in France, these prestigious schools flour-

[4] On the question of freedom of education see Louis Grimaud, *Histoire de la liberté d'enseignement en France*, 6 vols. (Paris, 1944-54), which covers the period from the old regime through the July Monarchy.

[5] Theodore Zeldin, "Higher Education in France, 1848-1940," *Journal of Contemporary History*, II, No. 3 (1967), 53-100; the standard work on French universities remains Louis Liard, *L'Enseignement supérieur en France, 1789-1889*, 2 vols. (Paris, 1888-94); see also Stephen d'Irsay, *Histoire des universités françaises et étrangères*, 2 vols. (Paris, 1933-35).

ished in the nineteenth century, and the traditional *facultés* dwelt in their shadow. The task of general education devolved upon the lycées, and it is these, and not the universities, with which this study is mainly concerned. For what occupied the attention of reformers was not university education, but the process of getting to a university in the first place.

A Napoleonic modification of the Jesuit *collège*, the lycée was the kind of establishment that always seemed to lead republicans apologetically to point out that France was, after all, a very old country indeed.

However congealed its revolutionary ardor may have been, the post-thermidorean Convention made some striking innovations in secondary education. The Ideologues, intellectual heirs of the Encyclopedists and representatives of a quasi-official brand of moderate republicanism, believed that proper schooling would produce a "nation of free men, unhampered by superstition and ignorance."[6] They cast aside the old classical curriculum and drew up a program based on the study of French grammar (under the Old Regime, French had been taught as an adjunct of Latin, if at all), history and the sciences. A decree of 3 *Brumaire An* IV (October 26, 1795), called for the establishment of one *école centrale* in each Department.

In a few Departments, the *écoles centrales* flourished. But their utilitarian air attracted a good many of the students, and the Ideologues had never meant the *écoles centrales* to be trade schools. Moreover, each one differed markedly from the next.[7] No provisions had been made to take on boarding students; children who lived a great distance from the schools could not attend them. Nor did there exist a system of primary or intermediate schools that effectively prepared one for entering the *écoles centrales*. The political leanings of their founders made them suspect in some eyes; even parents who had no

[6] L. P. Williams, "Science, Education and the French Revolution," *Isis*, XLIV (1953), 330. On the Ideologues, see Charles Van Duzer, *Contribution of the Ideologues to French Revolutionary Thought* (Baltimore, 1935).

[7] Williams, "Science, Education and the French Revolution," 319.

political reservations about them were put off by their lack of discipline and the apparent anarchy of the course of study.[8]

Of course Napoleon had a passion for order. Moreover, he had no interest whatever in the creation of a "nation of free men, unhampered by superstition and ignorance." But his regime did need able and loyal military officers, civil servants and members of the liberal professions, and the decay of educational institutions since the outbreak of the Revolution threatened to leave them in short supply. While still First Consul, Napoleon undertook the reform of secondary education. Because he had little interest in popular education, he left the responsibility for primary instruction to the communes, which showed predictably little zeal for establishing primary schools. But Napoleon intended to keep secondary education firmly under the control of the State. The law of 11 *Floréal, An* X (May 1, 1802), laid down that secondary education would be given in "lycées and special schools maintained at the expense of the public treasury."[9]

As a model for the lycée, Napoleon had in mind the Parisian "Prytanée français," formerly the *collège* Louis-le-Grand, and the only secondary school of the Old Regime to survive the Revolution. Indeed, his reform of secondary education was in large measure a reaction against the *écoles centrales*. In organization, in teaching methods, in spirit, the Imperial reforms marked a return to principles of education laid down by the Jesuits in the seventeenth century. French secondary education again took on a cloistered and authoritarian aspect that subsequent regimes were unable to efface.[10]

[8] Aulard, *Le Monopole universitaire*, pp. 19-38; see also the perhaps too generous view of the *écoles centrales* of Francisque Vial, *Trois Siècles d'histoire de l'enseignement secondaire* (Paris, 1936), pp. 71-154; a hostile view is E. Allain, *L'Oeuvre scolaire de la Révolution* (Paris, 1891).

[9] Aulard, *Le Monopole universitaire*, p. 49. The best history of French secondary education remains Georges Weill, *Histoire de l'enseignement secondaire en France* (Paris, 1921).

[10] Léon de Lanzac de Laborie, "L'Instruction publique pendant la période napoléonienne," *Revue de Paris*, XXXI (November-December 1924), 293.

The resolutely modernist Ideologues had given science an important if subordinate place in the curriculum. The Napoleonic reforms returned to a literary curriculum based upon Latin; science remained in the course of study, but only as a kind of afterthought. In part, the return to Latin responded to the wishes of parents, who were suspicious of the pedagogical experiments performed in the *écoles centrales*. Of course Latinists justified on pedagogical grounds the preeminence given Latin: "The principles of Belles-Lettres are not subject to the same revolutions as those of the sciences; they are drawn from the imitation of a model that does not change. Knowledge of the Latin language will always be the main part of education."[11]

A less edifying, if equally powerful motive for reestablishing the Latin curriculum seems to have been the necessity of competing for students with the religious schools.[12] But the force of tradition and habit should not be discounted. In the eighteenth century, every man with pretensions to culture knew Latin; it was not only a formal academic subject, but the bearer of a whole system of values that informed the thought of every educated man.[13] For all these reasons, the French language was again relegated to a subordinate role. The return to the classical curriculum became a source of incessant controversy over the next century and a half, the occasion for a new battle of ancients and moderns the ramifications of which only the initiated fully comprehended.

The atmosphere of the lycée was both military and monastic. The Jesuits constructed an extremely sophisticated educational philosophy based on the *internat*, or boarding school, in which they kept their students under constant surveillance, sealed off

[11] Quoted in Aulard, *Le Monopole universitaire*, pp. 99-100.

[12] On this competition in the nineteenth century, see Paul Gerbod, *La Condition universitaire en France au XIXᵉ siècle* (Paris, 1965), pp. 92-106.

[13] On the importance of classical antiquity in the cultural climate of the eighteenth century, see the brilliant discussion of Peter Gay, *The Enlightenment, An Interpretation; the Rise of Modern Paganism* (New York, 1966), especially pp. 31-126.

from the cares and temptations of the world.[14] Napoleon had a considerably more relaxed view of temptation than had the Jesuits, but his concern for discipline was no less rigorous than theirs, and he made sure that lycée students seldom had the chance to be tempted. Balzac recalled that once a child entered the lycée he did not emerge until he had completed his studies; visits home were not permitted.[15] At the end of the nineteenth century, conditions had not changed much. Objections to the rigor of the *internat* were a constant refrain. To Jules Isaac, the distinguished historian, five years of boarding at the Lycée Lakanal, in Paris, had meant "five years of imprisonment."[16] At century's end, Isaac recalled, Lakanal had been among the most fashionable of lycées. Nonetheless, "it still remained faithful to the Napoleonic conception from whence it had sprung, and of which it kept a strong imprint." Worst torture of all, Lakanal possessed a magnificent park of some thirty acres, but students were forbidden to use it.[17]

It must be made plain that for the first eighty years of its existence the lycée was an exclusively male institution. The state made no adequate provision for the secondary education of women until 1880. Even then, women's *collèges* were not the intellectual equivalent of the lycée. The law laid down that the *collèges* should offer a modernist curriculum, but for the first twenty-five years of operation they were really little more than higher primary schools. These provisions accurately reflected the subordinate position of women in French society. Secondary education, it was thought, would make of women good housewives, able to converse intelligently with their husbands and to raise their children well; it was not meant to encourage them to pursue careers of their own on an equal footing with men. Not until after the First World War had

[14] Georges Snyders, *La Pédagogie en France aux XVIIe et XVIIIe siècles* (Paris, 1965), pp. 35-48; Philippe Ariès, *Centuries of Childhood; A Social History of Family Life*, trans. Robert Baldick (New York, 1962), pp. 155-285.

[15] Cited in Vial, *Histoire de l'enseignement secondaire*, p. 181.

[16] Jules Isaac, *Expériences de ma vie* (Paris, 1959), pp. 35-37.

[17] Idem. See also Paul Gerbod, *La Vie quotidienne dans les lycées et collèges au XIXe siècle* (Paris, 1968).

drawn women into the labor market in great numbers did boys' and girls' secondary education become the same. Tradition and religious scruple inhibited the development of coeducation, but for the purposes of this study, no distinction seems necessary between boys' and girls' lycées.[18]

The founders of the *écoles centrales* had outlawed punishment; the Napoleonic reforms reintroduced into the lycée a scale of punishments precisely graded to fit the crime—from a ban on recreation to incarceration in a sort of "prison." Students wore uniforms; they changed classes to the beat of a drum; they ate their meals in silence; they were subjected to frequent inspections.[19] But the charge that the Napoleonic lycée was nothing more than a factory for the manufacture of an officer corps seems exaggerated. In the early years of the Empire, at least, a boy had more good reasons for becoming an officer than the dull routine of a school could ever drum into him.

For the lycéen the baccalaureate examination crowned seven years of study. Originally oral, after 1840 it became a long written examination, bearing on the major subjects of the lycée curriculum. Each year, it seemed to become increasingly complicated; for weeks before the examination there took place a frantic period of cramming known as *bachotage*. Above all, the baccalaureate examination required a precise understanding of the question set, copious documentation and a well-ordered statement of the argument ending in a definite conclusion. Inevitably, there arose cries that the *baccalauréat* was really not an indication of much of anything, that a clever boy could pass the examination with a minimum of effort. Critics called for its abolition.[20]

What gave the *baccalauréat* its enormous importance was its dual function. Not only did it signify successful completion of secondary education; it was at once the first university degree and a university entrance examination. Because it was

[18] On all this see Gaston Coirault, *Les Cinquantes premières années de l'enseignement secondaire féminin, 1880-1930* (Tours, 1940).

[19] Lanzac de Laborie, "L'instruction publique," p. 313.

[20] Weill, *Histoire de l'enseignement secondaire*, p. 198.

11

required for entrance into a university, the *baccalauréat* was clearly indispensable if one intended to enter any of the liberal professions. And a royal ordinance of September 13, 1820, required its possession for promotion into the higher ranks of the civil service.[21] Without it, one could scarcely hope to pursue the most prestigious careers in the republic. The *baccalauréat* acted as a mechanism of social selection whose importance can scarcely be exaggerated: "it divides the nation into two classes: the one which has parchments, the one which does not; the one which alone has entry into the liberal careers, the other which is rejected, and confined within the old commoners' professions: commerce and industry. The distinction is clear and decisive; either one belongs to the privileged class or one does not, and it is the baccalaureate which decides. The distinction is final and for life."[22]

The lycée was intended to educate an élite; it was a thoroughly bourgeois institution. On these two assumptions about secondary education, most articulate Frenchmen agreed. Disagreement came over how this élite should be educated and whether it should continue to be overwhelmingly bourgeois in social origin. For most of the nineteenth century, controversy centered on the nature of élite education, to which the social question was subordinated. Between 1802 and 1887, no less than seventy-five changes were made in the curriculum of the lycée,[23] and one observer was led to remark that in France programs of study had an even shorter life than constitutions.[24]

Regardless of these changes, the end of secondary education remained to teach adolescents how to think critically; introduction to *culture générale* remained the means by which this was done. One justification for liberal education has been that

[21] Paul Meuriot, *Le Baccalauréat; son évolution historique et statistique des origines à nos jours* (Nancy, 1919), pp. 4-5.

[22] Emile Boutmy, *Le Baccalauréat et l'enseignement secondaire* (Paris, 1899), p. 18.

[23] Emile Durkheim, *L'Evolution pédagogique en France*, 2 vols. (Paris, 1938), II, 172-73.

[24] Gabriel Compayré, *Etudes sur l'enseignement et l'éducation* (Paris, 1891), p. 215.

it prepares men for any eventuality. But at the same time, general education has long been considered a prelude to specialization in one of the liberal professions, for which the exercise of certain faculties of judgment and reflection is thought essential. The proponents of *culture générale* have always felt impelled to stress that it was the opposite of a utilitarian or technical education, despite its historical association with certain occupations. Disinterested, concerned with general moral and aesthetic principles, man-centered but designed to free man from his own limitations in space and time, *culture générale* has been the French variant of a Western educational ideal that grew out of the Renaissance.[25]

But when it came to devising a curriculum, the open-endedness of the idea of *culture générale* made it troublesome indeed. How could anyone know with certainty what subjects, in what combinations, best prepared one for "any eventuality"? No timeless principles underpinned the idea of *culture générale*. The classical curriculum that had so long seemed best to meet the requirements of disinterestedness had itself been historically determined. In the late Middle Ages, there emerged a leisure class whose members were more interested in culture than in annihilating each other, and Latin and Greek had been the vehicles by means of which they reestablished contact with classical civilization. When politics and literature came to rely upon vernacular languages, the study of Latin seemed increasingly disinterested as it became less useful. To the Jesuit founders of the *collèges,* Latin was doubly attractive, for it was not only the bearer of *culture générale*, but the language of the Church.[26]

[25] On this see Clément Falcucci, *L'Humanisme dans l'enseignement secondaire en France au XIXᵉ siècle* (Toulouse, 1931), p. ix; Antoine Cournot, *Des Institutions de l'instruction publique en France* (Paris, 1864), p. 39; Célestin Bouglé, *The French Conception of Culture Générale and its Influences upon Instruction* (New York, 1938), p. 8; Fernand Robert, *L'Humanisme; essai de définition* (Paris, 1946), p. 18; Durkheim, *L'Evolution pédagogique en France*, passim.

[26] See F. de Dainville, *Les Jésuites et l'éducation de la société française. La naissance de l'humanisme moderne* (Paris, 1940).

13

In the seventeenth and eighteenth centuries, concurrent with the Scientific Revolution, the idea had arisen that modern languages and science could, and indeed should, form an alternative basis for *culture générale*. The Ideologues had tried out this idea in the short-lived experiment with the *écoles centrales*. Limited to pedagogical considerations alone, the struggle between two different theories of *culture générale* would have been bitter enough.[27] But like most debates over what should be taught in the schools, the battle over the curriculum reflected social and economic change. It was intensely political. The lines of battle were confusing in the extreme. The controversy seemed to place the proponents of science and their allies, the champions of modern languages, on one side, with the classicists ranged against them on the other. At the same time, however, a debate raged between certain proponents of a predominantly literary culture—both classical and modern—and the champions of a predominantly scientific culture. Over the last third of the nineteenth century the modernists gradually did establish a foothold in the curriculum, until at the century's end they won a major victory.

The advance of industrialization had long since given rise to complaints that the classical secondary education failed to meet the new demands of an industrial society. It was pointed out that the lycée's continued neglect of science, for example, could only adversely affect French technological progress.[28] The men of the Second Empire, acutely attuned to the problems of industrial development, sought to meet these criticisms. Victor Duruy, who became minister of public instruction in 1863, and one of the greatest incumbents of that office, perceived that the advance in industrial and agricultural techniques had created the need for an education concerned with general ideas and theoretical principles, yet not divorced from practical matters.[29]

[27] Falcucci, *L'Humanisme*, p. xi; Gerbod, *La Condition universitaire*, p. 15.

[28] Weill, *Histoire de l'enseignement secondaire*, p. 134. On scientific education in nineteenth-century France, see the forthcoming Harvard University Ph.D. dissertation of John H. Weiss.

[29] *Ibid.*, p. 150.

In 1865 Duruy sponsored a law that founded *l'enseignement spécial*, a modern secondary education of three years' duration. But he failed to procure enough money to construct buildings to house this new form of secondary education; *l'enseignement spécial* was set up alongside the classical curriculum, where it remained a distinctly poor relation, disdained and shunned by the usual clientele of the lycée. Only a minority of the pupils enrolled actually completed the course; professors assigned to teach in the classes believed that they were being grievously put upon; the label *spécial* seemed somehow to brand it as second-rate. Finally, in 1891 Léon Bourgeois sought to rid modern education of this stigma by raising it to a level almost equal that of the classical curriculum. Bourgeois organized a modern section in the lycée; the term *spécial* was suppressed. The modern section lasted six years, one year less than the classical; modern languages replaced classical languages as the basis of its curriculum. The classicists were outraged. The modernists were unhappy that the modern section had been awarded a status almost, but not quite, equal that of the old classical curriculum.[30]

The reform of 1902 followed an extensive parliamentary investigation of secondary education. In 1899, at the height of the Dreyfus Affair, the education committee of the Chamber, under the chairmanship of Alexandre Ribot, collected depositions and heard testimony from nearly 200 witnesses.[31] For several years an especially intensive debate had raged on the curriculum of the lycée. The classicists had the advantage that Latin had been the heart of the curriculum since anyone could remember; pedagogical theory had often come along to justify some old and well-established practice.[32] Classical humanities and *culture générale* had once been one and the same; partisans of Latin held they still were and always would be: "From an educational standpoint, this absence of material usefulness,

[30] *Ibid.*, pp. 195-97.

[31] See *Enquête sur l'enseignement secondaire. Procès-verbaux des dépositions présentées par M. Ribot, président de la commission de l'enseignement* (Paris, 1899).

[32] R. Thamin, "La Réforme de l'enseignement," *Revue des deux mondes*, LXIII (1921), 169. Hereafter cited as *RDM*.

which masks a profound moral utility and is even the previous condition for it, accounts for the value of classical studies. . . . This incomparable instrument of culture has the privilege, both for teachers and students, of being directly useful only for culture itself."[33]

In the view of the classicists, the partisans of modern languages were clearly out to sabotage the traditional disinterestedness of the lycée: "in short, it is this utility which has inspired and still inspires the promoters of modern education."[34] The moderns replied that the study of modern languages and science was every bit as "disinterested" as the study of Latin; that the Latinists were reactionary snobs, out of step with their own times; that Latin had never been taught properly in the lycée anyway.[35] The partisans of science had in their favor the compelling argument that the rapid progress of scientific and technological development in the nineteenth century made ridiculous and dangerous this maintenance in a privileged position of a predominantly literary culture.[36]

The reform of 1902 was supposed to have been an attempt to satisfy all these claims at once, but it leaned toward the modernist position, by putting an end to the dualism that opposed classical to modern education. Henceforth, there was to be one kind of secondary education. Different sections of equal length would offer different courses of study; each would be presumed to possess an equal value. In short, these structural arrangements were intended to raise modern studies from their second-class status to a position equal in prestige to that of the classical humanities.[37] But proclaiming the unity of secondary education did not unify it; the reform did not put an end to the battle of ancients and moderns.

[33] Alfred Fouillée, Les Etudes classiques et la démocratie (Paris, 1898), p. 9.

[34] Ibid., p. 27.

[35] On the last point see Michel Bréal, Quelques Mots sur l'instruction publique en France, 5th edn. (Paris, 1886), p. 164.

[36] See, for example, Octave Gréard, Education et instruction, vol. IV, Enseignement supérieur (Paris, 1887), 210-11.

[37] J. B. Piobetta, Le Baccalauréat de l'enseignement secondaire (Paris, 1937), p. 249; Falcucci, L'Humanisme, p. 555.

It did, however, set up the curriculum of the lycée as it stood in 1918. The course of study lasted seven years; children entered the sixth class at the age of eleven. The reform divided the hitherto continuous program into two cycles: the first of four years duration, the second of three. In the first cycle, children could choose between two different sections, one that offered Latin and one that did not. The second cycle comprised four options; each with different subjects as the basis of its program.[38] The reform established a single *baccalauréat* that stood as the guarantee of the acquisition of *culture générale,* no matter what course a student had followed. The Baccalaureate remained both a secondary school diploma and a university entrance examination. The examination juries remained substantially as before, composed of members of the faculties of letters and sciences, and of active or retired lycée professors.[39]

IN THE report on his committee's inquiry, Alexandre Ribot had insisted: "To form a leadership élite [*élite dirigeante*], such is the role of secondary education."[40] No one would have disagreed. Republicans found the notion of an intellectual élite congenial, for it rested on a foundation of individual merit.[41] Unlike the old ascriptive élite of birth, and the newer plutocratic élite, the intellectual élite could be joined by anyone, so long as he had the ability. This was the meaning of the career open to talent. And it was only slightly embarrassing to repub-

[38] Luc Decaunes, *Réformes et projets de réforme de l'enseignement français de la Révolution à nos jours, 1789-1960* (Paris, 1962), pp. 48-51. Section A offered Latin beginning in the first year (sixth class), and optional Greek in the third. Section B offered neither Latin nor Greek, but gave more time to French, sciences and drawing; both sections had certain subjects in common. The four options in the second cycle were A (Latin-Greek); B (Latin-Modern Languages); C (Latin-Sciences); D (Sciences-Modern Languages).

[39] Piobetta, *Le Baccalauréat*, pp. 244-49.

[40] Alexandre Ribot, *La Réforme de l'enseignement secondaire* (Paris, 1900), p. 60.

[41] See Michalina Clifford-Vaughn, "Some French Concepts of Elites," *British Journal of Sociology*, XI (1960), 317-31.

licans that Napoleon Bonaparte had been the most notable French beneficiary of this principle. To be sure, democracy had as much need of an intellectual élite as any form of government did. Anyone, so the argument went, was permitted to become a lawyer, a doctor, an engineer, a high civil servant. All he needed was brains and a knack for passing competitive examinations, the very epitome of an egalitarian, yet individualist recruiting device. The lycée was the institution that selected and trained this intellectual élite. The *baccalauréat* was a badge of membership in the bourgeoisie. As Edmond Goblot remarked, "The unique function of the baccalaureate is to create a gap difficult to cross and to unite on the level of equality all who cross."[42] High culture was the mark of the republican aristocracy of merit. But the hitch in all this was plain to anyone: chances for the acquisition of the baccalaureate were by no means equal throughout French society.

In the first place, the lycées charged tuition. Most of them operated their own elementary classes. This meant tuition payments for a child from the age of six. The cost of tuition varied from establishment to establishment; it is impossible to obtain a precise idea of these costs. It has been calculated that in the period 1883 to 1913 a family had to spend each year the equivalent of 700 francs.[43] But that amount covered tuition alone. It did not include the cost of books, school uniforms, school supplies, tutors and boarding fees. It was not unusual for socially ambitious parents to spend 20 to 35 per cent of their annual incomes on the education of their children.[44]

Scholarships were available, but in short supply. In 1898, of a total of 52,372 students enrolled in the boys' lycées and *collèges,* 6,735 held some sort of boarding scholarship from the state, the departments and the communes; there were 2,346 day school scholarships.[45] By no means all of these were full

[42] Edmond Goblot, *La Barrière et le niveau* (Paris, 1925), p. 128.

[43] Marguerite Perrot, *Le Mode de vie des familles bourgeoises, 1873-1953* (Paris, 1961), p. 92.

[44] *Ibid.,* p. 105.

[45] *Statistique de l'enseignement secondaire des garçons, année 1900* (Paris, 1900), pp. 10-11.

scholarships. It is hard to see whom half-scholarships were meant to benefit, unless lower middle-class families, who could scrape together a certain amount to spend on education but not enough to cover all the costs. To the poor, a half-scholarship was as good as none at all. To remain in school until the age of eighteen meant the loss of earnings that simply could not be foregone.

In 1900 the government awarded 1,000 scholarships in the lycées and *collèges*. Only 275 of the scholarship holders came directly from the primary school system; 707 of the scholarships went to children enrolled in the elementary classes of the secondary establishments. In the years between 1901 and 1906 the number of scholarship holders who came directly from primary school each year fluctuated from a low of 196 to a high of 296. In 1900, of a total of 5,528 holders of secondary school scholarships, only 1,586 had come from the primary schools.[46] In 1911, nearly 80 per cent of the scholarship holders were of middle-class parentage. Only 14.2 per cent were the children of artisans, workers and small employers; 6.2 per cent the children of peasants.[47] There were only some 100 lycées and 240 *collèges* in all of France. Children who lived in remote rural areas could attend them only if their parents were able to pay for boarding school.

The bourgeoisie felt no guilt over its virtual monopoly of secondary education. Most of its members had worked hard; they believed they deserved what they could pay for. Indeed, for most of the nineteenth century, scarcely anyone but the planners of revolution challenged the assumption that a child would occupy the same rank in society as his parents, and should therefore receive an equivalent education. In 1859, back from a tour of continental schools, Matthew Arnold noted approvingly that "the boon conferred by the State, when it founded the lyceums, was not for the aristocracy; it

[46] Ferdinand Buisson, ed., *Nouveau dictionnaire de pédagogie* (Paris, 1911), p. 1149.

[47] These figures are cited from the *Journal officiel de la République française* by Ludovic Zoretti, *Education, un essai d'organisation démocratique* (Paris, 1918), p. 46.

19

was for the vast middle class of Frenchmen."[48] In the late 1870's Octave Gréard, a high official in the ministry of public instruction, did not find it extraordinary that the parents of 33.07 per cent of the students enrolled in the lycées and *collèges* of the Department of the Seine (Paris) followed no profession; the rest, he felt sure, belonged to "this middle class . . . which lives simply, not without privations now and then, by labor and probity."[49] Great was the temptation to believe that the republic and the middle class were one. Francisque Vial, another school official, argued that "the prosperity of our democracy, a work of the middle classes, is linked to the sound organization of secondary education."[50] Edouard Maneuvrier was less modest in his claims for the middle class. In spirit, he contended, the lycée remained a fundamentally aristocratic institution. School reform had therefore to begin with secondary education, "for it forms the bourgeoisie, and . . . it is the bourgeoisie which governs France."[51] Enraptured by his vision of the triumph of the bourgeoisie, Maneuvrier concluded "What epic poem equals the history of this middle class, which for ten centuries has not ceased to increase and which, fulfilling the celebrated saying, from nothing has become everything . . . the bourgeoisie which is nothing else, in sum, than the advent of the people itself; for what is a bourgeois, if not an *ouvrier arrivé?*"[52]

There was truth enough in Maneuvrier's peroration to provide the Third Republic with a comfortable myth. Of course there were bourgeois who had working-class origins. A ladder led upward into the bourgeoisie for all those individuals clever

[48] Matthew Arnold, "The Popular Education of France," in R. H. Super, ed., *The Complete Prose Works of Matthew Arnold*, vol. ii, *Democratic Education* (Ann Arbor, 1962), 22.

[49] Octave Gréard, *Education et instruction*, vol. i, *Enseignement secondaire*, 2nd edn. (Paris, 1889), 241.

[50] Francisque Vial, *L'Enseignement secondaire et la démocratie* (Paris, 1901), p. 73.

[51] Edouard Maneuvrier, *L'Education de la bourgeoisie sous la République* (Paris, 1888), p. 5.

[52] *Ibid.*, p. 378.

20

enough and lucky enough to grasp its lower rungs. But it was far easier to remain a bourgeois than to become one. What Charles Bigot wrote in 1875 remained essentially true in 1918: "Today real instruction, save for rare and affecting exceptions, is accessible only to children of the ruling classes; it guarantees, as it were, to the sons of a family of the bourgeoisie the inheritance of the social positions conquered by their parents, as the law guarantees them the inheritance of accumulated fortunes."[53] Besides, other arrangements had been made for the education of *Le Peuple*.

THE ESTABLISHMENT of a truly effective national system of primary education had to await the early years of the Third Republic. In the early 1880's, under the leadership of the moderate republican, Jules Ferry, a series of laws founded the free, compulsory and secular primary school. The campaign in its favor intensified the bitter struggle between the anticlerical Left and the Catholic and antirepublican Right. The demand for free, compulsory and secular primary education went back to the Revolution; so did the hostility of the Church toward Republicanism. The struggle between Church and State for the control of education was far older. The primary school became symbolic of the Third Republic itself, as it banished the ignorance that in republican oratory usually seemed to be the fault of the Church.[54]

The July Monarchy had undertaken the first great national effort in favor of primary education. In 1833, at the instigation of François Guizot, a law was passed that required every commune to establish a primary school, at its own expense or in combination with others.[55] The school was to give instruction in ethics and religion, reading, writing, grammar and arithmetic. The beneficiaries of the July Revolution expected primary education to inculcate in the people a sense of morality,

[53] Charles Bigot, *Les Classes dirigeantes* (Paris, 1875), p. 118.
[54] See Mona Ozouf, *L'Ecole, l'église et la République* (Paris, 1963).
[55] See Maurice Gontard, *L'Enseignement primaire en France de la Révolution à la loi Guizot, 1789-1833* (Paris, n.d.), especially pp. 443-548.

to provide a nascent industrial labor force with rudimentary skills, and to assure respect and obedience to the new social and political order—in short, to themselves. In Guizot's view, as his biographer has put it: ". . . far from education being a means of social change, education should rather reflect social distinctions and should accept to be limited by the divisions of society."[56]

The school was neither compulsory nor free; the Church retained considerable influence in primary education. Consequently, the extreme Left bitterly opposed the Guizot law; nor was the extreme Right appeased by the fact that the village curé had a voice in the operation of the school. Guizot reinforced the conservative bias of the system by leaving the schools under the control of local notables.[57] After 1833 most communes did found a school; illiteracy declined at a steady rate: in the period 1816-1820, 54.3 per cent of Frenchmen could write their names; by 1871-1875, that figure had risen to 78 per cent.[58] But this average was very unevenly distributed over France. In 1848, 4,000 communes still had not founded a school, and in 30 departments, half the boys of school age did not go to school.[59]

At the founding of the Third Republic primary education remained in all important respects faithful to the arrangements Guizot had laid down in 1833.[60] But it had become quite clear that so long as attendance at school was not compulsory, so long as the school charged fees, so long as hostile or indifferent local authorities retained control of the school, a truly universal primary education was beyond reach.

Even for conservatives, there existed compelling motives for

[56] Douglas Johnson, *Guizot; Aspects of French History* (London, 1963), pp. 111-12.

[57] Gontard, *L'Enseignement primaire*, pp. 503-4.

[58] Michel Fleury and Pierre Valmary, "Les Progrès de l'instruction élémentaire de Louis XIV à Napoléon III, d'après l'enquête de Louis Maggiolo, 1877-1879," *Population*, xii (January-March 1957), 78, 89.

[59] Maurice Gontard, *Les Ecoles primaires de la France bourgeoise* (Paris, 1964), pp. 25-26.

[60] *Ibid.*, p. 233.

reform. After the Franco-Prussian War, it became a common-place to attribute the stunning victory of the Germans to the Prussian schoolmaster; many Frenchmen believed France suffered from some grave flaw or deficiency in the national spirit.[61] The school, republicans thought, should become a crucible for the reshaping of national unity. At the same time, it would be a source of moral regeneration.[62] Moreover, republicans had long argued that universal suffrage would work properly only if a system of universal primary education backed it up. The short-lived Second Republic and the experience of plebiscitary democracy under the Second Empire seemed ample proof of how easily an ignorant electorate could be turned from the straight and narrow path of republicanism. The advance of industrialization demanded a better instructed and disciplined work force. In earlier times it had not much mattered whether factory hands could read, write and count: but as manufacturing techniques became more complicated, factories required workers with higher levels of skill. Finally, horrified by the Commune they had themselves so enthusiastically repressed and fearful of the recuperative powers of the Monarchists, the moderate architects of the Republic acutely felt that the new regime needed republicans. What better way to obtain them than to send out a loyal army of school teachers to carry the gospel of republicanism to every hamlet in the Republic?

Whatever differences in political philosophy may have separated them, François Guizot and Jules Ferry shared quite similar views on primary education: both intended it to dispense a form of common morality, to assist in the economic development of the country, and to assure respect and obedience to the new political order that each in his turn represented. Ferry parted from Guizot in the use he made of the egalitarian mystique that infused the popular movement in favor of pri-

[61] See especially Claude Digeon, *La Crise allemande de la pensée française* (Paris, 1959), pp. 364-83; M. Ozouf, *L'Ecole, l'église et la République*, pp. 15-23.

[62] Raoul Girardet, *Le Nationalisme français, 1871-1914* (Paris, 1966), pp. 70-71.

23

mary instruction, and in the anticlerical bias of himself and his followers.

Unlike many of his allies, Ferry did not regard a compulsory system of primary education as largely a means of individual emancipation. A student of Auguste Comte, the positivist philosopher, Ferry considered equality the surest guarantor of social order. He expected the free and compulsory education of the working class to imbue workers with a sense of discipline, and he believed that the expectation of acquiring an equality of rights and dignity within the existing society would at last put an end to the revolutionary impulse that had troubled France since 1789. By establishing the intellectual and moral conditions for cooperation between workers and employers, Ferry thought, equality in education would put an end to the class struggle.[63] As a good Comtean, he considered Christianity the vestige of a now superseded era. In the place of religion, science was to become the moral foundation of the new Positivist order, and the key to the mass education of a democracy.[64] "My goal," Ferry once said, "is to organize humanity without God and without a king."[65]

But even in the absence of such systematic assaults on Catholicism as Ferry's, the doctrine of *Laïcité* would have been one of the most bitterly contested issues in modern French history. As René Rémond has observed: "The notion of *Laïcité* is not an isolated one. It is linked to several others by logical relations. Because of this it is integrated into complex ideological systems. It implies in particular an idea of the State and its mission, a conception of the nature and content of truth, a philosophy of education and of the development of the mind. The notion of *Laïcité* is situated necessarily at the point of convergence of philosophies of knowledge, of philosophies of history, pedagogical systems, ethics and theology."[66]

[63] Louis Legrand, *L'Influence du positivisme dans l'oeuvre scolaire de Jules Ferry* (Paris, 1961), p. 124.

[64] *Ibid.*, p. 131.

[65] Quoted in Adrien Dansette, *Histoire religieuse de la France contemporaine*, 2nd edn. (Paris, 1965), p. 405.

[66] René Rémond, "Evolution de la notion de laïcité entre 1919 et 1939," *Cahiers d'histoire*, IV (1959), 72.

In order to assure freedom of conscience in a nation divided in belief, the minimal argument for *laïcité* runs, the teaching of religion must be excluded from any compulsory system of public education.[67] But the Catholic Church considers itself charged with watching over the eternal salvation of the faithful. All academic subjects must therefore be submitted to Christian principles. The state, responsible for the common good, must permit religious instruction in the public schools. Canon law enjoins all Catholics to see that their children receive religious instruction; they are forbidden to send their children to schools religiously neutral or open to non-Catholics.

Even on these legalistic grounds, the possibilities of conflict were endless. But republicans considered the Church their greatest enemy. In their hands, *Laïcité* became an aggressive and sometimes simple-minded *Laïcisme*. Convinced that once liberated from his enslavement to religion, man would become his own master, these anticlericals possessed a quasi-religious faith in the principles of the Great Revolution, a belief in the limitless possibilities of science, and a conviction that material progress and the perfectibility of mankind were one.[68] Their world view most certainly had no place in it for the teaching of religion in the schools. Catholics, both clerical and lay, returned in full measure the hostility of republicans. Except for an occasional maverick such as Lamennais, most had since the Revolution allied themselves with the Right; the most conspicuous champions of Catholicism were monarchists who detested the Republic. In these inauspicious circumstances, the free, secular and obligatory primary school was established.

Ferry, a cold, uninspiring and precise lawyer, had the political sense to know that he could not get all he wanted from parliament at once. Between 1881 and 1886, aided by a vast popular campaign in favor of primary education, he maneuvered the school laws through the Chamber and Senate. The

[67] On all this see A. Audibert *et al.* *La Laïcité* (Paris, 1960); Bernard Mégrine, *La Question scolaire en France* (Paris, 1960).

[68] Aline Coutrot and François Dreyfus, *Les Forces religieuses dans la société française* (Paris, 1965), pp. 21-24.

law of June 6, 1881, made primary education entirely free; that of March 28, 1882, made it obligatory for all children between the ages of six and thirteen, and over the bitter opposition of the Right it affirmed the religious neutrality of public education; finally, a law of October 30, 1886, laid down that in public schools the teaching personnel would be exclusively lay.[69]

Unlike the lycée, the primary school underwent no constant tinkering at the hands of the authorities. In all important respects, the curriculum of 1918 remained the same as that drawn up in 1887. The school had to equip a majority of the nation's children with all the formal instruction they would ever receive. The curriculum emphasized "facts to the detriment of the need for explanation, contemplative observation to the detriment of the exercise of judgment."[70] The relentlessly utilitarian program comprised "moral and civic instruction, the French language, arithmetic and the metric system, history and geography, especially of France, object lessons and the first scientific notions, principally in their applications to agriculture; the elements of drawing, singing, and manual training (needlework in girls' schools); gymnastic and military exercises."[71]

The recurrence of the same subjects over and over again in the course of study—the whole infused with a heavy dose of nationalist rhetoric—was intended to ensure that the rudiments of reading, writing, arithmetic and love of La Patrie were drummed into the most obdurate of heads.[72] At the age of thirteen, those children who wished to do so took the examination for the certificat des études primaires. Held each spring in the larger towns, it was by no means a formality. Indeed,

[69] See Ozouf, L'Ecole, l'église, et la République, pp. 53-96; Eleanor Acomb, The French Laic Laws (New York, 1941), pp. 163-82.

[70] Legrand, L'Influence du positivisme, p. 196.

[71] Octave Gréard, ed., La Législation de l'instruction primaire en France depuis 1789 (Paris, 1889-1902), vi.

[72] See Carleton J. H. Hayes, France, A Nation of Patriots (New York, 1929), pp. 35-63; 343-99; Emile Glay and Aléxis Léaud, L'Ecole primaire en France, 2 vols. (Paris, 1934), passim.

the *certificat* became a source of intense pride to the parents of those children who had passed the examination.[73]

For children who completed their obligatory schooling but desired additional formal instruction of a general and practical sort, there existed the *écoles primaires supérieures*, or higher primary schools. These were meant to train young people for certain industrial and white-collar jobs—shop foremen, book-keepers, government clerks and the like. In 1833, Guizot had made an abortive effort to establish schools of this kind.[74] But it was left to Jules Ferry to undertake their organization; under his guidance, the extremely popular *écoles primaires supérieures* proliferated. Ferry made clear that in character the *école primaire supérieure* was to remain a prolongation of the elementary school: "however high and far it should go, it is fitting that it always be based in some fashion on the popular school."[75] In no circumstances, he warned, should the *école primaire supérieure* become a copy of the modern section of the lycée. As a close associate of Ferry put it: "it is a demo-cratic education par excellence. It raises the level of instruction and of morality of the lower middle class; it summons and it will summon more and more the élite of the working popula-tion. Opening to everyone access to all careers in which sec-ondary studies are not necessary, it gives satisfaction to legitimate ambitions, without overexciting blind pretensions that are as disappointing for individuals as they are fatal to society."[76]

Designed as at least a two-year program of study, in some cases the *école primaire supérieure* offered three or four. The ministry of public instruction established schools under two arrangements: in larger cities and towns the *école primaire supérieure* was established in a building separate from the pri-

---

[73] On the persistence of this attitude see the brilliant study of Laurence Wylie, *Village in the Vaucluse*, 2nd. edn. (New York, 1964), pp. 55-97.

[74] Gontard, *L'Enseignement primaire*, pp. 501-2.

[75] Quoted in Decaunes, *Réformes et projets de réforme*, p. 40.

[76] Octave Gréard, *Education et instruction*, vol. I, *Enseignement primaire*, 4th edn. (Paris, 1904), 172.

mary school and under different administration; in rural areas, the *école primaire supérieure* was attached to the elementary school, and called a *cours complémentaire*. In the first year, the curriculum of the *école primaire supérieure* was truly encyclopedic. In the second and third years students had options among five sections. They could follow a general course that had little to distinguish it from the first cycle of the modern section of the lycée, or they could enter the agricultural, industrial, commercial or maritime section. Upon successful completion of the *école primaire supérieure,* various *brevets* opened access to a number of careers; they did not admit one to a university.[77] In method and course of study, the *école primaire supérieure* was little less utilitarian than the primary school: "it must be plainly oriented toward the pupils' future needs and awaken in them a taste for vocational employment."[78] But it did have the advantage of flexibility. In a *cours complémentaire,* a peasant child could prepare for another occupation without leaving home. School teaching, for example, was a favored means of social mobility among the peasantry. Indeed, throughout the life of the Third Republic, the *école primaire supérieure* was the main recruiting ground for primary school teachers, who went from there directly to the normal schools established in the *chef lieu* of each Department.[79]

It did not take long for the republican primary school to become a powerful symbol of popular emancipation from ignorance. With a sort of missionary fervor, thousands of *instituteurs* carried learning to the dullest, loneliest communes in

[77] For the curriculum of the *Ecole primaire supérieure* see *Plan d'études et programmes des écoles primaires supérieures de garçons. Décret et arrêté du 26 juillet 1909* (Paris, 1909), p. 78.

[78] *Ibid.,* p. 19.

[79] On this see the lively study, based on retrospective questionnaires of retired school teachers, of Jacques Ozouf, *Nous, les maîtres d'école; autobiographies d'instituteurs de la Belle Epoque* (Paris, 1967), passim. On school teaching as a means of social mobility see, for example, Ida Berger, "Contribution à l'étude de la mobilité sociale en France: les instituteurs," *Transactions of the Third World Congress of Sociology* (New York, 1956), pp. 45-50.

France. And emancipate the primary schools did, teaching the sons of peasants and workers and shopkeepers how to read, write and count. In 1876, on the eve of the Ferry reforms, 3,823,348 children attended 59,021 public schools. From 1876 to 1898, when the size of the French population grew scarcely at all, enrollment in the primary school increased by 1,443,212, or 61 per cent. In the same period the state constructed 35,145 new schools; the number of school teachers increased from 69,025 to 83,561. The percentage of illiterate army conscripts declined from 8.5 per cent in 1877 to 5.1 per cent in 1897. In 1877 81.2 per cent of Frenchmen and 70.6 per cent of the women could sign their own marriage contracts; in 1897 these figures had risen to 91.6 per cent and 90.6 per cent. In the 1912-1913 school year 4,969,402 children attended public primary schools; 699,849 were enrolled in private schools.[80]

BUT EGALITARIANISM and emancipation had their limits. In the educational system of the Third Republic there existed no structural connection between primary and secondary education. Public secondary education was not regarded as the next step in an educational ladder after the public primary school. The primary school and the lycée each had its own distinct past; each operated in isolation from the other. Primary and secondary education were under separate administrations that jealously guarded their every prerogative. The lycées operated their own elementary classes, whose program differed markedly from that of the public primary school (though perhaps not so markedly as the teachers of the elementary classes liked to claim). The primary system offered instruction beyond the school-leaving age in its *écoles primaires supérieures,* but these had no direct ties with the lycée. Indeed, after the reform of 1902 the general section of the *école primaire supérieure* nearly duplicated the modern section of the lycée, despite Ferry's insistence that it should not.

[80] Emile Levasseur, "Statistique de l'enseignement public primaire au xixe siècle," *Séances et travaux de l'académie des sciences morales et politiques,* CLIII (1900), 381-411; *Statistique générale de la France. Annuaire statistique,* vol. xxxiii (1913), 19.

The lycées charged tuition, operated boarding facilities, required their students to purchase their own uniforms, books and supplies. The primary system was free. The primary system recruited its own teachers from its own clientele and trained them in its own normal schools. Lycée professors received the same education as university professors, and might well become university professors themselves.

In short, over the course of the nineteenth century the design of men in power had made of primary and secondary education two separate worlds, unlike in purpose, spirit, methods, and in the social origins of their clientele. The accompanying table sets out the structure of the French educational system as it stood in 1918.[81]

Primary (Free)	Secondary (Tuition)
Ecole normale primaire supérieure	Entry to university faculties
Ecoles normales	Lycées et collèges
Ecole primaire supérieure	Classes élémentaires des
Ecole primaire	lycées et collèges

There is a regrettable lack of precise data on the social origins of French school children in the nineteenth century. But perceptions of class relationships have an importance of their own. For aspirations are related to perceived opportunity, not statistical data, and so is the breeding of discontent. The belief of Americans in the unlimited possibilities of individual ascent, for example, has in the past greatly contributed to the maintenance of social stability, however real those possibilities may have been.[82] In France it was harder to believe that any

[81] This table is adapted from one that appears in David Watson, "The Politics of Educational Reform in France during the Third Republic, 1900-1940," *Past and Present*, No. 34 (July 1966), 83. For differences between Mr. Watson and myself in the interpretation of reform see our debate in *Past and Present*, No. 36 (April 1967), 126-37.

[82] See Seymour Martin Lipset and Reinhard Bendix, *Social Mobility in Industrial Society* (Berkeley and Los Angeles, 1959), pp. 76-113; also Stephan Thernstrom, *Poverty and Progress; Social Mobility in a Nineteenth Century City* (Cambridge, Mass., 1964).

man had a chance to rise in the social order, regardless of his origins. The primary school was unmistakably the school of *Le Peuple*: workers, peasants and petty bourgeosie. The lycée was the preserve of the bourgeoisie, which here can be defined as those for whom it was not an intolerable burden to pay for a secondary education for their children. To Ferdinand Buisson, professor of education at the Sorbonne and former director of primary education, the facts were plain. In France, Buisson remarked to the Ribot Committee, secondary education could be quite simply defined: "it is the education accessible to families of a certain rank."[83]

If one's social background in large part determined the school he attended, the sort of education that he received in turn reflected his social position. One style of education was dispensed to a majority of the nation's children, another style was reserved, not necessarily for the able, but for those who could afford it. According to the census of 1911, there were in France 5,187,846 children between the ages of eleven and eighteen. In 1913, 133,485, or roughly 2.56 per cent of this age group were enrolled in the lycées and colleges.[84] Given the social dis-

[83] *Enquête sur l'enseignement secondaire*, p. 151. In the two decades prior to World War I, the number of students transferring from the école primaire supérieure to the lycée appears to have declined, despite an increase in enrollment in both institutions. In 1915 a parliamentary inquiry was held on the effects of the reform of 1902. Paul Lapie, director of primary education, stated that in 1892 410 students made the transition from the école primaire supérieure to the lycée. But in 1898 only 256 students transferred; in 1908, 387; in 1913, 215. In 1913, moreover, of the 1,588 students who entered the sixth class of the lycée in the Academy of Paris, only 360, or 22 per cent, had attended public primary schools. Lapie informed the committee that he considered this percentage "extrêmement faible." Throughout France, only three or four thousand of the 800,000 students who finished primary school in the spring of 1913 entered the lycée in the fall. *Archives nationales* C 7731 "Commission d'enquête sur les résultats de la réforme de 1902. Procès-verbaux." [Hearing of October 21, 1915] I am indebted to Professor Peter Larmour for this information.

[84] *Statistique générale de la France. Annuaire statistique*, vol. XXXIII (1913), 26-31.

tinctions between the primary school system and the lycée, it is not wholly an exaggeration to say that under the Third Republic the *sans-latin* was the social counterpart of the *sans-culotte* of the Revolution.

In effect, the structure of the educational establishment denied primary school pupils access to higher education. Admission to the universities required possession of the *baccalauréat*. The futures of the overwhelming majority of children were likely to be determined at the age of six, when they entered either the public primary school or the elementary class of the lycée. For the bright primary school pupil of limited means, one narrow and uncertain path to the university was open: he might obtain a scholarship to the lycée that would enable him to acquire the indispensable baccalaureate. But if not, he would go to work at the age of thirteen; or he might enroll in an *école primaire supérieure*; or perhaps he might attend one of the few existing public and private trade schools. Once a given course of action had been decided upon, it was very nearly irrevocable.

The Third Republic's educational system both reflected class distinctions and helped to perpetuate them. It maintained such a fine balance between the encouragement of limited social mobility, by means of the primary system, and the inhibition of social mobility, by means of the secondary system, that the effects of the lycée worked to cancel out the effects of the primary school. The bourgeoisie's quasi-monopoly of secondary education gave it a quasi-monopoly of positions of leadership in the Republic as well. Avenues of social ascent did exist, but they were avenues of individual ascent, too narrow to bear much traffic. By traversing the narrow passageway between the primary school and the lycée, one might become a member of the dominant social class, but on that class's own terms. The educational system was a sort of self-propelled engine of social control, acting as a brake upon social mobility and as a counterweight to civic and political equality. It was one more means by which the working class could be held at arm's length from the chief beneficiaries of the Third Republic.

The movement for educational reform that arose at the end

of the First World War was an attempt to end this state of affairs. Structural reform was intended to open access to secondary and higher education to able members of those social classes—the peasantry and the working class—whose members had previously been excluded from it. Every child was to receive an education commensurate with his ability, without regard for his social origins. Clearly, it was an ambitious undertaking. The more radical proponents of reform believed that a change in the educational establishment would cause fundamental changes in society. To be sure, a call for the transformation of the educational system was a challenge to the existing balance of social forces in French society.

Whether higher education should be made accessible to all the nation's able citizens, or remain restricted to some of them, was a political decision to be made by Parliament. Under the Third Republic, educational reform required an effort to effect social change by political action. This strategy meant conflict between political parties and interest groups that held incompatible ideas of how French society should be arranged, of the function of education, of the nature of the relationship that should prevail between the society and its educational system, and indeed, of human destiny. Beneath the clash of ideologies, the conflicts of class interest, the claims made on behalf of the welfare of the nation, and the long-standing quarrel between church and state that inevitably made its way into the dispute, the fundamental question at issue was about the individual: should a child be enabled to make his way in a democratic society on the basis of his own merit, or should he not?

Chapter ii. The Genesis of the Reform Movement

> Offrir à tous les individus de l'espèce humaine les moyens
> de pourvoir à leurs besoins, d'assurer leur bien-être, de
> connaître et d'exercer leurs droits, d'entendre et de
> remplir leurs devoirs; assurer à chacun la facilité de
> perfectionner son industrie, de se rendre capable des fonc-
> tions sociales auxquelles il a le droit d'être appelé, de
> developper toute l'étendue des talents qu'il a reçus de la
> nature, et, par là, établir entre les Citoyens une égalité
> de fait et rendre réelle l'égalité politique reconnue par la
> loi. Tel doit être le premier but d'une instruction nationale
> et, sous ce point de vue, elle est pour la puissance publique
> un devoir de justice.
>
> —Condorcet

I N LATE 1917, General Pétain's headquarters stood in
Compiègne. In the best of times Compiègne offered little
excitement; in 1917 it must have been a dreary place indeed, when off-duty hours meant only endless boredom.
A number of officers who had been teachers in civilian life
belonged to Pétain's staff. Thrown together by the war, and
further linked by peacetime experience, these young men saw
each other often in their idle moments. Long walks on the
streets of Compiègne revealed a common anxiety about the
effects of the war on the school system. No one could tell how
the parts of the old system would fit together, once the war
ended, and while the fighting dragged on few people gave it
much thought. But the little group at Compiègne had an idea,
grown out of endless discussion, that it did not want to see
evaporate in the tobacco smoke of an officers' mess. On February 9, 1918, a manifesto appeared in the weekly *L'Opinion*
signed *Les Compagnons de l'université nouvelle*.

The manifesto expressed a fierce resolution sprung from
the anguish of the war: "Let the dead bury the dead. . . .
Let us not lose precious time poking in the ashes of the con-
flagration that suddenly destroyed the old order. Let us not
write history. Let us make it." Like many other combatants,

34

the Compagnons dreamed of a France resurrected through reform. How else, they wondered, could the horrendous blood-letting of the past four years be justified? The essayist and critic Jean Guéhenno, himself a combatant, spoke for a generation when he remarked: "Never perhaps had anyone been dealt or inflicted so much suffering. Now martyrdom is a great ground for belief. And on the morrow of the armistice, credulous men hoped for some miracle. Why should life not have the same triumphs as death? They assured themselves these battles marked the opening of a new era."[1]

The demands of war seem to highlight in an especially harsh and intensive way the inadequacies of an educational system. Indeed, there is a tendency to fix upon formal education more blame for deficiencies in military conduct than seems fairly its share. If officers displayed a lack of intelligence in the conduct of military operations, could it not be attributed to some defect in the universities? If men broke and ran under fire, was there not some grave deficiency in primary education? If the enemy won an engagement, did they not owe their cleverness to their superior educational system? Had not morale in rear areas something to do with the quality of civic instruction in the schools? All these questions had been raised before, in other wars. In the humiliating aftermath of the Franco-Prussian War, Ernest Renan had declared: "The inferiority of France has been especially intellectual; what we have lacked is not courage but intelligence."[2]

This time the war had been won, but never had the French paid such a price for victory. The number of combatants killed and missing in action exceeded 1,310,000, or 16 per cent of the men under arms, and about 1,100,000 of the survivors were invalids for life. But the intellectual and cultural life of the nation suffered even more than these figures suggested, for the death rate had been much higher among officers than among enlisted men. Of every 100 army officers in service, 19 had been killed; the ranks had lost 16 men out of every 100. The ablest

[1] Jean Guéhenno, *L'Evangile éternel; étude sur Michelet* (Paris, 1927), p. 9.
[2] *La Réforme intellectuelle et morale*, 3rd edn. (Paris, 1872), p. 95.

young men had gone to the slaughter first. Of the graduates of the Ecole polytechnique 833 were killed, and 230 students and graduates of the Ecole normale supérieure.[3]

After four years of war, to the Compagnons the prewar educational establishment seemed a house without windows, closed off from the country. Not content with minor repairs, the Compagnons wanted it razed, and a new one built in its place. For the creation of "a new French spirit," the manifesto declared, France needed a totally new educational system: new in "ideas, programs, methods, and recruitment."[4]

The Germans' desperate lunge in the spring of 1918 cut short the Compagnons' own offensive,[5] and scattered them to meet the new threat. Moments snatched during lulls in the fighting, the hasty exchange of letters and finally, the war's end, gave them time more fully to work out their proposals for reform.

In early 1919, having founded an association to carry on in peacetime the work begun at Compiègne, the Compagnons revealed their identities in *La Solidarité,* a minor educational monthly they acquired for the expression of their ideas on reform. While in military service they were forbidden by regulations to sign their own names to articles that appeared in the civilian press. Moreover, they wished to convey a sense of collective effort; their extensive use of architectural terms led them to call themselves "Compagnons," after the builders of the Middle Ages. Seven teachers of different ages, backgrounds and interests made up the group at Compiègne: Albert Girard, professor of history at the Lycée Chaptal, in Paris; Henri Luc, professor of philosophy at the lycée of Alençon; Jean-Marie Carré, *chargé de cours* in comparative literature at

[3] Alfred Sauvy, *Histoire économique de la France entre les deux guerres,* vol. 1, *De l'armistice à la dévaluation de la livre, 1918-1931* (Paris, 1965), 22-23. For a breakdown of French losses by occupation, see Sauvy, Annex 1, 442.

[4] *L'Opinion*, February 9, 1918.

[5] In a note in *L'Opinion*, March 30, 1918, the Compagnons apologized for the sudden interruption in the publication of their articles.

the faculty of letters of Lyon; two *Normaliens,* Pierre Doyen and Robert Vieux, members of the promotion of 1912; Jacques Duval, professor at a Catholic faculty; and Edmond Vermeil, an historian who became *maître de conférences* at the University of Strasbourg after the war. None was more than forty years old; the youngest was twenty-six.[6] They shared a professional interest in Germany, and it may have been their knowledge of German efforts at educational reform that encouraged them to study the French situation. For wartime Germany had seen the beginnings of a reform of primary education strikingly similar to the proposals the Compagnons made for France.[7] In any event, Vermeil and Carré together drafted the manifesto of February 9, 1918; Carré then submitted it to Jean de Pierrefeu, editor of *L'Opinion,* who immediately asked for a series of articles on educational reform. On the day the manifesto appeared, the Compagnons sent a letter to friends and colleagues soliciting their help in the campaign for reform. Thirty-eight replied, and these, together with the seven at Compiègne, regarded themselves as charter members of the association. At the time, the only well-known figure among the original forty-five Compagnons was Georges Duhamel,

[6] On the original Compagnons see J. M. Carré, "L'Histoire des Compagnons," *Les Compagnons de l'université nouvelle* (Paris, 1920), pp. 5-10; Charles-Edmond Perrin, "Témoignage d'amitié," in *Connaissance de l'étranger. Mélanges offerts à la mémoire de Jean-Marie Carré* (Paris, 1964), pp. 40-47; Bernard Lavergne, "In Memoriam: Edmond Vermeil," *L'Année politique et parlémentaire,* xxxvii (June 1964), 242-43; Robert Minder, "Edmond Vermeil," *Annales de l'université de Paris,* xxxiv, No. 4 (October-December 1964), 606-9; on graduates of the Ecole Normale Supérieure see the yearly publication *Association amicale de secours des anciens élèves de l'école normale supérieure. Annuaire* (Paris). The ages of the Compagnons who were lycée professors were found in *Ministère de l'instruction publique et des Beaux-Arts. Direction de l'enseignement secondaire; 2e bureau. Tableau du personnel des lycées de garçons par ordre d'ancienneté au 31 décembre 1920* (Paris, 1921).

[7] See V. H. Friedel, *Pédagogie de guerre allemande* (Paris, 1917), pp. 85-118.

winner of the *Prix Goncourt* in 1918; but several, such as Carré and Vermeil, later had distinguished careers as university professors.[8]

In the year following the war's end, the Compagnons published *L'Université nouvelle*,[9] an audacious two-volume work that ranged over the entire school system, proposed new solutions to old problems, refurbished older proposals, and asked questions that the prewar generation had not had to answer. The importance of the work can hardly be exaggerated; indeed, the proposals outlined in *L'Université nouvelle* were to determine the nature of the reform movement throughout the interwar period, to furnish it with both its aims and its vocabulary. It is not too much to say that the basic principles of the ongoing reform of French education can be traced to the Compagnons' remarkable book.

The prewar educational system, the Compagnons charged, stood on a condemned foundation of "centralization and anarchy, apparent orthodoxy and profound individualism."[10] In a world transformed by the war, the excessive intellectualism of the old system had to give way to the development of the whole man, "body . . . will, and mind,"[11] and to the cultivation of a "social sense" in the individual.[12] In order to ensure the peace and repair her losses, France had to exert a great collective effort. Long before the war, the rate of growth of the population had begun to lag. A whole generation of leaders had been cut down in the war: France no longer had an élite. Production was the major problem of the postwar era; the educational system should serve as the wellspring of the productive forces of the country.[13] The better to prepare the French people for an intensified international competition, and

[8] *La Solidarité*, February 15, 1919. The group had an impressive war record. Thirteen wore the *Légion d'honneur*, 22 had been wounded in action and 33 received citations. Raymond Thamin, "La Réforme de l'enseignement," *RDM*, xci, 6ᵉ période (1921), 382.

[9] *L'Université nouvelle*, 2 vols. (Paris, 1918-19).

[10] *L'Université nouvelle*, I, 62.

[11] *Ibid.*, I, 29.   [12] *Ibid.*, II, 8.   [13] *Ibid.*, I, 18.

to help them in their tasks as citizens, *"everyone must be taught."* Moreover, "the *best must be drawn from the crowd and put in their real place, which is the first."*[14]

The demand that "everyone must be taught" meant mass education; that "the best must be drawn from the crowd" called for the preservation of an intellectual élite. The Compagnons had raised a question fundamental to every democratic society. How could equality be reconciled with the preservation of natural superiority? The Compagnon's answer was to create a formula by means of which, they believed, the maintenance of an intellectual élite became the inevitable consequence of mass education. Their plan for reform was a response to the question Charles Péguy, that tortured conscience of the *Belle époque,* had posed before the war, in one of those great outpourings to which he was given: "Why inequality in instruction, before culture; why this social inequality; why this iniquity; why [is] higher education almost closed; why high culture forbidden to the poor, to the miserable, to the children of the people; if only secondary education were forbidden, it would perhaps be only a demi-evil and a demi-fault; but in France and in modern society secondary education is the nearly inevitable path by which one ascends to higher education; why this fundamental inequality, and what remedies?"[15]

In 1918, of course, the educational establishment remained as Péguy had known it, with its rigid distinction between the free public primary schools and secondary education, each functioning as a self-contained unit. Clearly, the Compagnons pointed out, such an arrangement was contrary to "common sense, justice, and the national interest."[16]

Inspired by the rough social equality of the trenches, the Compagnons called for an end to the isolation of the primary

[14] *Les Compagnons de l'université nouvelle,* p. 16. Emphasis in original.

[15] Quoted by the Compagnons in *L'Université nouvelle,* I, 22. Péguy's question first appeared in *Cahiers de la quinzaine, 2e cahier de la 6e série* (1904), p. viii.

[16] *L'Université nouvelle,* I, 22.

system from the lycée. They asked for the carry-over of the wartime Sacred Union into the peace: "fathers have kept watch in the same trenches; wherever it is feasible, their sons can certainly sit on the same school benches."[17] To take the place of the public primary school and the elementary classes of the lycée, unlike in programs, methods, teaching staff and social composition, the Compagnons proposed one school, the *école unique*: "the primary school for everyone, son of bourgeois, of workers or of peasants, the free and public primary school, become the obligatory base of all education."[18] Despite their talk about bourgeois and worker seated on the same bench, the Compagnons were not convinced in 1918 that all children should receive primary education in the same building. They appeared content to allow the elementary class of the lycée to operate separately from the primary school, provided its curriculum was the same.[19] To be sure, practical difficulties stood in the way of suppressing the elementary classes. Of course their suppression was the more radical measure; this point was to cause trouble among reformers later. At the outset, in any case, the Compagnons' notion of equality of educational opportunity rested on the assumption that the removal of structural barriers to advancement would enable all children, whatever their social origins, to begin a highly competitive race on an equal footing.

The Compagnons did not intend to limit themselves to giving all children the same primary education. The key phrase in Péguy's remark was that "secondary education is the nearly inevitable path by which one ascends to higher education." The point in giving all children an equal start was to give them an equal chance at the next step. No longer should the primary school be a "closed cycle." Its task was not to cram small heads full of encyclopedic information, but "to open

[17] *Ibid.*, I, 26.

[18] *Ibid.*, I, 22-24.

[19] See, for example, *Les Compagnons*, "Le Lycée et l'école primaire," *Revue universitaire*, XXVII, part 2 (October 1918), 174: "L'Ecole unique n'est pas forcément le local unique, du moins pour le moment."

minds.... It is a preparation, not an end in itself that is merely better than nothing."[20]

At the end of the single primary school, designed to ensure equality, came selection, that part of the Compagnons' formula which they believed would guarantee the preservation of natural intellectual superiority. The Compagnons intended that only the intellectually able should receive secondary education. By secondary education they meant not only the traditional humanistic path that led to the universities, but also technical training. On the basis of his aptitudes and interests, a child would be directed either toward the lycée or to a vocational school.[21] It might well be wondered whether the Compagnons considered these alternatives equally attractive. They confessed their greatest preoccupation was with the clientele of the lycée: "the access to the humanities of the entire [intellectual] élite, and nothing but the élite; such is our program."[22] Clearly, a greater number of children would enter the vocational school, and a minority would prepare for the university. Those who did not go on to some form of secondary school were to receive obligatory "post-school training," by which the Compagnons meant a kind of night course for young apprentices and peasants.[23]

In order to implement the process of selection, in their early work the Compagnons proposed to divide the primary school into two parts. At the first stage, for children from six to eleven, the new program followed the pattern of the old primary school, mainly reading, writing and arithmetic. Observation and testing during the second stage, from eleven to fourteen,

---

[20] *L'Université nouvelle*, I, 23-24.

[21] Just prior to the war, of 3,000,000 adolescents who had left school at the age of thirteen, only 150,000 had received some kind of vocational training; many of them did not attend state schools, but private establishments whose standards varied considerably. Decaunes, *Réformes et projets de réforme*, p. 63.

[22] Louis Cazamian [president of the Compagnons] "Les Problèmes de l'université nouvelle," *Revue internationale de l'enseignement*, LXXIV (1920), 133.

[23] *L'Université nouvelle*, I, 32-33.

were to determine what kind of secondary education a child received. Upon the completion of an exhaustive aptitude examination, those destined for the lycée were to leave primary school at the age of thirteen; those headed for vocational training would remain until the age of fourteen, when they would take the examination for the *Certificat des études primaires*. Schools established in the larger centers of population would both provide general education and offer the beginnings of vocational instruction.[24]

This early scheme underwent considerable modification at the hands of the Compagnons and other reformers. For the forging of links between primary and secondary education posed a complicated technical problem; it raised difficulties among reform groups that reflected not only serious pedagogical differences—on the psychology of learning, for example—but quite different social objectives as well. Some reformers sought justice in a way that equally ardent supporters of reform considered a threat to the preservation of an intellectual élite; and the seekers after justice came to suspect the motives of some of the reformist defenders of traditional classical culture.

The common primary school, free secondary education and selection based on merit were the mechanisms that were to set in motion the remaking of the educational system. They were only the beginning. The Compagnons proposed major changes in the curriculum of the lycée and the duration of secondary study; a sweeping reform of physical education programs, which had scarcely existed before the war; the adaptation of the universities to modern scientific research; a drastic reform of teacher education, which reflected and reinforced the distinction between the primary and secondary systems. These problems, however, are outside the scope of this study; they had much less political importance than the major supports upon which the Compagnons' reform rested: *école unique, gratuité, sélection*.

There was little in *L'Université nouvelle* that someone had

[24] *Ibid.*, ii, 59, 68-70.

not suggested before, and the Compagnons were the first to admit it.[25] During the Revolution Condorcet had proposed a plan for an educational system that offered free and unobstructed passage from one level to the next.[26] In the prewar years, a number of leftist deputies had drawn up private member's bills that bore a family resemblance to the Compagnons' proposals.[27] In the Ribot Committee inquiry of 1899, the social question had been a persistent undercurrent to the discussion on curricular reform. Even so conservative an educationalist as Octave Gréard had called for the destruction of the "artificial barriers" that separated primary from secondary education.[28] And the no less conservative Gabriel Hanotaux, noted historian and diplomat, had argued before the Ribot Committee that all children should attend a common primary school up to the age of fifteen, when a system of selections would set them on the path that best suited their abilities.[29] But remarks like Hanotaux's remained an undercurrent; most of the testimony before the Committee took up more narrow curricular matters. At least one visionary study had proposed virtually all the reforms the Compagnons advanced.[30] But these activi-

[25] Louis Cazamian, "Les Problèmes de l'université nouvelle," *Revue internationale de l'enseignement,* LXXIV (1920), 124.

[26] "Rapport au nom du comité de l'instruction publique," *Archives parlementaires de 1789 à 1860,* première série, XLII. April 20, 1792, 192-95; April 21, 1792, 227-45.

[27] See, for example, the bill sponsored by the Radical deputy Henri Hervieu and 78 others, "Proposition de loi tendant à instituer l'instruction intégrale par voie de concours, . . ." No. 830. *Annexe au procès-verbal de la séance du 11 juillet 1890. Chambre des Députés. 5e législature. Session de 1890. Impressions; projets de lois, propositions, rapports, etc.* (Paris, 1890), pp. 2-6. The bill did not, however, suggest changes in the existing structure of the system. I am indebted to Professor Peter Larmour for pointing this *proposition de loi* out to me.

[28] *Enquête sur l'enseignement secondaire. procès-verbaux des dépositions* (Paris, 1899), p. 2.

[29] *Ibid.,* p. 394.

[30] Duprat, "L'Ecole et la démocratie au XXe siècle," *Bulletin du comité des travaux historiques et scientifiques* (Paris, 1902), 37-102. See also Alexis Bertrand, *L'Enseignement intégral* (Paris, 1898).

ties had been very much a sideshow to the religious question that held the center of the political stage.

The Compagnons came along at just the right time, in just the right mood, with a provocative synthesis of older ideas on democratic educational reform. The leadership of the prewar republic had not seriously addressed itself to the issue because it had not been forced to do so. The war changed all that. The Compagnons understood there would be trouble unless the politicians made some effort to build a society fit for decent men and their children to live in. Their great contribution was to make precise, clear and relevant to their own time a set of disparate ideas on education. *L'Université nouvelle* reflected an awareness of the acceleration of social change. Like many of their contemporaries, the Compagnons acutely felt the war had been a watershed in the French experience: "This war entails the failure of the élites of the past, of these bourgeois élites—honorable, thrifty, prudent, right-thinking but not very efficient—who managed to get along somehow in the comfort of mediocre platitudes and in the security of their savings. . . . These élites formed the principal clientele of our lycées. They are fading away . . . the common people is the great revelation of the war."[31]

The Compagnons knew that a hard task lay ahead of them. In the founding statute of their association, they called for "the most active propaganda, inside and outside of the University, with a view to leading public opinion and parliament toward the total reform of education."[32] They were a small band, but at the outset numbers mattered less than the ability to express a complex technical system in simple terms that could catch and hold the public imagination, lure the politicians and attract the big organizations that made reform their business. *Ecole unique*, which in *L'Université nouvelle* referred only to the common primary school, quickly became synonymous with democratic educational reform, a stirring symbol for all the

[31] Les Compagnons, "Le Lycée et l'école primaire," *Revue universitaire*, xxvii, part 2 (October 1918), 178.

[32] "Statuts de l'association," *Les Compagnons de l'université nouvelle*, pp. 36-37.

proposals of the reform movement. It was to prove an unfortunate choice of words.[33]

Any proposal to alter the status quo in the French educational system had to confront the so-called school question. The relationship between the confessional schools and the public schools was like that between two adjoining but unfriendly states; trouble at the border aroused the defenders of each side. So bitter had disputes been in the past that the school question was referred to as a kind of endemic civil war. For the accomplishment of their reform, the Compagnons needed a *paix scolaire*. Here they faced a difficult task. No matter how intellectually acceptable many of their arguments may have been, they ran the danger of not being heard in the clamor touched off by a revival of the school question.

In order to allay the fears of Catholics, the Compagnons emphasized that by *école unique* they did not mean a state monopoly of education: "what is unique is the *type* of school."[34] But the Compagnons knew that a state school system free at all levels might threaten the existence of the confessional schools. Forced to rely on private sources of income, the confessional schools could not stretch their budgets to provide free schooling beyond the elementary level. Faced with a choice between a free state lycée and an expensive confessional *collège*, Catholic parents on modest incomes might feel compelled to send their children to the lycée. That dilemma raised the question of freedom of conscience, because the confessional schools existed in the first place to provide children the religious instruction forbidden in the secular state schools. The confessional school risked becoming the preserve of a plutocracy if the poorer students abandoned it in favor of the free state school. The confessional school might also become the refuge of those who opposed democratization of the state system, and fled the influx of the poor into the lycée. Such a re-

[33] Because the use of the equivocal term *école unique* to designate the entire reform led to endless confusion about its content and the aims of its partisans, the term will be left in French throughout this study.

[34] *L'Université nouvelle*, I, 27.

shuffling ran counter to the Compagnons' intentions; they sought to avoid a class distinction between the state and confessional schools. Critics might argue that a class distinction prevailed already, with the Church allied to the rich in a kind of mutual defense pact. Perhaps, answered the Compagnons. The point was to change it.[35]

The solution seemed to lie in giving subsidies to the Church schools.[36] If both the confessional and public schools were free, poor Catholic parents would not be tempted by the free lycée; nor would wealthy parents who imagined their offspring contaminated by mere contact with working-class boys find an antiseptic refuge for them in private schools. If the confessional schools were free, working-class boys would be found on their benches, too.

Anticlericals, or just plain anti-Catholics, the Compagnons conceded, might object that to subsidize the confessional school was to give aid to the enemy. The Compagnons too lightly dismissed that objection as a feeble old battlecry drowned out by the harmony of the Sacred Union. If the State professed a certain philosophical doctrine that it wished to impose upon the country, and against which the religious instruction of a church competed, they argued, then to subsidize the confessional school would be foolish indeed. But the State claimed neutrality, and therefore indifference, in matters of religion.[37]

[35] *Ibid.*, I, 70-74.

[36] *Ibid.*, I, 72. There is some uncertainty about the personal religious attitudes of the original Compagnons. The eminent professor Charles Andler, who claimed to have known them well, remarked that "They [the Compagnons] were all Catholics . . . or crypto-Catholic protestants." *Vie de Lucien Herr* (Paris, 1932), p. 257. But J. M. Carré, one of the authors of the manifesto, claimed that the group at Compiègne was of diverse religious beliefs. *Les Compagnons de l'université nouvelle*, p. 6. At any rate, in view of the anticlerical bias of the teaching profession, it seems quite likely that practicing Catholics were a minority of the Compagnons at the time they formed their association. This was after the publication of the articles in *L'Opinion* and the first volume of *L'Université nouvelle*.

[37] According to Article 1 of the Law of 9 December 1905 on the separation of Church and State. On this see Axel Freiherr von Campenhausen, *L'Eglise et l'état en France* (Paris, 1964), pp. 21ff.

True freedom, the Compagnons pointed out, demanded that there exist both a neutral state education, and a confessional education. If free state secondary education threatened the existence of confessional schools, the latter needed state aid. A democratic education had to be obligatory, for the ignorance of individuals weakened the nation. The existing school attendance law did not specify the kind of education a child had to receive; it only required him to receive one. Insofar as a confessional school fulfilled a public obligation imposed upon all citizens by the State, the Compagnons argued, that school should receive a subsidy; for a private function—that is, religious instruction—it had to provide its own funds. In educational policy the State occupied a position analogous to the one it took toward the railroads, where private companies that fulfilled a public function received subsidies.[38]

The two slim volumes the Compagnons published at war's end called for a new kind of struggle. At first, they rejected involvement in politics: "Above all, we want to be educators."[39] But, in a parliamentary democracy, realistic reformers had to turn to the parliament for satisfaction. They had to excite the public imagination, to call attention to their demand, among all the others clamoring for the voter's approval. They had to show the need for educational reform to conscientious deputies and senators and convince some of the others that support for reform was at least worth their while. For the complex task of making a reform work, they needed the confidence and support of educational technicians who could shape broad demands into intricate structural changes in the University. And, finally, they had to overcome the opposition.

They did not have far to look for it. In a divided nation, in which educational problems had long been intensely political, simply to pose the question of the democratic reform of the educational system guaranteed formidable opposition. The *école unique* challenged the status quo, which was enough to antagonize those who liked things the way they were. It struck at class privilege; rarely do people give up privilege without a fight. It threatened to rekindle a religious feud that had already

---

[38] *L'Université nouvelle*, I, 72.   [39] *Ibid.*, II, 3.

consumed too much energy. It incorporated demands left over from the past because opponents had had the strength to deny them, or because reformers had given up the struggle. The *école unique* promised no immediately tangible benefit to anyone, and behind the catch phrase stood technical proposals that were hard to understand, and boring besides. The Compagnons claimed an indifference to ideology, but the *école unique* clearly stemmed from the Revolutionary tradition. The Declaration of the Rights of Man and the Citizen had laid down that "All citizens . . . are equally admissible to all public dignities, offices and employments, according to their capacity, and with no other distinction than that of their virtues and talents."[40] The *école unique* was a means of carrying out that promise. To be sure, the Revolutionary tradition had never lacked for interpreters; the meaning of the tradition was itself an inexhaustible source of violent disagreement. Consequently, the *école unique* became a many-handled political weapon, and the Compagnons perfectly understood its ambiguousness, even if they claimed an indifference to politics: "An enlightened bourgeois, a realistic socialist profit equally by our pedagogy. For it prepares, if one wishes it, bourgeois regeneration, but no less it paves the way for the advent of socialist democracy. It is for the future to decide which."[41]

The Compagnons reached their first objective: they created a stir. Even with the war raging, their articles in *L'Opinion* had provoked nearly forty comments in the Parisian and provincial press.[42] The articles had strongly affirmed the need for reform, but had less clearly shown how the Compagnons proposed to go about it. Most commentators, while praising the generous sentiments of the Compagnons, refrained from unequivocal endorsement of their proposals.

Watchful defenders of the confessional school immediately

[40] Quoted in Georges Lefebvre, *The Coming of the French Revolution*, trans. R. R. Palmer, Vintage Books edition (New York, 1957), p. 179.

[41] *L'Université nouvelle*, II, 16.

[42] *La Solidarité*, February 19, 1919. There is a fairly extensive reproduction of these comments in the appendix to *L'Université nouvelle*, I.

took notice of any proposal that might upset the relationship between their schools and the state. What position should Catholics take toward the Manifesto of the Compagnons? Despite the claims of people who traded in political myths, French Catholicism had never been a monolith. Quarrels within the fold were often more bitter than disputes with outsiders. There existed a kind of pluralism of Catholic attitudes toward the ancient perplexities of spiritual-temporal, or theological-political relationships, and Catholics who took up one of these attitudes might mentally exclude from the Church Catholics who adopted another. For the doctrine of the Church clearly and emphatically declares what Catholics are forbidden to think politically, but it much less clearly indicates what they *are* to think. French theology has often been intensely political, and politics passionately theological; even the separation of political from religious concerns required a theological justification.[43] The idea for the *école unique* lay in a penumbral area where Catholics would inevitably collide with one another. It might conflict with Church doctrine on education, or it might not. That depended not only on what form the *école unique* took in legislation, or what its backers proposed, but also on how a particular faction or *tendance* within the Church looked at it.

For the moment, all that Catholics had to form an opinion on were the imprecise statements of the Compagnons, which appeared to include a favorable attitude toward confessional schools. Catholic writers applauded the spirit in which the Compagnons undertook to reform the University, but advised an attitude of reserve until the Compagnons made their posi-

[43] On this see Etienne Borne's excellent article, "Ethiques politiques des églises: le catholicisme," in René Rémond, ed., *Forces religieuses et attitudes politiques dans la France contemporaine* (Paris, 1965), pp. 9-26. See also R. Rémond, "Droite et gauche dans le catholicisme français," *Revue française de science politique*, VIII (1958), 529-44; "Politique et religion," *Esprit* (March 1958), entire number; "Catholiques de droite? catholiques de gauche?: Une grande enquête auprès de l'opinion catholique française," *Chronique sociale de France* (December, 1956), entire number.

tion on the confessional schools more precise.[44] In *Etudes,* the influential Jesuit bi-weekly, Father Alexandre Brou remarked that the Compagnons were quite vague about the nature of the new relationship they proposed to establish between the public and confessional schools: "They only say no subjection to political aims or to religious aims. Perhaps that is easier said than done."[45]

The desire of the Compagnons to extend the Sacred Union into peacetime was admirable, but some conservative Catholic observers found a disturbing philosophical outlook behind it. Did not the Compagnons risk becoming the purveyors of a kind of socialism when they demanded equal rights for equal minds?[46] Their equating of inequality with injustice was the kind of rhetorical nonsense that had always plagued democratic political philosophy.[47] The classical conservative justification of the status quo appeared early in the discussion on the *école unique,* and the theme underwent constant elaboration and variation: hierarchies of wealth and influence were an immutable law of nature.[48] To persuade humble workers and peasants that their native abilities might carry them to the highest places in the republic risked depleting the countryside and emptying the factories.[49] There were already enough *déclassés* in French society; the project of the Compagnons only threatened to multiply them.[50]

The central concern of most Catholic writers, however, was the confessional school. The Compagnons' demand for a free public school system, as long as their attitude toward confes-

---

[44] See, for example, Alexandre Brou, "L'Université nouvelle: un manifeste," *Etudes,* 157 (1918), 21, 25; Paul Dudon, "L'Instruction intégrale et l'école unique des compagnons," *Etudes,* 160 (1919), 27; T. Mainage, "L'Esprit nouveau à l'école," *Revue des jeunes,* xviii (1919), 664-72; Robert Valléry-Radot, "Les Compagnons de l'université nouvelle," *Revue des jeunes,* xvii (1918), 551.

[45] Brou, *Etudes,* 157 (1918), 35.

[46] Dudon, *Etudes,* 160 (1919), 27.

[47] Brou, *Etudes,* 157 (1918), 30.

[48] Dudon, *Etudes,* 160 (1919), 47.

[49] *Ibid.,* 34.　　　　　　　　　[50] Brou, *Etudes,* 157 (1918), 31.

sional schools remained nebulous, appeared to threaten the Catholic system. Catholics seized upon this point from the beginning, and it became one of the most bitterly contested issues in the struggle over the *école unique*. Father Paul Dudon flatly stated that free secondary education meant a decisive step toward a state monopoly, repeating the Compagnons' own admission that poor Catholic parents might feel compelled to send their children to the "Godless [state] school." Even if monopoly were not legislated, the progressive abandonment of the confessional school would bring the same result.[51]

But the Compagnons had, after all, extended a hand, and if their early proposals aroused mistrust among some Catholics, they received a guarded welcome from others. One young Catholic intellectual pointed out that Catholics were no longer to be "excommunicated" from the public life of the Third Republic, for the Compagnons called upon them to participate in the construction of the New University. Therefore, "these young rebels are far from frightening us; what they want to tear from the national tree is the enormous parasitic vegetation which embraces it, preys upon it, and masks its true figure . . . , its grace and its majesty."[52]

Reactions of most Catholic spokesmen to the early proposals of the Compagnons were necessarily sketchy. Besides, in the unsettled conditions of the war's end, the *école unique* made a very small cloud on the horizon. There was a comfortable distance between the manifesto of a few idealistic young soldiers and legislative action. Still, one had to be watchful.

The noted Catholic editor Jean Guiraud made it his particular duty carefully to follow any proposal for the reform of education. Guiraud had attended the great Parisian lycée, Louis-le-Grand, had graduated from the Ecole normale supérieure, and had taught history for a time in a public university. At the Ecole normale, Guiraud had been a "Tala,"[53] and a rapt auditor of the lectures of the "green Cardinal," Ferdinand

[51] Dudon, *Etudes*, 160 (1919), 38-39.

[52] Robert Valléry-Radot, "Les Compagnons de l'université nouvelle," *Revue des jeunes*, xviii (1918), 553.

[53] "Ceux qui von*T A LA* messe."

Brunetière, a leader of the Catholic intellectual renaissance. As an editor of *La Croix,* Guiraud made himself a specialist in the school question, and in the course of his career his pencil had acquired a fine polemical point.[54] *La Croix* served as one platform for his intransigent kind of politically conservative Catholicism. In addition, he had helped to found the Association catholique des chefs de famille, that sought "the revision of all laws which, drawn up against the Christian principle of the family, accelerate its decadence and with it the ruin of society."[55] Because *La Croix* had the largest circulation of any Catholic publication, and because Guiraud was an enterprising and tireless worker, ready to give a speech at a moment's notice, he quickly became the chief spokesman for the Catholic opposition to the *école unique.*

Guiraud had little trouble making up his mind about the early doctrine of the Compagnons. He regarded it as a "Trojan horse, for it is presented under a slightly enigmatic appearance." Certainly the Compagnons attacked real vices in the existing educational system. But precisely because Catholics could agree easily with the Compagnons' critique, they should avoid "giving blind adherence to their positive program." They had better pay attention to what underlay the seductive formulas. The great question of educational reform was still at the level of discussion, but if Catholics were not vigilant, "it is beside, beyond, and undoubtedly against us that this great movement of reform would unfold."[56]

Moreover, Catholics, led by Guiraud, had demands of their own. They sought public subsidies for private schools by means of a scheme called *répartition proportionnelle scolaire*—the division of public funds between public and private schools in

[54] Jean Guiraud, *Pourquoi je suis catholique* (Paris, 1928), passim.

[55] *Ecole et famille,* 1 (1919), 43. On the ACCF see R. Talmy, *Histoire du mouvement familial en France,* 2 vols. (Paris, 1962), 1, 152-56. The ACCF was founded in 1905, but needed a thorough reorganization in 1919, for which Guiraud was almost singlehandedly responsible. In fact, Guiraud published *Ecole et famille,* the association's postwar organ, with little help from anyone else.

[56] *La Croix,* October 26, 1918.

proportion to the number of pupils in each school. An old demand, it was revived by the Association catholique de la jeunesse française at its congress of 1913.[57] The climate seemed favorable at the end of the war to a campaign for subsidies to confessional schools. Just as the Sacred Union inspired the Compagnons, it favored Catholics, by forcing a truce in the religious quarrel that had previously occupied the center of the stage in French politics.[58] But if defenders of the confessional school saw in the favorable conditions of 1919 an opportunity to take the offensive, they did not ignore the menace of the embryonic movement for reform of the public school system.

The Société générale d'éducation et d'enseignement, long a champion of the Catholic schools, heeded the warnings of Jean Guiraud.[59] It took little cleverness to see that a demand for subsidies could serve equally well to counter the movement for reform and to improve materially the position of the confessional schools. The Société d'éducation demanded this form of financial aid in a declaration of early 1919 that made clear its position on one aspect of the *école unique*: "In the event that 'free tuition' should be imposed on public schools of any order whatever, the Société générale d'éducation et d'enseignement demands, in the name of equity, an allocation from the

[57] *La Répartition proportionnelle scolaire. VIIe Congrès social national de l'A.C.J.F. tenu à Caen, le 18, 19, 20 avril 1913*. 3rd edition (Paris, n.d.).

[58] For the effect of the Sacred Union on the old religious struggle, see Adrien Dansette, *Histoire religieuse de la France contemporaine*, rev. edn. (Paris, 1965), pp. 710-12; and A. Latreille and R. Rémond, *Histoire du catholicisme en France*, III (Paris, 1962), 556-63.

[59] Founded in 1868, the Société d'éducation led the struggle in the 1880's against the establishment of the secular public primary school. For years the society was a kind of fief of Emile Keller, its founder; upon his death the presidency passed to his son, Colonel Prosper Keller. See Yves de La Brière, "Les Garanties de la liberté d'enseignement," *Etudes*, 171 (1922), 613-18. In intransigence and tenacity, Colonel Keller was Jean Guiraud's equal. Allied with Guiraud, he led the society into battle for *répartition proportionnelle scolaire* and against the *école unique*.

State, for free schools of the same order, prorated according to the number of pupils."[60]

Neither the demand for *répartition proportionnelle scolaire* nor for the *école unique* could be satisfied without action from parliament. The supporters of each believed that their chances for success depended upon great public campaigns that would exert sufficient pressure on senators and deputies to force action. And the necessary over-simplifications of public debate on complicated and sensitive issues threatened to obscure real problems that needed solution.

IF MOST commentators greeted the Manifesto of the Compagnons warily, one young politician showed no hesitation. On February 11, 1918, only two days after the appearance of their first article, Edouard Herriot sent a letter of support to the Compagnons.[61] Their proposals matched the former lycée professor's interests, and their undertaking suited his enormous energy. Herriot knew what it meant to be a poor student; scholarships had put him through the Ecole normale supérieure. The broad learning what was the foundation of his skill in debate had helped to push him into the front rank of the Radical party. He knew a good political idea when he saw one. Moreover, he had already acted along the lines suggested by the Compagnons. As mayor of Lyon before the war, Herriot established scholarships to open the local secondary schools to the best students from the primary schools.[62] Before the Compagnons published their Manifesto, Herriot had called upon the University to lead a renaissance of French energies: "In order to renovate a severely stricken country, education in France will offer to take its part in the common task. Should it not even direct that task?"[63]

[60] *Bulletin de la société générale d'éducation et d'enseignement*, 1 (1919), 283.

[61] J.-M. Carré, "L'Histoire des compagnons," *Les Compagnons de l'université nouvelle*, p. 8.

[62] Michel Soulié, *La Vie politique d'Edouard Herriot* (Paris, 1962), pp. 20, 39. On Herriot, see also P. O. Lapie, *Herriot* (Paris, 1967).

[63] "Le Rôle de l'école," *L'Ecole et la vie*, 1 (1917), 5. *L'Ecole et la*

By 1919, Herriot had made the Compagnons' doctrine his own. In a work entitled *Créer,* he undertook to provide the disjointed Radical party with a campaign machine retooled to meet the new demands of postwar politics. It is hard to say how much he borrowed directly from the Compagnons. In its outlines, however, the reform Herriot envisaged closely resembled theirs. As the Compagnons did, he argued that all children should go to the same primary school, and that secondary education should be reserved for the best students. He denied that the *école unique* implied a state monopoly of education. Of course he made the social aims of the Compagnons more politically incisive. Herriot regarded the *école unique* as a means of social reconciliation, and he held out its promise to the working class—a part of the electorate that doubtless made a good many Radical party workers sleep fitfully: "We will not have the right to invite the workers to consider themselves members of the common family as long as we have not put our children and their children side by side. . . . If the French people do not have the clairvoyance and the courage to assure regular social advancement by work and knowledge, we will lose any right to protest against revolutionary demands."[64]

With Herriot in their ranks, educational reformers had an ally who could lead the struggle in the political arena. If his emotional oratorical style sometimes spilled over into a kind of sentimental demagoguery, that was not necessarily a liability for advocates of change. In postwar France, the *école unique* appeared to be well worth the time of the Radical party.

For if the Compagnons called attention to the need for educational reform in a provocative manner, much of their program fitted in neatly with established Radical doctrine. The great ancestor, Léon Gambetta, had demanded in the Belleville

---

vie was founded in 1917 specifically to urge reform of the educational system, "for a closer union between the school and life," as the editors put it. The Compagnons met a warm reception from this professional journal.

[64] Edouard Herriot, *Créer,* 2 vols. (Paris, 1919), II, 136-38; 157-58.

Program of 1869 that the gates of the University be opened to the people. "Free, secular and obligatory primary instruction" had been the great republican accomplishment of the 1880's; "competition between the best minds for admission to higher courses, free as well,"[65] remained a hope. When the Radical party itself, suffering from one of its chronic attacks of doctrinal vagueness, had sought to reassert its principles at the Nancy congress of 1907, the party declaration had stated that "all the children of the people have the right to a complete education, according to their aptitudes."[66]

Herriot had served as *rapporteur* of the Radical program of 1907. In 1919 he took over the leadership of an enfeebled party. For the time being, at least, anticlericalism, on which the Radicals had made their political fortunes, counted for little against the Sacred Union.[67] At the party congress of 1919, held in view of the coming national elections, the Radicals struggled to build a platform for the postwar era. The declaration rephrased the 1907 position on education: "It is necessary to guarantee to everyone the encouragement of merit, without respect to conditions of fortune." Specifically, the party demanded the suppression of the elementary classes of the lycée.[68]

[65] The Belleville Manifesto is reprinted in Claude Nicolet, *Le Radicalisme* (Paris, 1957), p. 23.

[66] *Ibid.*, p. 50. Although the Radicals never had much interest in theory, the important place education held in Radical thought is exemplified in such works as Jules Simon, *La Politique radicale* (Paris, 1869); E. Vacherot, *La Démocratie* (Paris, 1860); F. Buisson, *La Politique radicale* (Paris, 1908); Léon Bourgeois, *Solidarité* (Paris, 1896); *L'Education de la démocratie française* (Paris, 1887); *Essai d'une philosophie de la solidarité* (Paris, 1902). See also J.E.H. Hayward, "Educational Pressure Groups and the Indoctrination of the Radical Ideology of Solidarism," *International Review of Social History*, VIII (1963), 1-17.

[67] See, for example, François Goguel, *La Politique des partis sous la IIIe République*, 3rd edn. (Paris, 1958), p. 219.

[68] *Le Radical*, September 23, 1919. There is no complete collection of stenographic reports of the congresses of the Radical party in any of the public libraries in Paris. One must therefore rely on the party press. *Le Radical* by 1919 expressed the views of the extreme right wing of the party.

Nevertheless, the declaration was a step backward even from Belleville, for it shied away from the question of an entirely free school system.

But vague declarations were a long-standing Radical practice. In an important campaign speech, Herriot more clearly showed how Radical support of educational reform could help to ease the party's adjustment to postwar politics. The purely political era of the republic was closed, Herriot remarked; the economic era had just opened. New tasks required a new education to prepare for them. Therefore, the Radical party had to "put the recasting of education in the first rank of its program." Economically wasteful class education was a scandal that had to cease, for "the ideal of a democracy is ascent through knowledge."[69]

As party leader, Herriot could wield considerable influence in a campaign for educational reform. But the Radicals' real schoolmaster remained Ferdinand Buisson, who had been Jules Ferry's chief assistant at the ministry of public instruction before Edouard Herriot entered primary school.[70] Buisson was seventy-seven at the end of the war, a wizened little man with pince-nez. He managed to be venerable ancestor and active politician at the same time. His symbolic importance, his technical understanding of the French educational system, and his political connections could contribute mightily to a reform movement. Buisson carried the message of the *école unique* to the Ligue de l'enseignement.

Like Buisson, the Ligue de l'enseignement could boast that

[69] *Le Radical*, October 17, 1919.

[70] As inspector-general of public instruction and director of primary education, Buisson helped draw up the primary school laws of the 1880's; an ardent Dreyfusard, he was a founder of the Ligue des droits de l'homme; as a deputy, he had a hand in suppressing the religious teaching orders, and he headed the parliamentary commission on the Separation of Church and State. He received the Nobel Prize for Peace in 1927. *Dictionnaire de biographie française*, VIII (Paris, 1956), cols. 645-46. No biography of this important Radical-Socialist politician exits. A Protestant by origin, and a pacifist, Buisson had been so heavily engaged in so many great Republican battles that he had himself become a kind of Republican institution.

it had been republican before the founding of the republic. Founded by Jean Macé late in the Second Empire, the League was the champion of public education, the "indefatigable propagandist of instruction and the secular school."[71] It had gradually declined after its great victory in the fight for free public primary schools in the 1880's, and had become moribund by the end of the war. Perhaps the militants of the League thought that the *école unique* might give it new life.[72]

At the first postwar congress of the League, held in Paris on September 23–24, 1919, Albert Girard, speaking for the Compagnons, shared the platform with Ferdinand Buisson on "The New Orientation of Education in France." Buisson urged the League to adopt the general principles of the Compagnons and to undertake a great campaign to bring the *école unique* to the attention of public opinion.[73] Though he had reservations about some aspects of the Compagnons' doctrine, Buisson praised their courage, and pointedly hoped that "the bourgeoisie was listening" to what they said.[74] He expressed dis-

[71] Clause Bellanger, *La Ligue française de l'enseignement* (Paris, 1938), p. 7. For an outline of the history of the Ligue, see Ozouf, *L'Ecole, l'église et la république*, p. 275. A study of this important republican pressure group remains to be made. An examination of the composition of its membership and its links with the Radical party would be particularly helpful for the period 1871-1914. The League had close ties with Freemasonry, too. See Hayward, *International Review of Social History*, VIII (1962), 5-9.

[72] In 1924, the League was to reorganize itself into the Confédération générale des oeuvres laïques. Some critical observers believed that the League's continuing ties with the Radical party made members as interested in place-holding and "traffic in indulgences" as in good works. See, for example, Pierre Frédérix, *L'Etat des forces en France* (Paris, 1935), p. 154.

[73] *La Ligue de l'enseignement depuis la guerre, novembre 1918-novembre 1920* (Paris, n.d.), p. 151. Stenographic reports of most interwar congresses of the League cannot be found in public libraries in Paris. The national headquarters of the League, 3 rue Recamier, Paris, possesses an incomplete collection of reports, a good share of its papers having been burned during the German Occupation of 1940-44.

[74] *Ibid.*, p. 141.

appointment at the failure of his own party clearly to favor a system free at all levels, and praised the educational program of the Confédération générale du travail.[75] At Buisson's urging, the Ligue de l'enseignement voted a resolution demanding free access to secondary and higher education for everyone who had the ability to profit from it, and called for an increase in the number of trade schools.[76]

Buisson's praise for the educational position of the CGT should have gone to Ludovic Zoretti. A *normalien,*[77] and mathematics professor in the science faculty of the University of Caen, Zoretti was a militant syndicalist and member of the Socialist party. To carry syndicalism into the upper reaches of the educational system, he founded the cumbersomely titled Fédération de l'enseignement aux 2e et 3e degrés, better known as the Zoretti Federation.[78] In 1918 he published *L'Education,* a book that, save for its more Leftist outlook, strongly resembled

[75] *Ibid.,* p. 151. Paul Lapie, director of primary education in the ministry of public instruction, and a member of the Radical party, followed Buisson on the rostrum. Lapie did not share Buisson's enthusiasm for the *école unique,* which he considered "a fairly ordinary and unimportant reform" underneath its revolutionary appearance. All it amounted to was the suppression of the elementary classes of the lycée (p. 196). Nonetheless, Lapie was soon to propose a reform remarkably similar to that of the Compagnons published under the pseudonym André Duval, "Esquisse d'une réforme générale de notre enseignement national," *Revue pédagogique,* LXXX (1922), 79-101.

[76] *La Ligue de l'enseignement depuis la guerre,* p. 171.

[77] There is need for a study that examines the relationship between the Ecole normale supérieure and politics under the Third Republic. Why, for example, did so many former students of the Ecole normale become political activists? For an impressionistic answer, see Albert Thibaudet, *La République des professeurs* (Paris, 1927). For a hostile view of this relationship see Hubert Bourgin, *De Jaurès à Léon Blum, L'Ecole normale et la politique* (Paris, 1938). On the role of the *normaliens* within the educational system itself, see the forthcoming Ph.D. dissertation of Richard Seabold, "Normaliens Fonctionnaires in the Lycées and Faculties of France, 1870-1918," University of California, Los Angeles.

[78] Perhaps the short form pleased Zoretti. A natural bent toward

L'Université nouvelle.[79] But the book also gave an early demonstration of the ambiguity of the *école unique*. For if there were certain broad principles on which the parties and pressure groups of the Left could agree, these same principles concealed others that could cause major trouble among reformers.[80]

Zoretti made his own position clear: "We are going to undertake a constructive study of the school system in the name of socialist principles."[81] Although he insisted on a socialist framework, the Compagnons still could have built their New University on Zoretti's scaffold of 1918. "It is for non-socialists that I am writing," he remarked. "I have tried to remain within the realm of immediate possibilities."[82] Like the Compagnons, Zoretti called for a common primary education, a diversified secondary education for those who could profit from it,[83] a school system free at all levels.[84] But he applied a distinctively syndicalist solution to the problem of a state educational monopoly. Zoretti professed no confidence in the bourgeois state, which he defied "to formulate a doctrine acceptable to the masses for an extended period." Besides, he did not think the question of great importance, and pointed out that the competition of the confessional school gave a healthy stimulus to the public school.[85]

---

self-importance was strengthened by his acute myopia, which made him appear more arrogant than he really was. Zoretti's intense pacifism took him down a dangerous path. Convicted of collaboration with the Germans, he died in prison in 1948. (Conversation of the author with a close associate of Zoretti's, October 18, 1965.)

[79] Zoretti and the Compagnons exchanged reviews of their respective books. Zoretti remarked that "We are truly in agreement, as much as one can be," and A. Micquelard, for the Compagnons, noted that "The points of contact are . . . numerous between M. Zoretti's ideas and ours." See Zoretti's "Lettre aux compagnons," *Revue du mois*, xx (June 1919), 196-99, and in the same issue, A. Micquelard, "Un Livre de M. Zoretti sur l'éducation," pp. 191-96.

[80] For the moment, Zoretti questioned the wisdom of granting subsidies to confessional schools. *Revue du mois*, xx (1919), 197.

[81] Ludovic Zoretti, *L'Education* (Paris, 1918), p. 131.

[82] *Ibid.*, p. xiv. [83] *Ibid.*, p. 138. [84] *Ibid.*, p. 151. [85] *Ibid.*

Probably few union delegates paid much attention to Zoretti when he appeared before the Congress of the CGT in 1919. Distracted by troubles that soon divided them against each other, and perhaps still dispirited by the disastrous metal workers' strike of that year, the delegates approved Zoretti's report without debate. Fernand Pelloutier[86] himself might have written the introductory statement, which dismissed the "outdated" educational system of the Third Republic, that had "only substituted a dogma of the State for the dogma of the Church and was simply preoccupied with maintaining the working class under the tutelage of the bourgeois class."[87] But the stuffiest bourgeois republican in the Ligue de l'enseignement might have accepted the CGT's major demand: "the absolute right for all children to have access to the highest degrees of culture, if their aptitudes are sufficient."[88] The CGT parted from the Ligue de l'enseignement only when it called for raising the school-leaving age to sixteen, which Zoretti called "the essential demand."[89]

Like the CGT, the Socialist party faced grave problems over the conclusions it should draw from the war and the Russian Revolution. That terrible decision interfered with hard thought about the problems of postwar France. The committee charged with drawing up an electoral platform could not agree on a common program. A minority report rejected the politics of reform.[90] But the will of Léon Blum, a newcomer to the party, prevailed. Yet another *normalien,* converted to socialism by Lucien Herr, librarian of the Ecole normale, Blum claimed that his interest in politics had been awakened at the age of

[86] On Pelloutier, see especially Alan Spitzer, "Anarchy and Culture: Fernand Pelloutier and the Dilemma of Revolutionary Syndicalism," *International Review of Social History,* VIII (1963), 379-88.

[87] *Confédération générale du travail. Compte-rendu des travaux. XXᵉ congrès national corporatif tenu à Lyon du 15 au 21 septembre 1919* (Paris, 1919), p. 326.

[88] *Ibid.,* p. 328.

[89] *Ibid.,* p. 328.

[90] Georges Lefranc, *Le Mouvement socialiste sous la IIIᵉ République* (Paris, 1963), p. 221.

fourteen, on reading that "fortune is hereditary, but intelligence is not."[91] Perhaps nothing could better have said what the *école unique* was all about.

Blum acutely sensed the vast social and economic changes effected by the war, and he meant the majority report to take them into account. Trying desperately to check the intrusion into the SFIO of notions borrowed from the Russian experience, Blum sought to preserve the idea of social revolution and at the same time to construct an immediate electoral program.[92] Blum and his co-authors intended to prepare the socialist order within bourgeois society. One step along the road was "a single department of national education, freely accessible at all degrees."[93]

When Blum rose to defend the majority report at the extraordinary party congress of April 21, 1919, he hurried through most of the section on "material and moral reparations," but he stopped at the question of national education, "for I believe it constitutes, in certain respects, a novelty and an original feature in the program of the party."[94] In fact,

[91] The remark was made by a character in Emile Augier's play, *Les Effrontés*. Léon Blum, "L'Idéal Socialiste," *Revue de Paris*, XXXI (May 1924), 93. The most recent biography of Blum—probably the best in any language—is Joel Colton, *Léon Blum: Humanist in Politics* (New York, 1966). For an excellent thumbnail sketch of Blum see Annie Kriegel's editorial comments in *Le Congrès du Tours, 1920; naissance du parti communiste français* (Paris, 1964), pp. 99-101.

[92] On this program see Annie Kriegel, *Aux Origines du communisme français, 1914-1920: contribution à l'histoire du mouvement ouvrier français*, 2 vols. (Paris, 1964), I, 327-30. Madame Kriegel observes that without reference to this "remarkable document . . . one cannot understand the political and economic thought of the French left between the wars." See also Robert Wohl, *French Communism in the Making, 1914-1924* (Stanford, 1966).

[93] *L'Humanité*, October 28, 1919.

[94] Léon Blum, *Commentaires sur le programme d'action du parti socialiste. Discours prononcé au congrès national extraordinaire, le 21 avril 1919* (Paris, 1933), p. 15. Because Blum faced a not entirely friendly audience, he probably realized that to many of the delegates, the majority report seemed an absurdly uneasy juxtaposition of reform

Blum considered the question so important that he believed "one could accomplish a large part of the social revolution solely through education and instruction."[95] He demanded a common rule for all so that "each child, whatever his birth, takes in the social army the exact post for which his personal temperament destines him." Moreover, he claimed that a common rule would act not just in the interest of the proletariat, but "in the interest of culture itself."[96] In his remarks on education Blum demonstrated his conviction that revolution did not require the building of barricades in the streets. He received an ovation, but the people who fervently believed in barricades looked ahead to the next party congress.

AMID THE excitement of the aftermath of war, demands for educational reform joined a whole catalogue of unfinished tasks that confronted a weary parliament and people. The Compagnons most dramatically sounded the call; perhaps the more optimistic among them believed that in the great movement of social idealism that was sweeping France some of their proposals, at least, stood a chance of passing quickly into law.[97] The two great political parties of the Left made demands that roughly matched the proposals of the Compagnons. In the case of the Radical party, the direct influence of the Compagnons on men like Herriot was clear. The once influential Ligue de l'enseignement had listened to the Compagnons; Zoretti's declaration to the CGT echoed their hopes; had Léon Blum been a staff officer at Compiègne, he might well have been a Compagnon.

---

and revolution. Though many of the points of the program obviously implied nationalization of the forces of production, which the extreme left-wing of the party opposed, Blum was careful never to mention the word, as Georges Lefranc notes in *Le Mouvement socialiste*, p. 222.

[95] Of course this remark raised a clamor. Blum, *Commentaires*, p. 15. Clearly, Blum was the intellectual heir of the great Jean Jaurès. For Jaurès' analogous views on education, see Harvey Goldberg, *The Life of Jean Jaurès* (Madison, 1962), pp. 84-89.

[96] *Commentaires*, p. 15.

[97] See Goguel, *Politique des partis*, p. 206.

But all the declarations were pretty vague. All agreed that there should be some kind of equality of opportunity in education. But none bothered to define just what "equality of opportunity" meant. It became abundantly clear later that none of the interested parties meant quite the same thing. Not all the declarations included so broad a demand as free secondary education. The Radicals hedged on that point. The Socialists' demand for "a single department of national education," phrased to meet necessities of the moment, left itself open to all sorts of interpretations. The program of the CGT, except for its demand to raise the school-leaving age, was little more specific. The Compagnons had shown in considerable detail how they thought equality could be reconciled with excellence, but had left a flank exposed on the Church-State problem. Besides, they were a tiny band of obscure teachers.

Nevertheless, the two largest parties of the Left carried demands for educational reform into the elections of 1919. The Socialists refused to form an electoral alliance with any other party; the Radicals fought among themselves; the CGT stayed out of the struggle. For once, the Right organized, behind the lurid placard of a Bolshevik with a knife between his teeth. The Left lost, and for the next four years a different group of men, with quite different ideas about educational reform, was to control the government.

CHAPTER III. The *Ecole Unique* under the Bloc National: Ancients, Moderns and Monarchists

> . . . il n'y a pas de question particulière qui puisse être résolue si l'on ne s'est entendu sur une philosophie générale.
>
> —JEAN JAURÈS

THE COLLECTIVE euphoria of the return to peace faded as men returned to private difficulties and the burden of private sorrows. On November 16, 1919, electors chose a new Chamber of Deputies, balanced further to the right than any since 1871. A new electoral law, a peculiar mixture of proportional representation and the majority principle, gave an advantage to electoral coalitions. The center-right Alliance démocratique called for an anticollectivist coalition, a *bloc national,* that momentarily attracted the Radicals, until they realized that no limits had been fixed to the right wing of the coalition. Cut off from their left by the Socialists' self-imposed isolation, the Radicals suffered an electoral disaster. The Socialists fared little better. The Bloc National took two-thirds of the seats in the new Chamber.[1] To educational reformers, the elections were a bitter disappointment.

For educational reform was not the sort of issue that could swing an election even in the best of times. Reformers had to depend upon the election of a parliamentary majority sympathetic to their aims; but so long as the two large parties of the left were divided against each other, as they were in 1919, the outlook for reform was dismal. Unable to expect much

---

[1] Goguel, *Politique des partis,* pp. 215-17; Bonnefous, *Histoire politique,* II, 63-70. In the elections of 1914, the Radicals had won 288 seats; in 1919 they fell to 138. The Socialists dropped from 101 deputies in 1914 to 72 in 1919. From left-center to right, the new Chamber counted 376 deputies.

65

action from the Bloc National, reformers had to continue, and to expand, their propaganda efforts outside parliament.[2]

Soon after the elections, the Compagnons felt obliged to alter their position on aid to confessional schools. Even before they published the second volume of *L'Université nouvelle*, they had apparently had second thoughts about the political wisdom of favoring subsidies. At their first general assembly, they resolved that the relationship between the confessional and public schools could be "arranged in rather different practical formulas."[3] Objections to subsidies continued, however, from quarters otherwise quite sympathetic to the Compagnons.

The well-known historian, Alphonse Aulard, denied that subsidies to confessional schools might help to resolve the troublesome school question, as the Compagnons claimed; instead, they would exacerbate it. Aulard, who had edited the papers of the Committee of Public Safety, was a kind of Jacobin himself, and a notorious anticlerical. He considered anticlericalism inseparable from true republicanism. Aulard enjoyed a good deal of prestige in the Radical party, and in the Radical press he asked the Compagnons for "clarification" of their position on subsidies to confessional schools.[4]

Louis Cazamian, president of the Compagnons, and a professor in the Sorbonne, immediately replied to Aulard: "Today we are limiting ourselves to applying our program within the framework of the existing regime." Gone was the idea for subsidies to confessional schools: "This part of the Compagnons' doctrine . . . has fallen like a dead branch from a tree."[5]

By dropping their support for subsidies, the Compagnons removed a barrier that held off possible allies on the left. But the decision was an admission that the effort to resolve the

[2] One commentator, noting the vagueness of promises on educational reform, observed that electoral programs contained not the briefest mention of how reform could be carried out. *L'Ecole et la vie*, May 29, 1920.

[3] *La Solidarité*, May 19, 1919.

[4] *L'Ere nouvelle*, January 4, 1920. *L'Ere nouvelle* was a new Radical newspaper, later considered to reflect the opinion of Edouard Herriot.

[5] *L'Ere nouvelle*, January 12, 1920.

troublesome school question had failed; and Cazamian knew that an attachment to the traditional left had its liabilities: "We've centered ourselves on the left. But have we done so without offending the preferences or ideas of any among us? Of course we hope not, but how can we be sure?"[6]

For the Compagnons' decision against subsidies allowed conservative Catholics like Jean Guiraud to claim that they had been right all the time: the *école unique* was a Trojan horse, constructed by all the forces that "conspire against the Church and contemporary society": Bolsheviks, Protestants, Freemasons, Radicals, Socialists and Jews.[7] Moreover, Catholics who associated with the Compagnons were surely in league with these forces.[8] Apparently the older generation of Aulard and Guiraud had prevailed over the younger generation of the Compagnons.

On June 10, 1920, when Edouard Herriot rose in the Chamber to advocate social reconciliation through educational reform,[9] most deputies probably had vividly in mind the great railroad strike that had just ended. As *rapporteur* on the budget for public instruction, Herriot had a vantage point from which to open the post-election campaign for the *école unique*. Herriot knew his suggestions had little chance of being acted upon by a conservative majority overwhelmed by other problems and disinclined to favor the *école unique*. But at least they were widely reported in the press[10] and, as *rap-*

[6] *La Solidarité*, April 15, 1920.

[7] *La Croix*, March 27, 1920.

[8] *Ibid*. Guiraud singled out Robert Valléry-Radot as an example of Catholics who foolishly lent their support to the Compagnons. Valléry-Radot replied that he entirely shared Guiraud's fears; the good intentions of the Compagnons had been thwarted by men like Aulard, the "gros potentats de la République laïque." *La Croix*, April 16, 1920.

[9] *Journal officiel de la république française. Débats parlementaires: Chambre* (1920), pp. 1984-89. Henceforth cited as *J.O.Ch.*

[10] *La Solidarité*, June 16, 1920; *Le Temps*, June 12, 1920; *L'Ere nouvelle*, June 11, 1920; *Le Radical*, June 13, 1920; *L'Oeuvre*, June 11, 1920. See also A. Darlu, "Le Budget de l'instruction publique devant la chambre," *Revue politique et parlementaire*, cv (1920), 15-26.

porteur, Herriot was able to note each year the Bloc National's inaction on the *école unique*—though he might have been chagrined had there been some action.

The same majority that was lamented by democratic educational reformers gave hope to the partisans of *répartition proportionnelle scolaire.* One bishop calculated that the new Chamber held over 200 deputies who could be considered sympathetic to Catholic demands.[11] But a specifically Catholic program stood little chance of success, as long as Catholic deputies remained unorganized. Past efforts at organization had failed, because of political antagonisms that a common religious conviction could not resolve.[12] Nevertheless, Jean Guiraud believed that the single issue of subsidies to confessional schools could unite Catholics and still leave them free to disagree on whatever else they wished. Catholic deputies had to forget the "excessive timidity that their past defeats had given them," and to take advantage of the religious truce imposed by the Sacred Union.[13]

It was true that the religious question had slipped into the background in the election of 1919. But fewer than thirty of the deputies elected to the Chamber had clearly spoken out in favor of subsidies to confessional schools.[14] And most of them, like Léon Daudet, of the Action française, were monarchists, beyond the pale of the Bloc National. The old alliance of traditionalist conservatism and Catholicism was the liability inherent in Jean Guiraud's scheme. Catholics had to count on picking up enough votes in the Chamber from a coalition of parties of the Right in order to make a strong demonstration

[11] Mgr. Caillot, bishop of Grenoble. *Documentation catholique,* III (1920), 165. Henceforth cited as *D.C.*

[12] See, for example, Alexander Sedgwick, *The Ralliement in French Politics* (Cambridge, Mass., 1965).

[13] *La Croix,* June 15, 1920.

[14] *Ecole et famille,* I (December 1919), 89-90. I have checked Guiraud's figures against the official "Barodet" [*Rapport fait au nom de la commission chargée de réunir et de publier les programmes electoraux des candidats aux élections législatives du 16 novembre 1919* (Paris, 1920)] henceforth cited as *Barodet,* with the relevant date.

in favor of *répartition proportionnelle scolaire,* if not to pass it outright.

But if the Bloc National was united against the Bolsheviks (a term which grew to include almost anyone conservatives did not like), it was far from united on the religious question. The Bloc was a coalition of two distinct traditions of conservatism. One component, the Fédération républicaine, contained a large number of Catholics who had made their peace with the republic, but who were nonetheless vigilant in the defense of religious interests. On the other hand, the Alliance démocratique, and some splinter groups like the Républicains de gauche, best represented by Raymond Poincaré, were resolutely laic, firmly attached to the traditions of the founders of the Third Republic.[15] A vague compromise on *laïcité* concealed the fissure between these two groups during the elections of 1919,[16] but the fissure threatened to reappear if anyone brought up the question in its most sensitive form, as Jean Guiraud and his allies intended to do.

For the demand for subsidies required a revision of the school laws. And if the war had blurred some of the old distinctions between right and left, *laïcité,* in the form of the school question, could still bring the dividing line sharply into focus.

If Catholics looked upon the *école unique* as an underhanded effort to bring about a state monopoly of education, the anticlerical left considered *répartition proportionnelle scolaire* simply one more maneuver calculated to reassert the political influence of the Catholic Church. The religious cleavage reinforced the division between those who supported a democratic reform of the University and those who opposed it. Reform required a middle ground upon which differences could be reconciled, but that middle ground was hard to find when differences were made into mutually exclusive systems.

The first confrontation in the Chamber over subsidies to Catholic schools was to come in early 1921. There had been

[15] See René Rémond, *La Droite en France,* 2nd edn. (Paris, 1963), pp. 196-208.

[16] Dansette, *Histoire religieuse,* p. 714.

a brief skirmish in the Senate, in July 1920, during the debate on the budget, but an amendment that opened the state scholarship fund to pupils in the confessional schools was easily turned back, 188 to 78;[17] the incident hardly created a stir in the press. Still, Guiraud was encouraged. Sixty senators inscribed in groups nominally on the Left had voted for the amendment, most of them newcomers elected the previous January. There was an even higher proportion of newcomers in the Chamber, and Guiraud figured that enough votes could be picked up from moderate republicans in the Bloc National majority to make a strong demonstration in favor of *répartition proportionnelle scolaire,* if it were not passed on the first try.[18]

Edouard Herriot's laconic introduction to the report on the budget of public instruction for 1921 merely noted the obvious: hope for immediate action on the *école unique* was dead.[19] But the prospects of securing subsidies for Catholic schools were not particularly bright, either. On January 16, 1921, Aristide Briand formed his seventh ministry. The Right now had an uncertain hold on the Chamber, for the Entente républicaine démocratique, though the largest group of the Right, with 183 deputies, received only three second-rate portfolios in the Briand cabinet.[20] Nonetheless, the partisans of subsidies to confessional schools pushed ahead with their demand. For those who were as interested in breaking lances against the republic as in securing subsidies, political realities mattered little.

On February 19, 1921, Baudry d'Asson, monarchist deputy from the Vendée, moved an amendment to the budget of public instruction that would provide "subsidies equivalent to scholarships" to pupils in private secondary schools.[21] To be sure, there was no law that forbade granting scholarships

[17] *J.O., Sénat* (1920), p. 1579.

[18] *La Croix*, August 3, 1920.

[19] *Journal officiel de la république française. Documents parlementaires: Chambre* (1921), annex no. 2101. Henceforth cited as *J.O. Doc. parl. Ch.*

[20] Bonnefous, *Histoire politique*, III, 207-10.

[21] *J.O.Ch.* (1921), p. 750.

to individuals who attended confessional schools.[22] But if Baudry d'Asson and his friends had jurisprudence on their side, opponents had republican tradition on theirs. Paul Doumer, minister of finance, rejected the amendment on behalf of the government. Herriot vigorously denounced it as an effort to rekindle the religious struggle, and to block the search for national unity by means of the *école unique*.[23]

The partisans of subsidies made a surprising show of strength; 200 deputies voted for the amendment, 344 against it.[24] But it was to prove the high point of their effort. The vote showed that *laïcité* remained one test of republicanism that most deputies did not care to fail. The "against" column extended far beyond the frontiers of the Radical and Socialist parties, which together had only 180 seats in the Chamber, into the Bloc National. It was one thing for moderate republicans to relegate *laïcité* to the background as an electoral convenience; for many of them, it was quite another thing to join in an assault upon it. But the partisans of subsidies persisted. When the budget of public instruction came round again in December 1921, Baudry d'Asson once more presented his amendment.[25]

Jules Isaac, minister of commerce and a noted Catholic layman, revealed a split in the Catholic camp that had not been apparent in February. Isaac feared that the effort to improve the status of the confessional schools might backfire and shatter the fragile religious truce that had prevailed since the war. Moreover, not only did Isaac himself oppose the effort to ob-

[22] Campenhausen, *L'Eglise et l'état*, pp. 138-40.

[23] *J.O.Ch.* (1921), pp. 751, 754.

[24] Guiraud called for a campaign to bring to the attention of public opinion those whom he called "defectors" from the Bloc National: "Let the fear of their electors reinforce the consciences of our deputies," *La Croix*, February 25, 1921. It is quite likely that the deputies who "defected" *did* have their electors in mind.

[25] Xavier Vallat, deputy of the extreme right, suggested in his memoirs that someone other than Baudry d'Asson, who "dédaignait la facile camaradérie de ses collègues," should have presented the amendment. *Le Nez de Cléopâtre* (Paris, 1957), p. 59.

tain subsidies, but—"I have advised my friends to abstain from the vote."[26]

An old Christian democrat, the Abbé Lemire, deputy from the Nord, supported Isaac. This tough and witty priest, who had spent a good part of his career scandalizing rightist Catholics, summed up his opposition in a proverb: "When you eat someone else's bread, you end up talking like him." The state had every right strictly to control the disposal of public money, and might be tempted to meddle in the religious instruction of the confessional school.[27]

Lemire and Isaac dealt a serious blow to the hopes of the supporters of subsidies. The opposition of a priest, even of a maverick like Lemire, gave Catholic deputies reason to vote against the amendment on religious grounds; Isaac's stand, according to one estimate, led 120 Catholic deputies to abstain from the vote.[28] Baudry d'Asson's amendment was defeated, 335 to 120. Nonetheless, the partisans of *répartition proportionnelle scolaire* did not resign themselves to defeat. Nor did the Left intend to drop an issue that the extreme Right had so obligingly handed to it.

In early 1922 the Société d'éducation formed a *Comité d'action pour la R.P.S.* to organize throughout the country[29] public meetings in favor of subsidies; the committee managed to hold several well-attended meetings in Paris, but it had difficulties in the provinces. In areas hostile to Catholicism, Catholics doubtless had little desire to risk offending their neighbors by such visible support for a provocative issue. Moreover, the Société d'éducation was in the control of hide-bound tradi-

[26] *J.O.Ch.* (1921), p. 4917.

[27] *J.O.Ch.* (1921), p. 4918.

[28] Vallat, p. 59. Vallat claimed that Baudry d'Asson's supporters had been fairly optimistic before the debate, and that he was astounded by Isaac's speech. Lemire's intervention "apaisa tout à fait les scrupules du centre, tout heureux d'avoir pour bouclier électoral en cette matière la soutane du prêtre." Paul Gay, deputy from the Haute Saône, who had proposed an amendment similar to Baudry d'Asson's, withdrew it immediately after Isaac's speech. *J.O.Ch.* (1921), p. 4918.

[29] *La Croix*, February 11, 1922.

tionalists such as Keller, who obviously did not speak for all Catholics, despite their claims. Cardinal Dubois, Archbishop of Paris, put his authority behind the campaign, but he warned against excessive optimism over its chances for success —an indication, perhaps, that some members of the hierarchy had reservations about the political wisdom of a vigorous campaign for subsidies at the very time the Church was seeking the reestablishment of the French embassy at the Vatican.[30] Nonetheless, the fourth general assembly of the French episcopate, publishing an official communiqué for the first time since 1919, renewed the support the hierarchy had previously given to the demand for subsidies;[31] and in individual episcopal letters some Church authorities argued that subsidies would go far toward resolving the religious question.[32]

But at the local level, where organization for electoral campaigns really counted, the campaign had not gathered much momentum, despite the support of the hierarchy and the exhortations of Catholic leaders in Paris. By Guiraud's own count, the departments of Finistère, Morbihan, Ille-et-Vilaine, Nord, Loire, and Rhône had strong organizations under way. But the first three of these departments, located in Brittany, were Catholic strongholds anyway; outside of these areas Guiraud had to admit that there was very little activity at all.[33]

The political impact of the drive for *répartition proportionnelle scolaire* was much greater than the real strength of the forces behind it. Two attempts in one year to wrest approval for subsidies from the Chamber, the approbation of the hierarchy for the campaign and Jean Guiraud's editorials in the largest Catholic newspaper in the country, were enough to arouse the Left, without regard for the real magnitude of the threat to the school laws. After the first debate on the Baudry d'Asson amendment, for example, the *Dépêche de Toulouse*,

[30] *La Croix*, February 21, 1922.

[31] *D.C.*, VII (1922), cols. 710-11.

[32] See, for example, the remarks of Mgr. Julien, Bishop of Arras, *D.C.*, VII (1922), col. 654.

[33] *La Croix*, March 3, 1922.

the voice of provincial Radicalism, sounded the alarm: "The war against secular education has been opened!"[34]

In early 1921, a good many Radicals acutely felt the danger of their party's continued involvement with the Bloc National. Problems of the peace settlement occupied most of the government's attention; the policy of wringing reparations out of the Germans seemed popular in the country, and on most important questions the majority of Radical deputies supported the government.[35] But continued isolation of the Radicals from their old allies, the Socialists, threatened a repetition of the disaster of 1919. Soon after the first skirmish over the Baudry d'Asson amendment, a few influential Radicals began an effort to reassert the old lines of division between Right and Left, and to build a bridge over the ideological ditch that separated them from the Socialists by means of *laïcité* and the *école unique*. Lack of discipline and loose organization made the Radical party a sort of political Janus that could look left and right simultaneously, so that some Radicals could woo the Socialists when most Radical deputies, in varying degrees of reluctance, supported the government of the Bloc National.

Alphonse Aulard professed to believe that the fence that had always marked the republic off from the Right needed mending, and that a barrier should be erected marked *"laïcité, social reforms,"* behind which all true republicans could unite.[36] In an open letter to Aulard, Edouard Herriot agreed on the necessity of collaboration among several parties, but as party leader he did not intend to make any firm commitment to Aulard's recommendation without consulting Radical colleagues. Nonetheless, he stressed that educational reform should be the backbone of any future alliance.[37] When Aulard called on the Socialists to respond to his suggestion on the formation of a leftist bloc, he emphasized Herriot's remarks on educational re-

[34] *La Dépêche de Toulouse*, February 22, 1921.

[35] Goguel, *Politique des partis*, pp. 187-88; pp. 218-19; Bonnefous, III, 237-38.

[36] *L'Ere nouvelle*, March 22, 1921.

[37] *L'Ere nouvelle*, April 4, 1921.

form.[38] The Socialists did not reply. But there existed other means of establishing a dialogue between Radicals and Socialists.

The Ligue des droits de l'homme was a kind of standing leftist alliance that functioned outside the party system but had strong ties with it. Founded at the time of the Dreyfus Affair, the League was a collection of intellectuals of the Left: politicians, members of the Institut, university professors, school teachers, civil servants and a number of doctors and lawyers. Sometimes the parties of the Left separately employed the League to achieve certain ends; sometimes the League served as a sort of study group with a view to the formation of coalitions between parties. At the outset Radicals predominated in the membership, but more and more Socialists joined the League, especially after 1924. The League had close ties, too, with the Ligue de l'enseignement. Since it collected under one roof so many fairly influential figures of the Left who might belong to more than one other leftist organization, the League served as a clearinghouse for ideas on educational reform, a meeting-ground for Radicals and Socialists and a pressure group for action.[39]

In 1921, Ferdinand Buisson was president of the League. For some months he had been urging an alliance between Radicals and Socialists; he knew that the League's support for educational reform would certainly not hinder such an alliance; accordingly, he drew up a long resolution on educational reform that included all the demands for which *école unique* provided a convenient label.[40] In a reference to the campaign for *répartition proportionnelle scolaire,* the resolution declared that "no subsidy, overt or disguised, should be granted to confessional schools." The League adopted all

[38] *L'Ere nouvelle*, April 8, 1921.

[39] This paragraph relies on Jean and Monica Charlot, "Un Rassemblement d'intellectuels: la ligue des droits de l'homme," *Revue française de science politique*, IX (1959), 995-1028.

[40] Buisson discussed the proposals he intended to present to the congress in an article "Droits de l'enfant," *Les Cahiers des droits de l'homme*, XXI (1921), 99-105.

of Buisson's suggestions at its congress in Paris, May 15–17, 1921.[41]

Not content to work within the established framework of parties and pressure groups, a group of Radicals, Buisson among them, undertook to create an *ad hoc* organization called the Ligue de la République, hoping to bring about a union of parties of the Left, and to rejuvenate the Radical party.[42] At a series of planning sessions in the summer of 1921, a committee drew up a minimum program which was published in October, shortly before the Radical and Socialist party congresses.[43] Clearly aimed at the Socialists, the program was a kind of updated Belleville Manifesto; the section on education followed almost word for word the educational platform of the Socialist party for 1919: "It [the League] demands a single department of national education."[44] Happily, there seemed no need to be any more specific about educational reform than the Socialists themselves had been.

At the Radical congress of 1921, held in Lyon at the end of October, the ubiquitous Ferdinand Buisson served as *rapporteur* for the committee on education. For the first time the party clearly endorsed free secondary education, and even called for allocations to low income families as an inducement to send their children to the lycée. In a patronizing tone, the final declaration hinted that educational reform might cement an alliance with the Socialists; it was clearly aimed at their working-class electorate: "those whom we wish to instruct also have the duty of understanding us and helping us."[45]

The Socialists faced the problem of rebuilding the old party, destroyed at the congress of Tours less than a year before. Although preoccupied with setting the *vieille maison* in order,

[41] *Les Cahiers des droits de l'homme*, XXI (1921), 150-51.

[42] The weekly *Progrès civique*, sympathetic to the left wing of the party, expressed the familiar postwar complaint that "for too long a time [the party] has practiced the policy of accommodation, of equivocation; no one believes in it any more." *Le Progrès civique*, October 23, 1920.

[43] The program was published in *L'Ere nouvelle*, October 21, 1921.

[44] *Ligue de la République: programme minimum* (Paris, 1921?).

[45] *L'Ere nouvelle*, October 29, 30, 1921.

in October 1921 the Socialists approved a five-point program for the elections of 1924. Neither their reaffirmation of the efficacy of revolution nor their program of industrial nationalization had anything in common with the aims of the Radicals, but point four of the Socialists' electoral program called for a free school system, based on selection by merit.[46] The Socialists shied away from the term *école unique,* but it was the *école unique* all the same.

Commenting on the two congresses, Yvon Delbos, then a young Radical journalist, remarked that doctrinal differences easily explained why neither party had overtly suggested an alliance. But, he noted, on at least two points—education and fiscal policy—their views were remarkably similar. Socialists and Radicals faced common adversaries; why should they struggle against each other?[47] Léon Blum viewed these similarities in a different light. On education and fiscal policy, he said, the Radicals had merely appropriated suggestions originally made by the Socialists, and "on all the other points [of the Radical program] I search in vain for a proposal or a project with real merit."[48] With an election more than two years away, Blum had plenty of time to see if an electoral alliance with the Radicals might prove to be a tactical necessity. But his backhanded admission that the Radical program had some merit hinted at his recognition of the potential political usefulness of the *école unique.* At the end of 1921, at least Radicals and Socialists were closer together than they had been in 1919.

They continued to be drawn together by the campaign for *répartition proportionnelle scolaire,* which provoked counter-demonstrations for the defense of secular education. These provincial meetings brought local Radical and Socialist militants together on the same platform, along with national leaders imported to raise the tone of the proceedings. At Angers, for example, in February 1922, the Ligue de la République sponsored a meeting in defense of the public school. Buisson came out from Paris as the representative of the Ligue des

[46] *Le Populaire,* November 1, 1921.
[47] *L'Ere nouvelle,* November 2, 1921.
[48] *Le Populaire,* November 3, 1921.

droits de l'homme; Paul-Boncour represented the Socialists; Emile Glay the militantly secular school teachers' union, the Syndicat national des instituteurs; and François Albert and Yvon Delbos the Radicals. This time it was a Socialist, Chevalle, secretary of the local federation, who called for an alliance with the Radicals, against RPS and for the *école unique*.[49]

At its congress of 1922, the Ligue des droits de l'homme linked the themes of RPS and the *école unique* together, calling on leftist opponents of the first to unite in support of the second. Proclaiming "the secular school in peril," the League urged its local sections "to make themselves the vigilant guardians of the fundamental laws that have instituted the secular school."[50] In July, the Ligue de l'enseignement gathered in Lyon and Herriot appeared to address the League at some length on the dangers of RPS and to urge League members actively to campaign for the *école unique*.[51] But of course his audience needed no persuasion.

The traditional rallying cry of republican defense had always made it easier for Radicals and Socialists to overlook their differences; but opposition to RPS was a sterile kind of policy, especially when it was not at all clear that a threat to *laïcité* really existed. Moreover, the government of the Bloc National had emphatically dissociated itself from the campaign for RPS. But Léon Bérard, who became minister of public instruction in January 1921, handed Radicals and Socialists an issue on which they could form a more constructive united opposition and could advance a clear alternative to government policy. For the elegant and learned Bérard made a serious political mistake: he sought to require Latin of all lycée students.

Latin was a symbol, as well as an intellectual discipline;

[49] *L'Ere nouvelle*, February 6, 1921.

[50] "Les Résolutions adoptées au congrès de la ligue," *Les Cahiers des droits de l'homme*, XXII (1922), 291-92; see also Henri Gamard, "L'Ecole laïque en péril," *Les Cahiers des droits de l'homme*, XXII (1922), 202. Gamard, a primary school teacher, and member of the central committee of the League, drew up the resolutions that the League adopted.

[51] *Le Progrès de Lyon*, July 29, 1922.

people were for or against its study as much for what it symbolized as for its intrinsic value, and for reasons emotional as well as intellectual. It had the support of snobs as well as classical scholars and clerics, and the antipathy of rough-handed workers who had never seen a Latin grammar as well as learned anticlericals and those who opposed on principle anything old. Partly as the mother of French, partly as the language of the Church, partly as a mental exercise, and partly, perhaps, just because it had always been taught, Latin had managed to survive each of the periodic struggles over the curriculum. Only at the end of the nineteenth century, it will be recalled, was a course of study that did not require Latin able to secure a toehold in the lycée. The Left was determined to keep it there.

Despite the formal equality established between classical and modern studies by the reform of 1902, the feeling widely persisted that a baccalaureate obtained without the study of Latin was somehow not quite legitimate. Consequently, the reform of 1902 was called into question in the postwar debate on educational reform. In *L'Université nouvelle* the Compagnons had suggested that Latin should be obligatory for all lycée pupils: "This devilish Latin is so mingled with our very substance by so many fibers, that we can dispense with it only to the detriment of our culture."[52] In April 1921, having undertaken its own study of reform, the Fédération nationale des professeurs de lycée voted by a large majority that Latin should be required of all pupils.[53]

In June 1921, encouraged by these signs of dissatisfaction with the reform of 1902, Léon Bérard submitted a questionnaire on the reform of the lycée curriculum to the Conseil supérieur de l'instruction publique.[54] More than half the re-

[52] *L'Université nouvelle*, II, 104ff.

[53] *Bulletin officiel de la fédération nationale des professeurs de lycée*, XVII (1921), 863. At the same congress, the lycée professors also endorsed the *école unique*, p. 824.

[54] The Conseil supérieur gave its opinion to the minister of public instruction on all projects concerning curricula, administrative and disciplinary regulations, and examinations, and served as a board of

sponses to the questionnaire favored obligatory Latin. At its December meeting, however, the Council reached no consensus on curricular reform.[55] Bérard went ahead on his own.

His intentions were soon clear: the study of classical languages would be obligatory, beginning in the first year of the lycée; the option of the reform of 1902 that required no Latin would be suppressed; choice between options would be postponed from the first year to the fourth.[56] Whatever its educational merits, Bérard's plan had social implications that the partisans of the *école unique* could not accept, as the Compagnons, erstwhile champions of Latin themselves, were quick to point out.[57]

The Left called on Bérard to account for his course of action. On June 8, 1922, interpellations on "the reform of national education," filed by Ferdinand Buisson and Hippolyte Ducos, Radicals, and Alexandre Bracke, Socialist, came before the Chamber.[58] The debate took up nineteen sessions and stretched over a year's time. A battle of ancients and moderns was a grand opportunity for displays of learned oratory and the debate proceeded at a leisurely pace, more appropriate, perhaps, to the Académie française than the Chamber of Deputies.[59]

---

appeal for disciplinary measures taken against University personnel. Richard, *L'Enseignement en France*, pp. 9-10.

[55] Most members wanted the modern option retained; some favored obligatory Latin; others wanted merely the rudiments of Latin introduced into the modern section. G. Beauvalon, "Quelques rémarques sur le rapport de M. Paul Crouzet," *Revue universitaire*, xxxii, part i (1923), 425-36.

[56] P. Crouzet, "Rapport à M. le ministre de l'instruction publique," *Revue universitaire*, xxxii (1923), 201. Crouzet was Bérard's technical adviser for the reform. Greek was also to be made obligatory for two years, beginning in the fourth class. In the lycée, class numbering begins with the higher numbers; that is, the sixth class is the first year of the lycée, and so forth.

[57] "The Bérard reform's social effects make it unacceptable," *La Solidarité*, July 19, 1921.

[58] *J.O.Ch.* (1922), p. 1683.

[59] François Albert, Radical senator, remarked, "La plus copieuse Académie des Beaux-Esprits reculerait devant un tel record." "Chronique politique," *Revue politique et parlementaire,* cxii (1922), 119.

Despite its high tone, the debate accomplished very little. It did, however, give Radicals and Socialists a chance to play off the *école unique* against Bérard and the Bloc National.

For the partisans of the *école unique,* the intrinsic merits of classical as against modern studies were not the real point at issue. As Alexandre Bracke, the Socialist party's spokesman on education, remarked: "The demarcation line that separates those who support the minister and those who distrust his projects doesn't coincide at all with the one that separates the defenders of classical humanities and the adversaries of classical humanities."[60]

Ducos, Bracke and Herriot bore the burden of the case against Bérard. Obligatory Latin in the first year of the lycée, they argued, would close its doors against primary pupils who sought to enter in the second or third year, and against transfer pupils from the *école primaire supérieure*; not having had Latin, they would be unable to catch up with lycée classmates who had already studied it for one or two years.[61]

What mattered most, Herriot argued, was the general cultural mission of the lycée, not the specific subject matter taught there.[62] Bérard's project would force bright children who had no desire to study Latin into the more utilitarian *école primaire supérieure*; unless the baccalaureate were dropped as a requirement for admission to the universities, all those who did not take Latin would be closed off from the universities, too. Bérard's conception of culture would thus impose upon all university students, no matter what discipline they pursued, a tradition whose relevance to modern society was open to considerable question.[63]

---

[60] *J.O.Ch.* (1922), p. 1724. The son of a Lille folksinger named Desrousseaux, Bracke used his mother's maiden name in politics. At the Ecole normale he worked up the skill that made him a distinguished Hellenist, and read Karl Marx in his spare time. He had become the fervent disciple of Jules Guesde, and then his right-hand man. See Claude Willard, *Le Mouvement socialiste en France, 1893-1905: les Guesdistes* (Paris, 1965), p. 607.

[61] See, for example, Ducos, *J.O.Ch.* (1922), p. 1687.

[62] *J.O.Ch.* (1922), p. 1881.

[63] *J.O.Ch.* (1922), p. 1883.

What was needed, as the Compagnons had suggested, was a coordinated system of secondary education that branched off into technical, modern and classical studies. But the Bérard plan focused on an institution and a style of culture historically associated with one social class.[64]

The debate in the press was less sedate than the debate in the Chamber. *Progrès civique* charged that Bérard's plan would completely close off access to secondary education to primary school pupils.[65] Léon Blum saw the opposition to Bérard as a defense of the rights of children, guaranteed by the Revolution, against the privileges of wealth.[66] A writer for the CGT lamented the lack of interest workers showed in the Bérard reform, for the real issue was not what kind of education should be given in the lycée, but who should receive it—a matter of the greatest concern to the working class.[67]

While the press of the Left vigorously denounced the social implications of Bérard's plan, the conservative press just as vigorously denied that it had such implications.[68] It was merely an effort to reinforce the intellectual content of the lycée curriculum; classical studies, that had passed the test of centuries, were better suited to the disinterested formation of the mind than modern studies.[69] This argument had the merit that it was impossible either to prove or to refute. Classical studies, conservatives claimed, would preserve the traditional cultural mission of the lycée; the *école unique,* supported by leftists bent on leveling the educational system, would destroy it.[70] The coordinated secondary level of the *école unique* was a

[64] *J.O.Ch.* (1922), pp. 1761-64. The Chamber adjourned for summer vacation in the middle of a speech of Georges Leygues, who, as minister of public instruction, had been responsible for the reform of 1902. Léon Bérard had not yet had a chance to respond to his critics.

[65] "Latin is the shibboleth that allows one to distinguish a little bourgeois from a little proletarian." *Progrès civique,* June 10, 1922.

[66] *Le Populaire,* June 10, 1922.

[67] *Le Peuple,* June 21, 1922.

[68] *Le Temps,* June 10, 1922.

[69] François Datin, "Où en est la Réforme de l'enseignement secondaire?" *Etudes,* 170 (1922), 361.

[70] *L'Echo de Paris,* June 12, 1922.

chimerical idea; nothing could be accomplished by "mixing together in the same mold manual workers and intellectuals," as *Le Temps* put it, for the mass of "the people" contained several kinds of "élites," much better served by distinct and separate kinds of education.[71]

On the eve of the debate on the Bérard reform, the Compagnons had rejoiced that the major parties and pressure groups of the Left had all declared themselves in favor of the Compagnons' general conception of reform; they undertook to stage a demonstration of this solidarity in support of the *école unique* during the interpellation of Bérard. To a meeting held in Paris in late June, the Compagnons drew an audience of more than a thousand: members of the political parties of the Left, *universitaires,* and representatives of the working class.[72]

Pressed to give the Chamber a clearer idea of his intentions, in October 1922 Bérard sent letters to the education committees of the Chamber and Senate. To counter the charge that obligatory Latin built a kind of Hadrian's wall around the lycée, Bérard proposed the creation of special Latin classes that would allow transfer students to enter in the fourth year of study. He proposed the unification of the programs of the elementary classes of the lycée and of the primary school; and in order to link the primary school to the lycée, he suggested dividing the final primary school examination into two parts: those who passed the first part of the examination, at age eleven, could enter the lycée in the sixth class. Stipends would be awarded to the parents of able children whose presence in the lycée utilized needed family income.[73]

It was true that the Compagnons had applied a similar solution to the problem of linking the primary school to the lycée. Buisson's report to the Radical Congress of 1921 had boasted

[71] *Le Temps,* June 15, 1922.

[72] *La Solidarité,* June 21, 1922. Among the speakers were Léon Blum and Marcel Sembat for the Socialists, Aimé Berthod for the Ligue de la République, and Jammy Schmidt for the Radicals, all of whom avowed their organizations' support for the *école unique* and denounced the Bérard reform.

[73] *Quinzaine universitaire,* November 15, 1922.

of its progressivism in demanding subsidies to families. But if Bérard intended his new proposals to make his reform more palatable to opponents, he failed, for he still aimed to make Latin obligatory.

In January 1923, the Conseil supérieur gave a hostile reception to Bérard's detailed presentation of his reform project, and refused to accept responsibility for it.[74] In April the Fédération nationale des professeurs de lycée reversed its earlier resolution in favor of obligatory Latin, and demanded the retention of the modern section from beginning to end of the lycée.[75] Despite this opposition, however, Bérard went ahead with his plans. Changes in curriculum were made by decree; they did not require the approval of parliament. The interpellation of 1922 had ceased abruptly when vacations suddenly seemed vastly more appealing than a discussion of the merits of Cicero. Bérard understandably tired of waiting to see whether the debate might be resumed. On May 3, 1923, he published a decree on the reform: henceforth, all lycée students would be obliged to take Latin.[76]

The Left professed to be outraged by Bérard's action. With his usual penchant for hyperbole, Herriot charged that Bérard's methods resembled those of the Duc de Broglie, under the government of Moral Order;[77] in an editorial he demanded an immediate discussion of what he called the "defiance of the University and the Parliament."[78] But the government suc-

[74] A declaration signed by a majority of the Council agreed to approve Bérard's reform because of some good things it contained, but stated that the reform in no way corresponded to the wishes of the majority. Georges Beauvalon, "La Session du Conseil supérieur de l'instruction publique," *Revue universitaire*, xxxii, part 1 (1923), 120-33. Bérard's lengthy speech to the Council was reprinted in his *Pour la Réforme de l'enseignement secondaire* (Paris, 1923).

[75] *Bulletin officiel de la fédération nationale des professeurs de Lycée*, xix (1923), 715.

[76] Bérard's explanation of the reform and the provisions of the reform itself are most accessible in Decaunes, *Réformes et projets de réforme*, pp. 247-51.

[77] *J.O.Ch.* (1923), p. 1776.

[78] *L'Oeuvre*, May 8, 1923.

ceeded in taking up the interpellation where it had left off the year before.

In his defense, Bérard repeated his view that the essential goal of secondary education was "to form the faculties of judgment." Classical studies best served that purpose; anyone who wanted a more utilitarian education belonged in the *école primaire supérieure*. Bérard claimed that Latin was no more a barrier to the poor than algebra, and he reviewed the steps he had taken to assure communication between primary and secondary education.[79]

Herriot admitted that the links Bérard had established between primary and secondary education were a progressive step.[80] But on the Left the feeling persisted that obligatory Latin rendered ineffective Bérard's adoption of some aspects of the *école unique*. If, for example, Bérard had taken steps to make entry into the sixth class easier for students from primary school, he had multiplied the difficulties of entering in higher classes, by throwing up the roadblock of special Latin classes that would discourage all but the most intrepid transfer students.[81]

One lycée professor argued that the heart of the misunderstanding between Bérard and his opponents lay in the refusal of the classicists, on the one hand, to recognize any other kind of humanistic study as the cultural equivalent of Latin; and the insistence of the Left, on the other hand, that primary school pupils wanted to enter the lycée only if it had a modern section.[82] But the misunderstanding was greater than that. For if Bérard's reform theoretically made it easier for primary pupils to enter the lycée, it made it no easier for them to stay once they had entered. As Bracke pointed out, even a reformed scholarship system was too uncertain to induce parents on low

[79] *J.O.Ch.* (1923), pp. 3389ff.

[80] *J.O.Ch.* (1923), p. 3111.

[81] *L'Oeuvre*, May 5, 1923; Raymond Figéac charged that the workers would be the greatest victims of the decree. *Le Peuple*, May 13, 1923.

[82] Henri Boivin, "La Réforme de l'enseignement secondaire devant la presse," *Revue universitaire*, XXXII, part 2 (1923), 314-30; 411-19.

incomes to commit their children to the lycée.[83] Parents on low incomes could not afford to make long range plans; to them, six years of lycée study without obvious practical benefit must have seemed an intolerably long time.

Nevertheless, Bérard had the conservative majority on his side. The interpellation resumed in May dragged on into July; an order of the day that merely approved his decree was adopted, 307 to 216, with 25 abstentions.[84] Shortly afterward, the Chamber adjourned for the summer.

On the eve of the adjournment, Herriot wrote that the vote on the Bérard decree had the gravest implications of any taken in the entire legislature. The decree would have "monstrous" results: "An indigent pedantry, and a narrow spirit of social conservation take us back to the most superannuated school system . . . to the great joy of the stupid Bloc National." The Left, Herriot declared, would carry to the electorate the battle that it had lost in the Chamber.[85]

RADICALS and Socialists stood together in opposing the educational policy of the Bloc National; they stood together in opposing the campaign for *répartition proportionnelle scolaire*; they mutually supported the *école unique*. Since 1921 they had together held political rallies where it had been constantly repeated that educational reform could be the basis for an alliance. The apparent simplicity of the issues involved enhanced their electoral appeal: the *école unique* was democratic; the Bérard reform was undemocratic; RPS was an assault on the lay laws. None of these issues required the splitting of doctrinal hairs between Radicals and Socialists, for each evoked emotional responses that stemmed from the shared republican tradition. By the middle of 1923, Radicals and Socialists had acquired the habit of standing together on educational policy, but each party retained its independence from the other.

For despite all the oratory about the vital importance of education, the *école unique* obviously was not a question in it-

[83] *J.O.Ch.* (1923), p. 3389.   [84] *J.O.Ch.* (1923), p. 3340.
[85] *L'Ere nouvelle*, July 14, 1923.

self attractive enough to unite Radicals and Socialists in the absence of other, more compelling reasons for union. The cause of reform may have suffered from its very attractiveness as a minor electoral issue. Easily embraced when circumstances suited, it could be as easily forgotten when they did not.

Though the Radicals supported the *école unique* against the educational policy of the Bloc National, they were still in an equivocal position. For most Radical deputies voted with the government on important questions. Raymond Poincaré, who had become premier in January 1922, had taken a position above party struggles, the better to deal with the German problem which occupied most of the government's attention. The Radicals had generally gone along with him, at the same time adroitly keeping a line open to the Socialists. But the Left's dislike of the occupation of the Ruhr, together with growing economic difficulties for which the government received the blame, and the approach of the elections, made the Radicals increasingly uneasy in their support of the government. Moreover, the Radical party's flirtation with the Socialists angered most of Poincaré's majority. In June 1923, the Radicals definitely entered into opposition.[86] One barrier to alliance with the Socialists had been removed.

THE Cartel des gauches was largely a marriage of convenience, made necessary by the maintenance of the absurd electoral law of 1919 (which favored electoral coalitions) for the election of 1924. Educational reform, having already allowed Radicals and Socialists to carry on a sort of dialogue under the Bloc National, helped to make the marriage of convenience bearable during the elections. In these circumstances the two parties displayed the accuracy of the Compagnons' remark that both bourgeois and socialist could profit from their doctrine.

To be sure, Radical educational experts regarded the *école unique* as bait to lure the working class into their own camp, as well as a bridge to the Socialist party apparatus. Claiming the *école unique* as their own invention, at the party congress

[86] On the circumstances surrounding this move, see Bonnefous, *Histoire politique*, III, 371-76.

of October 1923 the Radicals declared that "No emancipation of the workers is possible without the development of instruction. The unequal distribution of material wealth seems still less scandalous to us than the unequal distribution of intellectual wealth."[87] But the party did not show just how it proposed to redistribute this "intellectual wealth" (whatever that meant); it merely repeated the old statement that all children should have equal access to instruction—a goal systematically thwarted by the Bloc National.[88]

At the end of January 1924, the Socialists agreed to an electoral alliance with the Radicals. There was considerable opposition to this move within the party, but the electoral law seemed to offer no alternative, short of another disaster at the polls. Nonetheless, the doctrine of antiministerialism prevailed: the alliance would be for the duration of the elections only.[89] Announcing their decision, the Socialists stated: "The experience of the past obviously shows that the support of socialist deputies will certainly be accorded to any sincerely democratic and innovative work of reform undertaken by other parties."[90] The *école unique* fitted that prescription neatly. The Socialists retained the electoral program drawn up for the

[87] *Le Rappel*, October 21, 1923.

[88] Herriot was little more precise about the *école unique* in an essay he contributed to a Radical campaign tract aimed at the intelligentsia; he took up a good deal of his space protesting against the Bérard decree. It was time, Herriot wrote, for French democracy to create an educational system that corresponded socially to the political definition of the regime. But even in this tract meant for a readership presumably familiar with the University, Herriot said little that he had not already said in *Créer* five years earlier. E. Herriot, "L'Enseignement," in *La Politique républicaine* (Paris, 1924), pp. 389-416.

[89] One very feeble *tendance* in the party favored a coalition with the Communists; another recommended that the party fight the elections alone; still another suggested a far-reaching common program with the other parties in the Cartel. A centrist *tendance*, led by Blum, prevailed, and accepted the Cartel as an unhappy necessity for only the duration of the electoral campaign. Nonetheless, 23 federations presented lists made up only of Socialists. Lefranc, *Mouvement socialiste*, pp. 261-62.

[90] *Le Populaire*, February 4, 1924.

election of 1919 that included the vaguely-worded demand for a "single department of national education, accessible to everyone at all levels."

At the end of March 1924, 15,000 militants of the CGT gathered at the Bourse du Travail to demonstrate in favor of the "minimum program" of the CGT. Ludovic Zoretti harangued the crowd on the importance of the demand for educational reform, which "shows that workers don't always have just demands that concern their bellies, but know how to defend aspirations as noble as they are legitimate." The demands of the CGT had not changed since 1919: the raising of the school-leaving age to fifteen; "education accessible to everyone, at all levels."[91]

In April, the CGT held meetings all over the country to mobilize working-class support for the minimum program.[92] There could be little doubt of the singular importance that the syndicalist leadership attached to educational reform; on May Day, when *Le Peuple* called on militants to down tools for the traditional demonstration of working-class solidarity, its front page proclaimed that "the working class will demand the end of the [present] iniquitous regime of education, a class regime that automatically eliminates proletarian youth from it."[93]

Most Radical militants had no desire to put an end to this "iniquitous regime." Nor would they have favored the Socialists' "single department of national education," had they known what it meant. The content of the educational platforms of the Radicals, the Socialists and the CGT had changed scarcely at all since 1919. Neither the Radicals nor the Socialists had any clearer idea what they would actually do about educational reform, if elected, than they had had in 1919. But under the government of the Bloc National, the question of education —through the campaign for subsidies to confessional schools, the long and heated debates over the Bérard reform, the espousal of democratic reform by most of the great pressure

[91] *Le Peuple*, March 24, 1924.
[92] *Le Peuple*, April 15, 1924.   [93] *Le Peuple*, May 1, 1924.

groups of the Left—had received enough public attention to make the *école unique* the common ideological property of the Left against the Right. A fraction of the Right had sponsored an attempt to revise the school laws that no man of the Left could tolerate; the "party of Order" had approved an educational reform whose intent appeared contrary to the aims of democratic reformers. Against these efforts, the *école unique* symbolized the egalitarian and secular mystique that Radicals, Socialists and trade unionists shared, despite their differences.

At the end of 1923, a sudden financial crisis took the country by surprise, and upset a number of prior calculations about the elections. Poincaré hastily proposed a 20 per cent increase in all taxes and cuts in government expenditures. However necessary these measures may have been, they were politically onerous. The elections of 1924 hinged upon the high cost of living and the financial policy of the government.[94] Opposition to the financial policy of the Bloc National may have been enough to hold the Radical and Socialist electoral coalition together. But the Radicals opposed high indirect taxes, supported the income tax and were not quite sure how they could do things differently from Poincaré, while the Socialists considered the capital levy the cure for all financial ills. The most important issue of the campaign could not be squarely met by the Cartel des gauches with clear practical alternatives to Poincaré's policy.

The Cartel actually worked in fifty-seven out of eighty-one metropolitan departments, for in a number of departments, Radicals and Socialists ran on separate lists. Therefore in most departments Radicals and Socialists demanded educational reform together; but in others they demanded it separately, as competitors. In still other departments in which they ran as competitors, candidates of one party included educational re-

---

[94] Bonnefous, *L'Histoire politique*, III, 396-409; Jean-Paul Charnay, *Les Scrutins politiques en France de 1815 à 1962* (Paris, 1964), pp. 110-12. That the elections hinged upon the high cost of living and the financial policy of the government was the opinion of contemporaries, as well. See, for example, André Chaumeix, "La Nouvelle chambre," *Revue de Paris*, XXXI (1924), 710-20.

form in their *professions de foi,* candidates of the other did not. In the Haute-Garonne, for example, the Socialists' *profession de foi* made no mention of the school, but the Radical list, on which Hippolyte Ducos was elected, called for the *école unique.* Most electoral declarations of Cartellist candidates employed some variant of the formula "equality of all children with regard to instruction," and demanded a free school system. Some mentioned selection by merit, others did not.[95]

To find out precisely to what degree and in what fashion candidates of the Cartel talked about educational reform would require examining the campaign in each electoral district. It is doubtful that the isolation of a secondary electoral issue would yield enough information to justify such an examination. Nonetheless, some general observations can be made about the *école unique* and the elections.

The statements of Herriot, as party leader, indicate how the *école unique* helped to obscure absence of agreement on important questions between the partners in the Cartel after having eased the way to the coalition. In an article in *Progrès civique* on "the essential traits of the Radical party's doctrine," Herriot referred in passing to the need for a "just fiscal policy"; but he swept that problem aside to declare that "the first condition of liberation in the modern world is the diffusion of knowledge," attainable through the *école unique.*[96] In an important speech at Périgueux, Herriot declared that all republicans should consider educational reform the most pressing business at hand.[97] A few days later, he charged that Poincaré, who had ridiculed the idea of a Radical-Socialist alliance, had nothing to propose in place of the social reforms that knit Radicals and Socialists together: "nothing on the diffusion of instruction, which I think is the most urgent task."[98]

Herriot's reticence on economic problems suggests that he

[95] This paragraph is based upon an examination of the *professions de foi* published in the *Barodet* for 1924.

[96] *Le Progrès civique,* April 26, 1924.

[97] *Le Quotidien,* April 24, 1924.

[98] *Le Quotidien,* April 27, 1924.

skirted issues that he knew could embarrass Radicals and Socialists, in favor of the one issue that more closely bound them together than any other. More personal considerations may also have led him to place such emphasis on the *école unique*. Like most of the educated politicians of his generation, Herriot had received a classical education; he simply did not know much about economics.[99] Though it would be difficult to prove, perhaps his case was symptomatic; perhaps the fervent support that he and bourgeois intellectuals like him gave to the *école unique* betrayed their reluctance to face up to harsh economic problems that nothing in their backgrounds had prepared them to handle.

At any rate, Herriot's appeals struck a responsive chord in the circles for which he intended them. The *école unique* was not, after all, simply a gimmick, a convenient cover-up for disagreement between Radicals and Socialists. It has always been easy to take the Radicals to task as opportunists whose only aim in life was to cling to their seats in the Chamber, as windbags who never kept a promise. Doubtless that indictment contains some truth, but it is no less a caricature than the noble image many Radicals had of themselves. There is no reason to doubt that a good many Radical politicians sincerely believed that the existing school system discriminated against the poor, and that they believed as sincerely as the Socialists that it was in their power to do something about it.

There is no way to tell how many voters thought about the *école unique* when they mulled over their ballots, if they thought about it at all. But that Herriot had struck the right note in his appeal was confirmed by Francis Million, former wood-turner and editor of *Le Peuple*, in an editorial he published on the eve of the election: "Ignorance must be conquered first in order to allow the proletariat to free itself, and when instruction becomes the property of everyone, a pro-

[99] See Peter Larmour, *The French Radical Party in the 1930's* (Stanford, 1964), p. 71. Two leading Radicals told Larmour that when they talked to Herriot about economic questions, "he [Herriot] would hold his head in his hands in despair and tell them to do what they thought right."

found and lasting revolution will have been accomplished in the world."[100]

In his own election-eve article, in which he recapitulated the program of the Cartel des gauches, Herriot began with an admission of the fragility of the coalition: "We Radicals and Socialists struggle together in common respect for each other's doctrines." The Cartel, he said, campaigned for "fiscal equality" and for "lowering the cost of living," but he did not indicate how either of these might be achieved. First of all, the Cartel defended the public school, "a little temple of concord raised in the center of each village." Finally, "we desire the emancipation of the people through instruction." And he cited Million's remarks to insist that there was no more urgent revolutionary task than the instruction of the proletariat. "Worker, what would you do with this factory that you're promised, if you didn't know how to run it?"[101]

The Cartel was victorious. Many moderate candidates merely attached themselves to the coattails of Raymond Poincaré, in the belief that his prestige alone was enough to elect them. But Poincaré himself did not conduct a vigorous campaign, and except in the realm of foreign affairs his government did not have a clearly defined policy. The electoral law worked in favor of the Cartel, just as it had worked in favor of the Bloc National in 1919; the Cartel won fifty more seats than it might have won under a system of strict proportional representation. The displacement of votes from the Right to the Left was quite small. Perhaps voters who had sought a change in 1919 had been disappointed with the change they had received, and sought another change in 1924. Indeed, many doubtless voted against the Bloc National instead of for the Cartel, against high prices and high taxes instead of for the vague remedies that the Cartel proposed.[102]

[100] *Le Peuple*, May 10, 1924.

[101] *Le Quotidien*, May 10, 1924. It was not Herriot, of course, who was promising factories to the workers.

[102] See Georges Lachapelle, *Elections législatives du 11 mai 1924* (Paris, 1924); François Goguel, *Géographie des élections françaises de*

The campaign for *répartition proportionnelle scolaire* had helped to throw the Bloc National into some disarray. On the eve of the election, Guiraud complained that few candidates had dared to include the demand for subsidies to confessional schools in their electoral declarations.[103] Indeed, explicit demands for subsidies appeared in the *professions de foi* of candidates in only eight departments. But in several other departments—the Basses-Pyrénées, for example—the existence of two lists, one of moderate republicans, the other of Catholics, suggests that the school question may have prevented the formation of a single list.[104] But the elections were a severe blow to the hopes of Guiraud and his allies; in early 1926, he lamented that "this demand [RPS] has been put to sleep. Alas, today the campaigns that are conducted in its favor are rare."[105]

Partisans of the *école unique* now had the favorable parliamentary majority that they believed to be their first requirement. It remained to be seen whether the doctrine of the Compagnons had not better served the parties of the Cartel than they, in turn, would be able to serve the Compagnons. For the main business of party leaders is to see that their candidates get elected. A little mystique went a long way in an election campaign, but it did not go far toward the solution of concrete problems. Perhaps there was more than the usual amount of electoral irresponsibility in the promises of the Cartel on educational reform. Herriot, for example, had not sug-

---

1870 à 1951 (Paris, 1951), pp. 45, 69; Charnay, *Les Scrutins politiques*, pp. 110-12; Bonnefous, *Histoire politique*, III, 431-37; Goguel, *Politique des partis*, pp. 224-26.

[103] *La Croix*, May 6, 1924.

[104] The departments were Allier, the second circonscription of Loire-Inférieure, the second circonscription of Maine-et-Loire; Morbihan, Moselle, Vaucluse, and Vendée, according to an examination of the *professions de foi* in *Barodet* for 1924. Only those candidates who clearly demanded subsidies are included; some, for example, demanded that "liberty of education should be truly respected," which may have been a disguised demand for subsidies. With the exception of Allier and Vaucluse, these are traditional Catholic strongholds.

[105] *Ecole et famille*, VII (April 1926), 186.

gested that reform might be a long and difficult task, nor that the financial crisis inherited from the Bloc National might interfere with that task. No one had suggested that between the aspiration for the *école unique* and its fulfillment lay a thicket of technical problems as tangled and impenetrable as the thicket of political opposition. And if the *école unique* had covered over differences between Radicals and Socialists, it did not in the least resolve them.

Chapter iv. Failure of Hopes: The *Cartel des Gauches* Experiment

> Si seulement les deux enfants, le pauvre et le riche,
> avaient été assis aux bancs d'une même école . . . ils
> feraient plus entre eux que toutes les politiques, toutes les
> morales du monde.
>
> —Jules Michelet

I N THE exhilaration of the victory of the Cartel des gauches, Léon Jouhaux, secretary-general of the cgt, declared: "Now, more than ever, we must give proof of a robust will, and remember that in the institution of new social cadres and in the elevation of the masses by education reside the safeguards of the results attained, and the guarantee of their development."[1]

Now the Cartel faced the responsibility of government. No matter how helpful the *école unique* had been as a weapon in the electoral arsenal of the Cartel, educational reform was a secondary issue, contingent above all upon the resolution of the continuing financial crisis. But Radicals and Socialists were at odds as to how the crisis should be surmounted. The hard task of building the *école unique* required money, plans and time. As it turned out, the Cartel des gauches had none of these.

Nonetheless, the composition of the new Chamber seemed to augur well for the accomplishment of educational reform: the new majority contained a number of deputies familiar with the technical problems of education. Ferdinand Buisson had failed of reelection, and Alphonse Aulard had been defeated. But within the ranks of the Cartel, there were thirty *universitaires*.[2] It was, indeed, a republic of professors; and Edouard Herriot, the best known professor, headed the new government.

---

[1] *Le Peuple*, May 13, 1924.
[2] *L'Ere nouvelle*, May 18, 1924; *La Solidarité*, May 20, 1924.

Just before he became prime minister, Herriot had the municipal council of Lyon establish fifty-two lycée scholarships for primary school pupils, a gesture of his intention to act on the electoral promises of the Cartel des gauches: "I wish to lay the foundations of the *école unique*."[3]

But he needed the help of the Socialists to undertake any sort of reform, and he sought their participation in the government. In a letter to "mon cher Blum," whose propriety raised the eyebrows of those fastidious about propriety, Herriot urged the Socialists to share responsibility for his program; on education he declared, "We will revoke the Bérard decree; we will work to bring about the *école unique,* as we have defined it."[4] But the Socialists, faithful to the doctrine of antiministerialism, and under violent attack from the Communists for having anything to do with the bourgeois Radicals, refused participation and offered instead their "support."[5]

Spurned by the Socialists, Herriot formed a government for the most part composed of Radicals.[6] François Albert, Radical senator, an old hand at political journalism, and an associate of Clemenceau, became minister of public instruction. Herriot's choice symbolized the Radicals' equivocation on the relationship between their old standby, anticlericalism, and their educational reform program. For François Albert was a notorious anticlerical who had loudly opposed the reestablishment of the French embassy to the Vatican, had attacked the Bérard reform mainly on the ground that it favored confessional schools, and had recently become president of the Ligue de l'enseignement.[7] His appointment was hardly calculated to soothe the fears of Catholics over the *école unique.*

In his ministerial declaration on June 17, 1924, Herriot made

---

[3] *La Croix*, May 21, 1924.

[4] *Le Temps*, June 2, 1924.

[5] Lefranc, *Mouvement socialiste*, p. 267.

[6] Bonnefous, *Histoire politique*, IV, 386.

[7] Conversation of the author with former associates of Albert, 1965. On Albert's attitude toward the confessional schools see, for example, his article "Un plan de campagne contre l'enseignement d'état," *Progrès civique*, May 21, 1921.

no specific reference to the *école unique*. He merely declared that the government intended to suppress the Bérard decree, and that democracy in France would not be secure, "so long as . . . accession to secondary education is determined by the wealth of parents, and not, as it should be, by the merit of children."[8] Moments before, Herriot had stated that his government intended to withdraw the French embassy at the Vatican, to enforce the laws against the teaching orders, and to extend the lay laws to the recovered provinces of Alsace and Lorraine. After a stormy debate that led to actual blows, the Chamber voted confidence in Herriot's government.

It was not surprising that some Catholics linked the government's announced religious policy and the *école unique*. Father Yves de La Brière, political commentator for the Jesuit bi-weekly, *Etudes*, called Herriot's declaration "an official enterprise of public demolition."[9] And Guiraud described François Albert as the worst anticlerical in the government.[10] Other Catholics, however, believed the *école unique* was less an anti-Catholic maneuver than a deceitful promise made to attract the support of the masses.[11] *L'Ere nouvelle* urged Herriot to face reality, now that the election was over: he should make clear that only minor changes in the educational system could be expected until the government overcame the financial crisis.[12]

It seemed easy enough to rescind the Bérard decrees, however. On August 9, 1924, François Albert began to restore the modern section to the lycée,[13] marking a return to the path laid out by the reform of 1902. Section B, which had offered modern languages and science and dispensed with Latin, was

[8] *J.O.Ch.* (1924), p. 2306.

[9] "Les Premiers exploits de la chambre du 11 mai," *Etudes*, 180 (1924), 102.

[10] *La Croix*, June 17, 1924.

[11] *Dossiers d'action populaire*, June 25, 1924.

[12] *L'Ere nouvelle*, June 13, 1924. It is possible that the inspiration for this editorial came from Herriot himself. After he had assumed power, the imprudence of his electoral promises may have led him to prepare a retreat.

[13] *J.O., Lois et décrets* (1924), p. 7458.

restored to the curriculum throughout the course of study. The reform abandoned the division of the lycée into two cycles. The option Latin/modern languages was dropped. Henceforth, the last four years of the lycée offered three options instead of four: A (French, Latin, Greek); A' (French, Latin, science, one modern language); B (French, Latin, two modern languages). For the first time, certain of the basic disciplines—French, history, geography and sciences—were to constitute a common program for pupils of all sections. The reform was a greater innovation than appeared at first sight. A *culture générale* based on the study of French and science became for the first time the fundamental characteristic of secondary education; the study of classical languages, keystone of the old classical curriculum, now became simply one option among others.[14]

The final arrangements for the reform were not made until September 1925, when François Albert had left the ministry. After two months in office the Cartel des gauches had settled one score with Léon Bérard and the Bloc national, but it had not moved very far toward the *école unique*. In September 1924, François Albert ordered preparations made to place the elementary classes of the lycée under the authority of the primary inspectors. In addition, available places in the elementary classes were to be opened to able pupils from primary school.[15] He intended these measures as steps toward unification of the primary system, but the first angered the teachers in the elementary classes of the lycées, who resented being placed under the same administrative authority as the primary school teachers to whom they considered themselves superior; the second dashed the hopes of those who expected the elementary classes to be abolished outright.[16] It appeared that building the *école*

[14] Piobetta, *Le Baccalauréat*, pp. 263-64.

[15] *Information universitaire*, November 11, 1924.

[16] *L'Ere nouvelle*, December 6, 1924. Emile Kahn, primary school teacher, Socialist and a prominent member of the Ligue des droits de l'homme, wrote that François Albert's circular was an infringement of the rights of the professors of the elementary classes, who had appealed to the Conseil d'état, on the ground that administrative arrangements made by decree could not be altered by a circular.

unique was not so simple as it had looked from the perspective of opposition.

François Albert found his work complicated by the Freemasons—embarrassing allies in the circumstances. The nature of the relationship between Freemasonry and the parties of the Left is embarrassing to the historian, too. For the Masons were, of course, a secret society. Most books about them are unreliable. In the early years of the century, at least, through membership in local committees, Masons dominated the Radical party.[17] No one knew exactly who the Masons were, unless they admitted it themselves, but there was no more damning charge that Catholics such as Guiraud could bring against political enemies.

The Grand Orient de France, most militantly anticlerical of the Masonic organizations, had discussed educational reform at every postwar congress, or *convent,* since 1918, and the resolutions it passed on reform closely resembled those of the political parties that supported the *école unique.* What was particularly important about its *convent* of September 15–20, 1924, however, was that the Grand Orient passed a resolution in favor of a state monopoly of education, just at the time the Cartel des gauches undertook a new anticlerical offensive. A. Debierre, Radical senator and university professor, presented the case for monopoly that best expressed the hostility of many Masons toward the confessional schools: "We must choose! We must choose between belief and superstition on the one hand, scientific culture and human reason on the other."[18]

In August 1924, A. G. Michel undertook to bring statements such as Debierre's to the attention of Catholics. The title of Michel's tract, *La Dictature de la franc-maçonnerie sur la France,*[19] pretty well explained his aim. By publishing excerpts

[17] See Daniel Bardonnet, *L'Evolution de la structure du parti radical* (Paris, 1960), pp. 228-42; also Frédérix, *L'Etat des forces en France,* pp. 123-28.

[18] "Compte-rendu des travaux de l'assemblée générale du grand orient de France du 15 au 20 septembre 1924," *Bulletin du Grand Orient de France,* p. 148. The resolution in favor of monopoly appeared on pp. 118-19.

[19] Paris, 1924.

of the deliberations of recent Masonic *convents* on subjects that Herriot dealt with in his ministerial declaration, Michel tried to show that the Cartel des gauches was a vast Masonic conspiracy. It was not a convincing demonstration.

But the tract itself was less important than the circumstances in which it was published and the patronage it found. Herriot had made clear that he intended to carry out the religious policy outlined in his ministerial declaration: the withdrawal of the French embassy at the Vatican, the enforcement of the laws against the teaching orders and the extension of the lay laws into Alsace and Lorraine. Each of these problems had a long and complicated history.[20]

The important point here is the entanglement of the religious policy of the Cartel des gauches with the problem of educational reform: the government assured Catholics that the *école unique* posed no threat to the confessional schools, and at the same time it undertook to revise a religious settlement that had apparently been made in favor of Catholics. This action seemed to give further weight to the arguments of right-wing Catholic activists who detested the *école unique* and for some time had fought against it.

Catholic agitation against the government's course of action began in Alsace-Lorraine in July 1924, and spread to the rest of France. It soon became clear that the government had more on its hands than it had bargained for. Michel's tract against the Freemasons was part of the embryonic resistance. Even if the tract was nonsense, it had the patronage of General Edouard de Castelnau, perhaps the most prestigious Catholic layman in France. Called the "booted Capuchin" by his enemies, Castelnau combined politics and Catholicism in a way that might have made him a *Chevalier de la foi* under the Restoration. Castelnau wrote an introduction to Michel's book and circulated it among the hierarchy. He seemed to be just the man to organize resistance to the religious policy of the Cartel des gauches.[21]

[20] See Dansette, *Histoire religieuse*, especially book eight, ch. III, 413-30, and book nine, chs. I-IV, 565-624.

[21] An excellent field commander, Castelnau had been, with Pétain,

In the meantime, Jean Guiraud had already been doing some organizing. On October 6, at La Roche-sur-Yon, in the Vendée, the Associations Catholiques des chefs de famille sponsored a demonstration against the government that, by Guiraud's count, drew 18,000 Catholics. Guiraud singled out François Albert as a symbol of the Cartel's religious policy: "uniting in his person the action of masonry and official action in national education"; the *école unique* was simply "a sectarian enterprise that aims at establishing the monopoly of the atheist state."[22]

La Roche-sur-Yon was only the beginning of Catholic resistance. At the end of October, in *L'Echo de Paris,* General Castelnau called on Catholics "to create a national federation of all Christian groups,"[23] an appeal which led to the establishment of the Fédération nationale catholique. With the support of the French hierarchy and of the papacy, local chapters of the FNC proliferated. It was the first time Catholics had successfully organized on a national scale for the defense of religious interests.[24]

---

a defender of Verdun. But he received no marshal's baton, a disappointment that must have rankled. He lost three sons in the war. Some Catholics, and perhaps Castelnau himself, believed his failure to become a marshal was because of his Catholicism. See Yves de La Brière, "La F.N.C. et les organisations de défense politique et sociale," *Etudes,* 182 (1925), 101. Dansette suggests, however, that Castelnau had had a dispute with Foch that probably had a good deal to do with his remaining a general. Dansette, *Histoire religieuse,* p. 728. In the preface to Michel's book, Castelnau wrote: "Les religieux hors la loi, la rupture avec le Vatican, l'Alsace-Lorraine sous le joug laïque, l'école unique prélude du monopole d'enseignement, tous ces mots que répéte M. Herriot, . . . ce sont les ordres donnés par la secte maçonnique, depuis deux ans et plus, pour le jour attendu, préparé, ou les serviteurs seraient les maîtres du pays. Tel est l'objectif immédiat. Le but plus lointain est la révolution internationale dans le triomphe de l'athéisme vainqueur du Christianisme." *La Dictature de la franc-maçonnerie sur la France,* p. 4.

[22] *La Croix,* October 7, 1924.

[23] *L'Echo de Paris,* October 31, 1924.

[24] At its founding, the FNC laid out a broad mandate for itself: "the

The FNC carried on the technique of the mass demonstration. Each Sunday, regardless of the weather, throughout the fall and winter of 1924-1925, thousands of Catholics flocked to hear speakers such as Castelnau and Guiraud denounce the Cartel des gauches.[25] Given Guiraud's obsession with the *école unique,* it is safe to assume that thousands of Catholics heard it condemned as an important aspect of the antireligious policy of the government. Most of those who attended the meetings probably had no idea what went on in Paris, and did not much care. Theirs was an emotional response to an apparent threat to their religion. In the minds of many of them, the *école unique* inevitably became associated with that threat.

At the Radical congress of Boulogne-sur-Mer, in mid-October 1924, Herriot asserted that his government's religious policy was only a response to "a violent offensive directed against the lay spirit." He charged Guiraud with a calculated attempt to confuse the issues of educational reform and the defense of *laïcité*: "Our efforts in regard to the *école unique,* interpreted not only with malicious intent, but also with a complete ignorance of the subject, are represented as an attempt to enslave consciences."[26] But *Le Temps* failed to understand Herriot's distinction, and professed to see in the *école unique* an assault on religious freedom, "a form of intolerable

---

reform of all laws which are in contradiction with Catholic liberties." Yves de la Brière, "La F.N.C. et les organisations de défense politique et sociale," *Etudes*, 182 (1925), 96-107. Cardinal Dubois, archbishop of Paris, gave his adherence to the FNC in a public letter of November 29, 1924; Pope Pius XI added his support on December 18, 1924. See Georges Coquelle-Viance, *La Fédération nationale catholique* (1939?), pp. 10-15.

[25] Among the largest meetings were: Pau, 18,000; Bayonne, 20,000; Rodez, 7,000; Montpellier, 12,000; Montauban and Cholet, 10,000 each; La Rochefoucauld, 12,000; Quimper, 20,000; Folgoët, 50,000; Bordeaux and Nancy, 12,000; Saint-Brieuc, 30,000. Frédérix, *L'Etat des forces en France*, p. 141.

[26] *Le Temps*, October 21, 1924.

oppression."[27] And despite Herriot's effort to distinguish between his government's religious policy and the *école unique*, his own ministers furthered the confusion. On November 1, the Ligue de l'enseignement gathered at Valence for its annual congress. François Albert's double capacity as minister of public instruction and president of the league gave a quasi-official air to the meeting. In an interview with *Le Quotidien*, François Albert had said that he considered the *école unique* an effective means of competing with the confessional schools.[28] Ostensibly, the League met to make suggestions on the *école unique*. François Albert's major address, however, was a tirade against the Jesuits—"a certain company nearly as powerful and eternal as the Church herself," that intended to suppress the University.[29] The Société d'éducation called Albert's speech a "solemn and striking affirmation of the school policy of the Bloc des gauches";[30] and the Jesuits of *Action populaire* warned Catholics: "the Sacred Union is indeed dead . . . the struggle over the school is beginning again with implacable energy."[31]

[27] *Le Temps*, October 29, 1924. The Cartel's friends took the occasion of the Radical congress to remind the government that they expected some action on the *école unique*. Zoretti warned that disappointment would be great if the government did not act on its electoral promises. If opening the elementary classes to primary pupils was a gesture of François Albert's good intentions, it was scarcely an audacious measure; with the Radicals in control of the government and the Socialists in support, the government could afford some audacity. *Le Peuple*, October 25, 1924.

[28] *Le Quotidien*, October 13, 1924.

[29] *L'Homme libre*, November 3, 1924.

[30] *D.C.*, XIV (1925), col. 128.

[31] *Dossiers de l'action populaire*, December 10, 1924. Yves de La Brière, who often mixed shrewd comment and exaggerated fears in equal doses in his articles for *Etudes*, was more amused than alarmed by Albert's speech. Camille Pelletan, he remarked, had been the professional blunderer in the Combes cabinet; François Albert seemed to have taken over that role in the Cartel des gauches. "L'Enlèvement de la redoute, ou M. François Albert à l'assaut du Gésu," *Etudes*, 181 (1924), 612-13.

The government of the Cartel des gauches was deeply in trouble. Herriot's conciliatory foreign policy had angered conservatives. Across the country Catholics agitated against the government. The Communist party became bolder in its attacks.[32] Ominously, on November 2, the Socialists voted only "reserved support" of the Radical government.[33] Five months after they had assumed office, the Radicals had done very little about the *école unique.* Zoretti considered a request for advice Herriot made to the Ligue de l'enseignement an indication of the government's intention to persevere in educational reform, but he wondered why Herriot had not asked for help from the CGT as well.[34]

In the meantime, members of Herriot's own party publicly called for a state monopoly of education. Alphonse Aulard wrote in the influential *Dépêche de Toulouse* that "the confessional schools are a great war machine against the lay Republic. We will only have the *école unique* when all young Frenchmen, at some time in their schooling, are fraternally associated on the benches of the national school."[35] Senator Debierre repeated in the press what he had said at the *convent* of the Grand Orient in September: the *école unique* could not be reconciled with liberty for confessional education.[36] Edmond Dumesnil, editor of *Le Rappel,* a Radical newspaper, maintained that he "boldly hoped" for a state monopoly.[37]

Disturbed by signs of the government's temporizing on reform, the Compagnons sent François Albert an open letter. The so-called first step toward the *école unique*—opening the elementary classes of the lycée to the poor—actually con-

---

[32] Bonnefous, *Histoire politique,* IV, 46.

[33] *Le Populaire,* November 3, 1924.

[34] *Le Peuple,* November 18, 1924.

[35] *La Dépêche de Toulouse,* October 30, 1924.

[36] *Le Rappel,* November 9, 1924.

[37] *Le Rappel,* November 19, 1924. Jean Guiraud professed a preference for Dumesnil's "frankness" to the "hypocrisy" of others on the *école unique,* "the grand idea of the Radical and Socialist reign," *La Croix,* November 21, 1924.

tradicted the spirit of democratic reform, by sanctioning the alleged superiority of the elementary classes over the primary schools. Pleas for patience were an old conservative dodge: "You have everything you need—a convinced opinion that supports you, a decided majority." Failure to act would be a "great and woeful disappointment for . . . all those who believe in the efficacy of parliamentary methods."[38]

Edouard Herriot had a sure touch when it was a matter of appeasing impatient allies. Parliamentary investigating committees often afford the chance for a sort of political sleight of hand; they make motion appear to be action. It was true, too, that the government had not explored the technical problems of educational reform. In order both to silence friendly critics, and to seek needed information, Herriot decided to set up a committee on the *école unique*. In a speech at Roubaix, December 7, 1924, Herriot announced that a committee would be forthwith established under the presidency of Ferdinand Buisson; the Chamber, he declared, would act immediately on the committee's recommendations.[39]

François Albert lost no time selecting a committee, balanced between representatives of the Cartellist majority and technical experts from the University.[40] At the first meeting, December 23, 1924, he laid down guidelines for the investigation. He expected immediately practicable suggestions by April 1, 1925, he said, but the committee should also concern itself with long-range goals. Though François Albert had done a good deal himself to confuse reform with the religious question, he warned the committee that its deliberations should have nothing to do with the question of monopoly of education. Above all, the committee should remember that the *école unique* was a great democratic symbol.[41] *Le Temps* agreed that the *école*

[38] *La Solidarité*, November 25, 1924.

[39] *Le Peuple*, December 8, 1924.

[40] *Le Temps* assailed the decision to form a committee: "It is inevitable that under the Cartellist reign peace is obstinately prepared at the Ministry of War, and war is obstinately prepared in the Ministry of Public Instruction." *Le Temps*, December 20, 1924.

[41] *L'Ere nouvelle*, December 24, 1924.

unique was a symbol, all right, but the symbol of a "struggle engaged against the enlightened and republican bourgeoisie."[42]

The first meetings of the committee attracted a good deal of attention in the press, but as time went on, reports were buried in the back pages, if they appeared at all. The committee had no practical recommendations ready for François Albert in April 1925; when it did finish its work, at the end of July, he no longer occupied the ministry on the rue de Grenelle. Some critics charged, perhaps rightly, that the committee had never had a clear idea of what it was supposed to do.[43]

While Buisson's committee, sheltered from party strife and admonished to keep away from the question of monopoly, sought a way to build the *école unique,* agitation against the religious policy of the government continued in the streets.[44] The hierarchy had actively encouraged the resistance to the government. At the end of their annual meeting, March 10, 1925, the Cardinals and Archbishops of France published a "declaration on the so-called lay laws and on the measures to take in order to combat them." In the most violent language the episcopate assailed the school laws that enabled the public school to "delude the intelligence of children, pervert their wills, and warp their consciences." The hierarchy called on Catholics everywhere "to sound the same note of reprobation against the injustices of this legislation," and it specifically associated the *école unique* with those injustices.[45] *La Croix* called the declaration "the most notable act in the history of the Church in France in fifty years."[46]

[42] *Le Temps*, December 30, 1924.

[43] Some of the strongest criticism of the committee came from the Compagnons, who may, indeed, have been hypercritical. See "A propos de la commission officielle de l'école unique," *L'Université nouvelle,* July-August, 1926.

[44] From October, 1924, to January, 1925, the FNC held nearly 400 meetings. Frédérix, *L'Etat des forces,* p. 143; it soon claimed it had over one million members. Coquelle-Viance, *La F.N.C.,* p. 15. A meeting held in Marseilles in February, 1925, provoked a street battle between Catholics and elements of the left; two rioters were killed.

[45] *D.C.,* XIII (1925), cols. 707-12.

[46] *La Croix*, March 12 and 13, 1925.

Tension between Catholics and the Cartellist government had reached its highest point. It is difficult to assess the impact of the declaration upon Catholic laymen who had little interest in politics. The Vatican, embarked on a conciliatory policy toward the republic, later disavowed the declaration, and even forced the signatories to retract; nonetheless, individual prelates continued publicly to express the same opinions.[47] And the extreme position of the hierarchy was, temporarily at least, a vindication of Catholics of the Right such as Castelnau and Guiraud, who could use an official statement of the Church to support their own opinions on educational reform. Moreover, Herriot's effort to exploit the declaration, in order to increase his majority, failed.[48]

Herriot faced serious political difficulties from other sources. The financial crisis inherited from the Bloc National had worsened. The Treasury could meet its obligations only by resorting to inflationary loans from the Bank of France. But the rapid decline of the franc and fear of the intentions of a left-wing government alarmed the government's lenders; the Bank hesitated to make further advances to the Treasury. Capital fled the country. Prices mounted. The financial crisis destroyed the façade of Radical and Socialist unity created by such measures as educational reform: the Socialists wanted a capital levy and a reduction of the interest rate on government bonds; the Radicals, aware that a good share of their clientele had some kind of savings, opposed these tactics. Herriot was desperately seeking a solution to the crisis when, on April 10, the Bank of France revealed that the legal limit on the amount of currency in circulation had been exceeded. The Senate, professing alarm at this "breaking of the ceiling," overturned the Herriot government.[49]

[47] See René Rémond, "Evolution de la notion de laïcité entre 1919 et 1939," *Cahiers d'histoire*, IV (1959), 74-75.

[48] Bonnefous, *Histoire politique*, IV, 64.

[49] For a detailed discussion of the financial crisis, see Bonnefous, *Histoire politique*, IV, 72-79; for a clear and comprehensible picture of the continuing financial crisis of 1919-26, see Goguel, *Politique des partis*, pp. 192-205.

The fall of Herriot broke the *élan* of the Cartel des gauches. Though Socialists and Radicals continued their alliance, the high hopes of May 11 had been dashed against the largely mythical *mur d'argent*. April 10, 1925, marked the beginning of a search for a stable majority that was not found until July 1926. The financial crisis steadily worsened as new ministerial combinations were tried out and found wanting. The Cartel cracked, and was mended several times until it broke at last.[50]

From April 1925 until July 1926, the succession of ministers to the rue de Grenelle resembled nothing as sedate as a waltz. In fifteen months there were six ministers of public instruction, counting Edouard Daladier's second turn at the post— for one day.[51] Long tenure in office by a political minister did not guarantee action on reform, but François Albert's successors scarcely had time to learn their jobs. And with no money in the Treasury, the prospects of the *école unique* looked dismal indeed. Paul Painlevé, "eminent mathematician and mediocre politician,"[52] succeeded Herriot. His promise to carry on with his predecessor's program earned him the support of the Socialists.[53] But he broke off the anticlerical offensive begun by Herriot; Catholic resistance had been rewarded. Perhaps another measure of Painlevé's effort to appease Catholics was his appointment of Anatole de Monzie as minister of public

[50] Goguel gives the best discussion of the confused and complicated search for a stable majority. *Politique des partis*, pp. 231-35.

[51] The ministers were Anatole de Monzie, under the second Painlevé government, April 17, 1925 to October 27, 1925; Yvon Delbos, under the third Painlevé government, October 29, 1925 to November 22, 1925; Edouard Daladier, under the eighth Briand government, November 28, 1925 to March 6, 1926; Lucien Lamoureux, under the ninth Briand government, March 9, 1926 to June 15, 1926; Nogaro, under the tenth Briand government, June 24, 1926 to July 17, 1926; Daladier once again under the ephemeral second Herriot government, July 20, 1926 to July 21, 1926. All of the ministers were Radicals, with the exception of de Monzie, who belonged to the important left splinter group, Gauche radicale.

[52] Denis Brogan, *The Development of Modern France*. Harper torchbook edn. (New York, 1966), II, 588.

[53] Bonnefous, *Histoire politique*, IV, 82.

instruction. De Monzie, whose bulbous brow made him look very much the intellectual that he was, had vigorously defended the maintenance of the embassy at the Vatican.[54]

In a speech at Cahors in June 1925, de Monzie revealed that he planned to continue with educational reform.[55] He made some new appointments to the committee on the *école unique,* the composition of which had come under fire; among them were the noted physicist Paul Langevin (who twenty years later would head his own government committee on educational reform) and the eminent writer Paul Valéry.[56] He busily set to work on a vast reform project of his own, based on the committee's report,[57] but he left office when the Painlevé government fell in October.

It had been seven years since the Compagnons had published their manifesto. *Ecole unique* had become a catchphrase; the ideological associations that it evoked had become as important as the specific content of the reform proposals. As one writer on educational reform put it: "everyone builds his system of the *école unique* as he pleases, according to his

[54] See Louis Planté, *Un grand seigneur de politique: Anatole de Monzie* (Paris, 1955).

[55] *Le Temps,* June 16, 1925.

[56] See Ducos' report on the budget for 1926, *J.O. Doc. parl.* (1925), annex no. 1965.

[57] By a narrow margin, the committee voted to retain the elementary classes of the lycée. It recommended that the *certificat des études primaires* should serve as the examination for selection for the lycée. The committee divided secondary education into two distinct levels: the "second" and "third" degrees, which were each divided into four sections. The committee disbanded before it had had time to consider the problem of university education. *J.O. Doc. parl.* (1925), annex no. 1965. Few of the suggestions made by the committee were incorporated into later reform programs. According to Hippolyte Ducos, the report was never discussed by the committee on education of the Chamber, of which Ducos was a member. (Conversation with the author, October 13, 1965.) De Monzie drew up a long private member's bill on reform that got nowhere, like most private member's bills. Louis Planté, "110 rue de Grenelle—Léon Bérard, de Monzie, Edouard Herriot, Jean Zay," *Hommes et mondes,* no. 48 (July, 1950), 395-96.

inclinations . . . or his aversions."[58] While the Chamber of Deputies groped toward a stable majority, outside of parliament the debate on the *école unique* continued.

The debate, as a contemporary noted,[59] became monotonous and at times confusing, as the same men on each side repeated the same arguments. In an effort not to compound the confusion, some of the general themes that underlay the opposition to the *école unique* will be discussed here; the views of its supporters, who quarreled among themselves, will be explored later. Greater clarity may compensate for the arbitrariness of this arrangement.

FRANÇOIS ALBERT once again reformed the lycée curriculum. He tried to put the primary schools and the elementary classes of the lycée under the same administrative direction. He opened the elementary classes to able primary school pupils. In January 1925, he unified the scholarship examinations for the secondary level, so that a scholarship student who wished to transfer, for example, from an *école primaire supérieure* to a lycée did not have to apply for another kind of scholarship; instead, his original scholarship followed him.[60]

With such meager accomplishments to seize upon, the opposition to the *école unique* fell back upon speculation. Opponents dwelt upon a handful of themes, and were not at all hesitant to repeat over and over the same criticisms. There was, after all, a limit to ingenuity, and the *école unique* was a fairly simple idea.

But it was true, as Albert Thibaudet remarked, that "the *école unique*, under its plain and simple look, struck at a nerve center that involved our entire social structure."[61] Opponents sought to maintain a kind of hierarchical conception of society against this egalitarian thrust. In an extreme form, it was a

[58] Jean-Albert Bédé, "Le Problème de l'école unique en France," *Etudes françaises*, 24e cahier (April, 1931), 3.

[59] Henri Boivin, "L'Ecole unique devant la presse," *Revue universitaire*, xxiv, part 2 (1925), 322-23.

[60] *J.O. Doc. parl. Ch.* (1925), annex no. 1965.

[61] *La République des professeurs*, p. 180.

matter of keeping the rich man in his castle and the poor man at his gate, the son of the rich man in the lycée, the son of the poor man in the primary school.[62] Most opponents, however, argued that the existing school system provided avenues of social ascent as broad as the society could bear. Somehow, a bright boy could make his own way, no matter what his background. Most adversaries of the *école unique* were quite willing to admit that adjustments in the existing system might be necessary. Indeed, François Albert had done little more than carry out suggestions already made by Léon Bérard, who was actually an opponent of the *école unique*.[63] But a wholesale remaking of the school system, adversaries argued, had dangerous educational and social implications. Defense of educational tradition and defense of the existing social structure went hand in hand.

The partisans of the *école unique,* according to both political and pedagogical conservatives, sought a kind of "primarization" of the school system. It was chimerical to think that the primary school, devoted to furnishing rudimentary notions of reading, writing and arithmetic to future voters, could also prepare some children for the rigors of the lycée curriculum. Instead, a common primary school would eventually lower the quality of lycée studies, as legions of inadequately prepared primary students invaded the lycée.[64]

[62] See, for example, the rightist Paul Bourget's "Réflexions sur l'école unique," *L'Illustration*, July 31, 1920; also Abel Bonnard, *L'Eloge de l'ignorance* (Paris, 1925). As its title suggests, the whole book was an argument for the virtues of ignorance: "Il faut . . . que ceux qui étudient se dévouent sans réserve à leur grand objet, mais il faut aussi que les ignorants, s'il est permis de le dire, ignorent bien (p. 32). . . . La fonction des ignorants n'est pas seulement nécessaire, elle est pleine de grandeur et de poésie (p. 35). Il est bon, il est régulier, il est profondément juste et salutaire, que la haute instruction soit entourée de beaucoup d'obstacles" (p. 29).

[63] Léon Bérard, "Ce que j'ai voulu faire," *RDM*, xciv, 7e période (1924), 513-26.

[64] See, for example, P. Lahargou, "L'Ecole unique," *Enseignement chrétien*, xliii (1924), 570; "Primarization" was a constantly repeated theme of *Le Temps*: see, for example August 15, 16, 1924. J. Delvolvé,

By lowering the quality of lycée studies, the *école unique* would impose a stifling uniformity upon the country.[65] The existing system, in which specific educational functions were parceled out among distinct and separate establishments, better suited the needs of the nation, which needed good butchers, bakers and candlestick makers as well as doctors and lawyers. There was no point in stuffing the heads of workers and peasants with fancy ideas they could not use. The *école unique* would encourage them to abandon the workbench and the plow and drift into the cities, there to become a rootless intellectual proletariat.[66] In pursuing this argument, opponents of the *école unique* ignored the fact that reformers had never suggested that all secondary students should receive the same kind of training. Moreover, there was a possible contradiction in the argument that the *école unique* would destroy the high intellectual level of the lycée and would at the same time unleash a horde of unemployed intellectuals upon the streets. Nonetheless, fears of unemployed intellectuals were not groundless: idle intellectuals had often been a threat to social stability in the past. It is doubtless quite unwise for any gov-

---

"L'Ecole unique et éducation intégrale," *Revue de métaphysique et de morale*, xxxv (1928), 430, suggested that the *école unique* had actually been borrowed from the Americans, "a people without intellectual tradition." A lycée professor, Henri Bernès, "A propos de l'école unique," *RDM*, xcv, 7e periode (1925), 595, expressed the reservations of a number of his colleagues: "Ils [les Compagnons] donnent . . . à cette première école, dominée naturellement par les besoins de l'immense majorité de ses élèves, l'influence décisive sur la création des habitudes de pensée, sur la formation des esprits." Even partisans of the *école unique* had similar reservations; for example, Henri Boivin, "Où en est l'école unique?" *Revue universitaire*, xxxvi, part 2 (1927), 97.

[65] *Le Temps*, May 15, 1925; Albert Bessières, *L'Ecole unique* (Lyon, 1925), p. 13. The *école unique*, Bessières charged, would be a "conscription of intelligence that reminds one of Napoleon militarizing the lycée."

[66] An editorial writer in *L'Echo de Paris*, June 18, 1925, argued that what the country really needed were "braves gens, *capables de sacrifier leur vie à la patrie en temps de guerre, et d'élever une famille nombreuse en temps de paix* [emphasis in original]."

ernment to encourage the training of a group of talented and highly-skilled individuals, without reasonable certainty that there will be enough of the proper sort of jobs to go around. But it is also true that when opponents of the *école unique* hurled the charge that reform would create a mass of *déclassés,* they revealed their conviction that the social and economic order was static and unchanging. There was no room in their calculations for the idea that an expanding economy would create more jobs that would require higher levels of skill, or that education was itself an investment. In the eyes of many conservatives it was strictly a form of consumption that should be limited to the enjoyment of one social class.

Any method of selection based on merit, opponents charged, would be an unconscionable interference of the state with the right of parents to make decisions for their children. The argument against selection clearly showed how the defense of privilege intermingled with more disinterested pedagogical criticism and with religious objections, just as the charge of "primarization" could be hurled by those who simply wanted to maintain the hegemony of a social class over the lycée, as well as by those who felt that the methods of the primary school would undermine the high intellectual level of secondary studies. No fair and reliable method of selection could be devised, they declared. Selection by examination at the age of eleven would be artificial and premature; it would measure only a bookish sort of intelligence. The favorite cautionary tale of opponents of selection was that of Louis Pasteur, the tanner's child, who had appeared quite dull as a boy. Selection might thwart any number of Pasteurs.[67] It was also true,

[67] G. Daumas, "Ceux qui sont contre l'école unique," *Revue apologétique,* XLI (1926), 567; A. de Barandarian, *L'Ecole unique* (Paris, 1925), p. 11. Léon Bérard, "L'Ecole unique," *Revue hebdomadaire,* XXXIX (January, 1930), 268, called selection "la chimère majeure de l'école unique"; Hippolyte Parigot, "L'Ecole unique," *RDM,* CII (November, 1932), 65ff; J. Mora, *Le vrai visage de l'école unique* (Paris, 1931?), p. 97; Bessières, *L'Ecole unique,* p. 14; Yves de La Brière, "Pourquoi il faut combattre l'école unique," *Revue apologétique,* XLI (1926), 567.

however, that selection posed a threat to those whose parents could afford the lycée, but who were something less than Pasteurs.

Some of the other arguments against the *école unique* more starkly revealed class bias. Father Albert Bessières, a Jesuit contended that the liberal professions suited only certain kinds of people, who had the proper family background for them. To seat the son of a bourgeois and the son of a worker on the same school bench would merely stir the latter to hatred and envy of the former as they both grew up. It would be far better to keep the two classes separated from the beginning.[68]

The charge that the *école unique* meant a state monopoly of education droned on as a steady accompaniment to the chorus of criticism directed against the reform. There were, however, two distinct positions on monopoly taken by opponents. Liberal critics like those in *Le Temps* held that the *école unique* would lead to a bourgeois exodus from the public schools to the confessional schools; in self-defense, the state would then be driven to abolish the confessional schools, a measure contrary to republican principles.[69] François Albert lent some credence to this charge when he opposed the suppression of the elementary class of the lycée, on similar grounds. Catholics, on the other hand, continued to maintain that the *école unique* would force the confessional schools to close, because they could not compete with a free lycée. And some Catholics, of course, argued that monopoly would be not merely a side effect of the *école unique* but its overriding purpose, as the support of the Masons attested.[70]

Father Marc Dubruel, a Jesuit, at least contributed some

[68] Bessières, *L'Ecole unique*, p. 14.

[69] For example, *Le Temps*, August 15, 1924.

[70] That the *école unique* meant a state monopoly of education was a favorite theme of Guiraud, constantly repeated in editorials in *La Croix* and *Ecole et famille*; see also his tract, *L'Ecole unique et monopole de l'enseignement* (Paris, 1926); J. Mora, *L'Ecole unique et le bien commun* (Paris, n.d.), p. 32; F. Datin, "Le Dangers de l'école unique: une étape vers le monopole," *Etudes*, 181 (1924), 385-402; 539-53; Pierre Dufrenne, *L'Ecole unique* (Paris, 1932), p. 34.

originality to the Catholic opposition. He scoffed at the idea that the *école unique* necessarily meant a state monopoly of education. The real danger lay in the "seizure by a caste— the professors—of the entire life of the nation."[71] By means of the process of selection, the mandarins of the University would control the destinies of all the nation's children. Moreover, the reform was anti-democratic: the *école unique* would deprive the working class of its leaders, because a lycée education was a notorious means of *embourgeoisement*.[72] Here Dubruel's criticism echoed reservations that some partisans of the *école unique* shared.[73]

THE Compagnons had learned that catch-phrases could be deciphered any number of ways, by friend and adversary alike. Dismayed by the tenor of the public debate, they made a restatement of their essential aim: "What, at bottom, is the real point of the unification of the school? It is to knock down the pedagogical barriers between students from different social classes." What mattered most were analogous programs in schools of the same educational level. Everything else, such as the question of the suppression of the elementary classes, was secondary.[74] It was too late, however, for the Compagnons to retreat to what they conceived to be technical ground. Besides, the "essential aim" of 1925 was a big enough order.

The parties of the left that had promised bold measures on educational reform were in disarray in the face of the financial crisis.[75] Inflation worsened. Social unrest grew as the franc weakened. Right-wing leagues agitated in the streets against parliament. The *école unique* seemed a luxury indeed as prices soared out of the reach of all but the most capacious pocket-books. Perhaps the best measure of the fortunes of the educational reformers was the temporary collapse of the Compagnons; in the spring of 1925 they had 32 francs in their treasury.

[71] *Le Règne des pédagogues: l'école unique* (Paris, 1926), pp. 28-29.
[72] *Ibid.*, pp. 33-35.
[73] See Chapter v.
[74] *La Solidarité*, November 25, 1925.
[75] Bonnefous, *Histoire politique*, iv, 100-101.

La Solidarité belied its name by collapsing.[76] Organized groups of the Left continued to press for reform, but they were singularly vague about just what could be done.[77]

By the end of 1925, there must have been many partisans of reform who recalled how beautiful the *école unique* had looked under the Bloc National. Little by little, Radicals moderated their enthusiasm for a reform they had so eagerly embraced as an electoral slogan. François Albert insisted the reform would be carried out despite financial difficulties, but it would have to be done in stages, "a little more slowly than we would like."[78] In December, Herriot presided over a demonstration in honor of Condorcet and the *école unique,* attended by numerous Radical notables; he had a good deal more to say about Condorcet than about the *école unique.*[79] In his report on the budget of public instruction for 1926, drawn up at the end of 1925, Hippolyte Ducos could say little more about government initiative in educational reform than Herriot had been able to say in his report in 1920.[80] On the floor of the Chamber, Edouard Daladier, then minister of public

[76] *L'Université nouvelle,* December, 1926. This new publication of the Compagnons began to appear in April, 1926.

[77] The Ligue des droits de l'homme again turned to educational reform at its congress in La Rochelle, November 1-3, 1925. The League's resolution on "The Democratic Organization of Education," though it rejected "piecemeal reforms," merely restated support for the *école unique,* and called on parliament to draw up a project "as soon as possible." *Ligue des droits de l'homme. congrès national de 1925. compte-rendu sténographique* (Paris, 1925), pp. 348-49. The Grand Orient de France found it advisable to send its resolution on reform back to local lodges to study "the financial means that will permit the realization of the *école unique.*" *Bulletin du grand orient de France,* LXXXI (1925), 132. At its congress of 1925, the Ligue de l'enseignement declared that attenuations would have to be made in the great principles of the reform, "while awaiting a period of budgetary elasticity more favorable to social improvements." *Action laïque* (February, 1926).

[78] *Progrès civique,* October 10, 1925.

[79] *Le Quotidien,* December 10, 1925.

[80] *J.O. Doc. parl.* (1925), annex no. 1965.

instruction in Briand's eighth government, referred to the *école unique* as a "generous dream" and wondered if assuring better attendance at primary school was not a more imperious duty for the moment.[81]

The one practical measure in favor of the *école unique*—the admission of able pupils from the primary school to free places in the elementary classes—had not worked out as its proponents hoped it would. In the first place, the measure had drawn fire from reformers, for it seemed to imply that the elementary classes really were superior to the primary school, at a time when reformers, for social as well as pedagogical reasons, sought to abolish the elementary classes outright. Moreover, François Albert made public his decision only in September 1924—too close to the opening of the school year for the measure to have much effect. Only 383 primary school children entered the elementary classes in the school year of 1924-1925. But the reasons for this lack of response to the measure lay deeper than the failure of the ministry of public instruction adequately to publicize it. In the 1925-1926 school year, 22,524 children enrolled in the elementary classes of the lycées and *collèges*. Free places were made available to 7,716 children from the primary school; only 1,184 took them, despite information made available in the primary schools by the primary inspectors and notices inserted in the press. In the 1926-1927 school year, 1,510 primary school children entered the elementary classes free, an increase of only 326 over the previous year. And in the 1927-1928 school year, the last year for which statistics of this kind were kept, only 1,415 primary school children enrolled in the elementary classes, a decrease of 95 from the previous year.[82]

Opponents of the *école unique* were quick to claim that the failure of the experiment merely showed that there was no demand for reform, that those excluded from the lycée by

[81] *J.O.Ch.* (1925), p. 4336.

[82] Archives nationales F[17] 13951. *Essai d'école unique: admission à titre gratuit d'élèves de l'enseignement primaire dans les classes primaires élémentaires des collèges et lycées; statistique d'entrée en 6e. 1924-1928.*

financial barriers were somehow happy with their lot. But the truth was much more complicated than that. In a report to the minister of public instruction, Sébastien Charléty, noted historian and rector of the Academy of Paris, sought to explain the failure of the experiment. His remarks bear quoting in full:

"Concerning the pupils admitted free to the primary and elementary classes, I must point out that the choice of these pupils is not always made as would seem suitable; indeed, it seems that the Directors of the primary schools voluntarily allow only their average or mediocre pupils to leave; moreover, the material condition of the primary classes is often superior to that of the elementary classes of the secondary establishments; so is their pedagogical organization, since in the primary schools there are at least four classes for children between the ages of six and twelve, while there are only three or two of them in the secondary establishments; finally, free school supplies in the primary schools are yet another obstacle to the entry of poor primary school children into the primary classes of the lycées and *collèges*; the municipalities are asked to grant them free supplies, but that does not happen without some friction.

"Selection being for these reasons imperfect, it happens that a rather large number of children designated under such conditions fail at the scholarship examination and do not enter the secondary classes, so that their admission [to the primary classes] has served for little or nothing."[83]

The Ligue de l'enseignement held its congress for 1926 in the predominantly working-class city of Saint-Etienne. In order to make a demonstration of support for the *école unique,* Radicals arrived in force. In this industrial area, Edouard Herriot assured his audience that "to emancipate a people is above all to instruct them." But he cautioned that the day of emancipation had not yet come—material problems had to be

[83] Archives nationales, F[17] 13951. Le Recteur de l'Académie de Paris à M. le ministre de l'instruction publique et des beaux-arts, 30 novembre 1927.

resolved before the work of reform could proceed.[84] Lucien Lamoureux, minister of public instruction in Briand's ninth government, laid the hopes of the reformers to rest. The *école unique,* Lamoureux claimed, had already substantially been created.[85]

It was true that in February 1926 Lamoureux had established a common curriculum for the primary school and the elementary classes of the lycée. But even taken together with François Albert's work, these measures hardly constituted the *école unique* as the Radicals understood it. The barriers of tuition stood. The structure of secondary education, the real concern of partisans of the *école unique,* remained substantially unaltered. The links established between the primary school and the lycée were weak indeed; nothing had been done about selection.

But the Radicals knew that they could not deliver on their electoral promises; Lamoureux, as a Radical minister, probably felt moved to put the best face on what had been done. In the spring of 1926, Radicals found themselves in the familiar position of disagreement over tactics: some wanted to continue to work with the Socialists; others wanted to form a government of concentration—a coalition with center parties that would exclude the Socialists.[86] In July, Herriot's effort to form a ministry lasted one day.[87] The Cartel des gauches was pronounced dead, though it had actually expired over a year before.

As for educational reform, Lamoureux's address the previous May had reduced the *école unique* from a sweeping scheme for the remaking of the University to a handful of readjustments of the existing system. When Raymond Poincaré formed a government of national union on July 23, 1926, it was not at all certain that the *école unique* had not been buried along with the Cartel des gauches.

[84] "L'Ecole unique," *Revue de métaphysique et de morale,* xxxiii (1926), 260.

[85] *L'Oeuvre,* May 5, 1926.

[86] Bonnefous, *Histoire politique,* iv, 141.

[87] *Ibid.,* pp. 156-59.

> En l'état actuel des choses, ces actions concertées delimitées
> à des points précis réalisent le meilleur moyen pratique
> pour aboutir à un résultat.
> —HENRI BARBUSSE

THE CRUSHING of their exalted hopes taught educational reformers that reform was a much more complicated business than they had once thought. They had expected the Cartellist majority to bring them gratification. But that majority collapsed without giving serious consideration to the *école unique,* and now reform seemed postponed indefinitely by the financial crisis. Caught up in the game of politics, the *école unique* had become a collection of vague propositions that had the advantage of sounding impressive and the disadvantage of not meaning much. Little new thinking had been done about the structure of democratic educational reform since 1918, when the Compagnons published *L'Université nouvelle.* Confronted with the meager accomplishments of the Cartel des gauches, reformers undertook to draw up a new blueprint for the *école unique*; the initiative briefly held by the government returned to private hands.

The work of the Compagnons continued to inspire these new initiatives; indeed, the Compagnons participated in them. But after 1924 there was a kind of leftward shift in the vocabulary of the discussion on reform. Most important, although the structure of the *école unique* remained substantially the same, a new understanding of the idea of equality of opportunity began to take shape. The most active participants in this discussion were affiliates of the new syndicalist movement within the University; most of them were unknown outside their own professional circles, though at least one of them— Marcel Déat—became notorious later. The initiative in reform passed from the Radical party, which never moved much

121

beyond the devising of slogans, to the CGT, whose plan became the basis for the reform later undertaken by Jean Zay
under the Popular Front.

The political parties and pressure groups that supported the
école unique together approached the problem of educational
reform from ideological angles that did not fit neatly together.
Through 1924, these differences were concealed under the
vague formulas that served as reform programs; after 1924, to
be sure, ideological differences never got in the way of common support for steps taken in parliament, doubtless because
these few measures were not of the sort that could cause difficulties. Nonetheless, differences among the partisans of the
école unique were considerable; each had his own vision of
what he expected it to accomplish.

In the fall of 1925, diverse groups interested in educational
reform undertook to redefine what they meant by *école
unique* by forming a committee to hammer out a synthesis of
their aspirations. The initiative for the creation of this committee came from the Groupe fraternel de l'enseignement, a
collection of Masonic school teachers presided over by A.
Ziwès, a Parisian school teacher. Ziwès, though president,
stood in the shadow of Marceau Pivert, a most extraordinary
member of the group. Pivert, thirty years old in 1925, had
followed the conventional path of many bright peasant boys
who sought escape from the farm: he became a school teacher,
then a professor in an *école primaire supérieure*, and then a
socialist—but an unconventional socialist. Pivert attached himself to a revolutionary *tendance* of the party, where he vented
his love of the grand gesture, his romantic notion of the class
struggle and his hatred of the Church, a sort of *enragé* per-
petually in search of some barricade to mount.[1]

Pivert probably had a hand in a pamphlet on the *école
unique* published by the Groupe fraternel de l'enseignement
in the still hopeful days of the Cartel. Along with a number of

[1] On Pivert, see Donald N. Baker, "Revolutionism in the French
Socialist Party between the World Wars: The revolutionary *tendances*."
Unpublished doctoral dissertation, Stanford University, 1965, pp. 66-74.

fairly precise and unexceptionable recommendations, the Groupe fraternel demanded the "socialization of national education" and the "rational distribution of social functions."[2] The tract failed to draw much attention. The Groupe fraternel better served the *école unique* when it suggested that the associations interested in reform should combine their efforts.

A coordinating agency, the Comité d'étude et d'action pour l'école unique was formed late in 1925. Thirty-one organizations made up the Study Committee, a mixture of teachers' professional groups, trade unions, political parties and great republican associations such as the Ligue des droits de l'homme.[3] The Socialist party did not take part in the committee's work, but individual Socialists did, men such as Marceau Pivert and his brother Charles, and Ludovic Zoretti. Maurice Weber, *normalien*, lycée professor and syndicalist, represented the Compagnons, and shouldered a good share of the work of the Committee. Each group retained its autonomy; the Committee acted as a sort of cartel limited to drawing up a common program that fairly well satisfied all of the participants. Mindful of the complications thrown in the way of reform by the religious question, the Committee avoided the problem by resolving not to talk about it.[4] The Committee worked within the framework of *L'Université nouvelle,* but its point of view differed in an important respect from that of the original Compagnons. The Compagnons had stressed the qualitative aspect of their formula: *gratuité, sélection.* They had been preoccupied with the problem of extricating from the mass of children an élite capable of receiving a rigorous liberal education. The Study Committee, on the other hand, insisted that popular education deserved at least as much attention as the recruitment and education of professional élites: "The first duty of a democracy is to get rid of ignorance and

[2] *L'Ecole unique: les principes, le système, le budget* (Paris, 1925), p. 4.

[3] The groups ranged from the obscure *Association de propagande laïque et d'éducation sociale par le cinéma* to the Grand Orient de France.

[4] *L'Université nouvelle,* April 1926.

123

to struggle against the enslavement of the workers to thought-killing economic disciplines. It is necessary to raise the level of instruction of the masses."[5] The Compagnons felt an obsession with mass education might lead to that "primarization" of secondary education a good many lycée professors feared: "A misguided attempt at a general unification of culture and of the mentality of youth."[6] In the Study Committee the Compagnons, probably because of the considerable influence of Maurice Weber, managed to maintain the balance between concern for mass and concern for élite education, despite Pivert's enthusiasm for the former.[7]

The deliberations of the Committee extended over a year and a half. In early May, 1927, the work was finished; the final report, *An Organic Statute for Public Education*, was adopted on June 9 and presented to the "parliamentary group on national education"; then, as far as the deputies were concerned, it promptly disappeared from sight. Marceau Pivert, released from the burden of cooperating with bourgeois reformers, declared that "only socialism could fully carry it [the plan] out."[8]

The *Organic Statute* reduced the welter of ideas on reform to a number of concise articles.[9] The influence of the Compagnons was clear. Free secondary and university education, selection based upon aptitude, remained the foundation upon which the whole structure rested. The educational system was

[5] *Ce que doit être l'école unique d'après les grandes associations démocratiques*; *Rapport présenté au nom de la commission composée de MM. Zoretti, Weber, Bascan, Roussel, M. Pivert* (Paris, 1927), p. 4.

[6] "Ecole unique et école unique," *L'Université nouvelle*, November 1926.

[7] Obviously the representatives of 31 organizations meeting in plenary sessions could not accomplish much. The work was divided among subcommittees. Maurice Weber had charge of the important section on secondary education. See his "Rapport sur l'organisation de l'enseignement du second degré," *L'Université nouvelle*, May-June 1926.

[8] *Le Populaire*, June 23, 1927.

[9] The text of the *Statut organique* can be found in *Bulletin officiel du syndicat national des professeurs de lycée*, XXVI (1930), 863-69.

to be organized under one ministry of national education into three successive and coordinated levels. The Statute called for a common primary school, allocations to families which could not afford to lose a wage earner to studies beyond primary school, and the raising of the school-leaving age to fifteen.

The Statute handled the difficult problem of selection in a harsher manner than had the Compagnons in *L'Université nouvelle*. The Compagnons had proposed that selection for secondary education should be made at the age of thirteen or fourteen; the Statute lowered the age to eleven. Primary school grade averages, written and oral examinations designed to discern aptitude rather than acquired knowledge, and psychological tests were to be the means of selection. Doubtless there was a good deal of truth in the charge of opponents of the *école unique* that it would be risky to apply such methods in any rigorous fashion to eleven-year-old children.

The Committee proposed to ease the apparent harshness of this mode of selection, however, by means of a common program of general studies in the first year of the secondary level; only at the end of the year would students be directed toward one of three sections—scientific, literary or technical. After the first year, each section would continue a program of general studies common to all of the sections; in order to rectify possible errors in orientation, transfer would be made from one section to another with little difficulty. The orientation class was designed to discover which of the three sections a child's aptitude best suited him to enter and, through its program of general culture, to postpone specialization for as long as possible. And the idea of the orientation class also reflected the conviction of most reformers that a unity of cultural values should weld the secondary educational establishment together, despite the diverse kinds of education that it offered. Technical students, for example, should have access to the liberal humanistic tradition that the lycée tended to monopolize, for the first task of education was not to form adjuncts of machines, but human beings.

But in the Statute there was a contradiction between the concepts of orientation and selection. The idea of selection

125

fastened attention on the most intellectually able children; it had no concern for the fate of the average or the dull. The point of orientation, however, was to match each child's interests and abilities to the style of education that best suited him, whether he was clever or not. It was therefore much more inclusive than selection, for a child was not abandoned on the ground of low intellectual capacity.

Perhaps the Study Committee's deliberations were surpassingly dull; its communiqués had none of the lyric tone that had suffused the earlier work of the Compagnons; nor did the Committee range over as many problems as the Compagnons had covered. Perhaps disappointments were too recent and the financial picture too dark to permit a rekindling of the fires of *L'Université nouvelle*. Nevertheless, prior to the Committee's work, the reform movement had had no program that could serve as a legislative text; the *Organic Statute* became the basis for subsequent efforts to press a reform upon parliament. As a synthesis of the desires of most of the organized supporters of the *école unique,* perhaps the text represented, as Marceau Pivert claimed, "the dominant aspirations of democracy in the matter of education."[10] Beneath the bare bones of the document that declared what the *école unique* should *be*, however, there lay contradictory ideas among its supporters what it should *do*.

In *La République des professeurs*, written as a kind of occasional piece on the failure of the Cartel des gauches, Albert Thibaudet suggested that the *école unique* had become the main plank in the platform of the Radical party.[11] The party, Thibaudet argued, was a party of ideas, in the sense that the battle it led over separation of Church and state had been a battle of the lay idea against the Catholic idea. Unable to elaborate a coherent economic doctrine of its own,[12] and helpless in the face of a financial crisis, the party prospered only

[10] *Ce que doit être l'école unique*, p. 2.

[11] *La République des professeurs*, pp. 181-82.

[12] *Ibid.*, p. 289; for a vivid example of the Radicals' difficulties in the face of economic problems see Larmour, *French Radical Party*, p. 73.

when its program appealed to those whom Thibaudet called, after Alain, the "idealists of the provinces": professors and school teachers who were notables at home, but nobodies in Paris. These idealists gave their allegiance to a program that expressed: "an idea of a spiritual but nonrevolutionary order that one finds fitting smoothly into the bourgeois order, as the separation of Church and state did."[13] But the battle over separation had long been over, and in order to survive, the Radical party needed a new idea: "The *école unique* and its consequences can appropriately provide it for a few years with a myth that is made to order."[14]

Thibaudet may have exaggerated the importance that a good many Radicals attached to the *école unique*; perhaps he underestimated that party's ability to survive without an "idea." But it was true that in the 1920's, at least, the *école unique* was a major plank in the party platform. If the Radical party was a party of ideas, in Thibaudet's sense, it was not, as countless others have pointed out, a party of systematic doctrine. The Radical version of the *école unique* was at once an example of the poverty of Radical theory and an unusually consistent expression of what usually passed for theory among Radicals. The party never worked out its own program for educational reform, but party spokesmen on education tirelessly repeated the same set of ideas about it. Pieced together, they constituted a fairly coherent Radical doctrine on education, which was repeated in more or less standard form by rank and file party workers. Indeed, these ideas were less a doctrine than a rationalization of the instinctual desires of the lower middle class in the matter of education. The position of the Radical party on the *école unique* was a perfect expression of what an English historian has called "The perennial schizophrenia of the radical ethic—hovering between two sets of

[13] *La République des professeurs*, pp. 195-96, 260.

[14] *Ibid.*, p. 262. Thibaudet himself had little enthusiasm for the *école unique*: "C'est comme 'républicain' individualiste, anticonformiste que je manque d'amitié pour l'école unique" (Albert Thibaudet, interviewed by Frédéric Lefevre). *Les Nouvelles littéraires*, November 5, 1932.

127

unstated assumptions about social structure, seething at in-equality, yet cherishing property and individual achieve-ment."[15]

Jacques Kayser has suggested that if the Radicals were not philosophers, they were historians; their most characteristic mode of expression was the historical parallel. The Great Rev-olution was the yardstick by which all things were measured.[16] For Radical candidates who included the *école unique* in electoral promises, the reform was a body of received ideas, handed down from the Revolution. In *Pourquoi je suis radical-socialiste,* Edouard Herriot wrote: "our [the Radicals'] con-cern for democratic justice leads us back to the ideas of the Revolution, to its effort to establish a rational education, to the principles of Talleyrand and Condorcet. . . ."[17] Herriot con-stantly returned to this theme in speeches to the Chamber. In a book on the *école unique,* Hippolyte Ducos declared: "The *école unique* translates into the modern world a truth re-vealed by the dialectic of the eighteenth century, confirmed by the Declaration of the Rights of Man, that has become the law of our democracy."[18] In a kind of Radical handbook, Albert Bayet, influential member of the Ligue de l'enseignement, described the *école unique* as an "intellectual '89."[19] Bayet apparently did not feel that he could safely call the reform an "intellectual '93."

But if the Revolution was the source of all good things, it was also, as Kayser pointed out, a refuge.[20] In their advocacy

[15] J. R. Vincent, *Pollbooks; How Victorians Voted.* (Cambridge, 1967), p. 25.

[16] Jacques Kayser, "Le Radicalisme des radicaux," *Tendances poli-tiques dans la vie française depuis 1789* (Paris, 1960), pp. 70-71.

[17] *Pourquoi je suis radical-socialiste* (Paris, 1928), p. 178.

[18] *Pourquoi l'école unique?* (Paris, 1932), p. 237. Ducos managed to squeeze the Radical view of the revolutionary tradition into one sen-tence: "Qu'on le veuille ou non, le mot d'école unique renferme à l'heure présente, ce que la logique ardente de Condorcet, la foi du Carnot de 1848, l'enthousiasme de Michelet, le réalisme passionné de G. Clemenceau, au temps du programme de Montmartre, la fougue idéaliste de Jaurès ont revendiqué pour la démocratie" (p. 11).

[19] *Le Radicalisme* (Paris, 1932), pp. 153-54.

[20] Kayser, *Tendances politiques,* p. 74.

of suggestions that Condorcet had made in 1792, the Radicals did not find it necessary to examine the relevance of these suggestions to the twentieth century. They looked over their shoulders for precedents on the *école unique*; they did not look ahead, or even at the society about them to see what sort of educational system changing economic and social patterns might demand. Their view of reform was a sort of political wish fulfillment, unencumbered by any economic or sociological data. Like most of the left, the Radicals tended to think about complicated technical problems in narrow political categories; they deluded themselves and their clientele into believing that it was possible to obtain a parliamentary majority that would effect fundamental structural changes in the educational establishment.

Drawing upon the fraternal urge of the revolutionary tradition, the Radicals considered the *école unique* a means of social reconciliation. They never tired of repeating Michelet's conviction that class antagonism would give way to brotherhood if all French children were seated on the benches of the same school. In 1920, introducing the *école unique* to the Chamber, Herriot had declared: "The point of departure of all of my preoccupations is to bring about French brotherhood by means of the school."[21] The Radicals hated to admit that social classes existed, and they clung as tenaciously to Michelet's mid-nineteenth century romanticism as some Marxists clung to mid-nineteenth century Marxism; indeed, they scarcely changed Michelet's phraseology.[22] Constant references to the concept of *le peuple,* which implied a belief in a kind of natural solidarity of peasants, workers and petty bourgeois, betrayed the Radicals' reluctance to admit the existence of an industrial labor force that had interests different from their own.

The *école unique,* Radicals thought, would be a ladder for individual social ascent.[23] The reform was a kind of safety valve for the alleviation of material discontent: it promised

---

[21] *J.O.Ch.* (1920), p. 1985.

[22] See, for example, Bayet, *Le Radicalisme,* p. 172.

[23] Ducos, *Pourquoi l'école unique?* p. 44; Herriot, *Pourquoi je suis radical-socialiste,* p. 74. Jammy-Schmidt, *Les Grandes thèses radicales* (Paris, 1932), pp. 318-19.

that one could lift himself out of a precarious existence by the strength of one's own brain. By dint of hard work, a worker's son could become a member of one of the liberal professions, and therefore a member of the middle class. Herriot declared that "democracy is not a regime which promises men an artificial and impossible equality in the distribution of material goods. It is the regime which gives everyone the same means to climb toward the summits of knowledge."[24] The Radicals' idea of equality of educational opportunity exemplified what C. B. MacPherson has called "the classical liberal vision of the market society."[25] Everyone, Herriot and his colleagues believed, should have an equal legal right to enter the competitive race.[26]

Herriot built his conception of the *école unique* on a kind of republican folk ideal, an ideal that contained a good deal of truth, as his own experience showed. Under the Third Republic, countless peasants' sons had become school teachers and many school teachers' sons had become professors—this had been the path to a sort of social eminence for people without money. The Radicals conceived the *école unique* as a means of making this process more certain, of reducing its element of chance and of broadening the avenues of social ascent: more careers would be opened to talent. From the point of view of working-class leaders, however, the myth of individual ascent, as Stanley Hoffmann has remarked, seemed a betrayal of working-class solidarity.[27]

[24] Herriot, in the preface to Ducos, *Pourquoi l'école unique?* p. 7.

[25] C. B. MacPherson, *The Real World of Democracy* (Oxford, 1966), p. 47.

[26] On this and related matters see Raymond Williams' brilliant study, *Culture and Society* (New York, 1960), p. 331.

[27] Hoffmann *et al.*, *In Search of France*, p. 7. Hoffmann fails to point out, however, that the idea of working-class solidarity might have been as great a myth as the idea of individual social ascent. On the teaching profession as a means of social mobility in the prewar republic see Gérard Vincent, "Les Professeurs de l'enseignement secondaire dans la société de la 'Belle époque.'" *Revue d'histoire moderne et contemporaine*, XIII (1966), 49-86; also, by the same author, "Les Professeurs

Radicals did not question the traditional assumption that the lycée should be reserved for a small elite. The *école unique* was a more efficient and more democratic means of seeking out those best suited to undertake the traditional broad program of humanistic studies that led to specialization in the universities.[28] Unlike some of their leftist allies, the Radical spokesmen did not wonder whether this form of intermediate education was entirely adequate to furnish the increasingly diversified kinds of knowledge and skill that an industrial society required.

Some Radicals desired a state monopoly of education, but the official party view held that the *école unique* had nothing to do with monopoly.[29] Nonetheless, party spokesmen did little to alleviate the fears of Catholics on this point. In 1924, Ducos declared in the Chamber that the *école unique* and monopoly were quite distinct problems. But if the reform could be carried out only by means of a state monopoly, then he preferred monopoly to not carrying it out at all.[30] Radicals made no effort to clear up the confusion that arose from trying to square their professed belief in freedom of education with the demand that all French children should be seated on the benches of the same school. Given the Radicals' anticlerical past, it is understandable that many Catholics considered the *école unique* a weapon directed against themselves.

And it is doubtless true that many Radicals would not have been grieved to see the confessional schools disappear, even if they did not intend the *école unique* as a weapon against them. Their defense of the liberty of education was not an active defense; the confessional schools were merely tolerated. They were an affront to the Radical sense that the public school was the best cement of national unity. And for those to

---

du second degré au début du xxᵉ Siècle," *Le Mouvement Sociale*, No. 55 (April-June 1966), 47-74; Ozouf, *Nous, les maîtres d'école*, pp. 63-85.

[28] Ducos, *Pourquoi l'école unique?* p. 63; Herriot, *Pourquoi je suis radical-socialiste*, p. 73.

[29] Ducos, p. 120; Herriot, pp. 176-78; Bayet, p. 164; Jammy-Schmidt, pp. 318-19.

[30] *J.O.Ch.* (1924), p. 3640.

whom *laïcité* was not a juridical arrangement assuring freedom of conscience in a divided nation, but a system of belief in the limitless possibilities of science, the confessional schools were still a dangerous rival.[31]

The *école unique* of the Radicals, constructed out of commonplaces drawn from the revolutionary tradition, was an expression of the Radical vision of the ideal society: individualist and respectful of property rights, where intellectual virtue was rewarded, conflict did not exist, and everyone belonged to the middle class. But it was also an expression of the Radicals' perpetual embarrassment; with hearts on the left, pocketbooks on the right, but a good share of their electorate in the center, almost all that they could promise workers was that their children could become members of the middle class —if they were clever enough.

IN SUPPORTING the *école unique,* the CGT and the Socialist party faced a dilemma that tormented Jean Guéhenno, who described himself as "a sort of hybrid—neither a bourgeois nor a proletarian. Everything would have been easier for me if it had been possible to forget."[32] Proletarian by origin, but made bourgeois by his education, Guéhenno wondered how a man from a social class historically denied access to liberal education could become well educated without betraying his origins in the process.[33] As Michelet had put it: "The difficult thing is

[31] For the best postwar expression of this attitude see Albert Bayet, *La Morale laïque et ses adversaires,* 4th edn. (Paris, 1925), p. 103. "La vraie laïcité c'est la science. . . . La science étendra sans fin ses conquêtes et sans fin fera réculer l'ombre qui nous environne. Nous croyons qu'attentive aux choses sociales elle projetera tôt ou tard sur le monde humaine les mêmes lueurs qu'elle a déjà projetées sur le monde physique. Nous croyons au fur et à mesure qu'elle étendra nos connaissances, elle offrira des armes plus solides à la justice et à l'amour. Nous croyons que, grâce à elle, il sera possible un jour de balayer de cette terre les misères, les laideurs, les crimes, les haines qui aujourd'hui la déshonorent . . ." (p. 205).

[32] *La Foi difficile* (Paris, 1957), p. 46.

[33] "Success," Guéhenno argued, "is in its essence bourgeois," *Caliban parle* (Paris, 1928), p. 90.

not to rise in the world, but, while rising, to remain oneself."[34]

Despite the Radicals' veneration for Michelet they were not very much concerned with this difficulty, but Guéhenno's dilemma was of great importance to Socialists and syndicalists. The working-class movement needed educated leaders. But what would happen to the movement if the brightest working-class boys became *embourgeoisé* by the lycée and turned their backs on the working class? Aware that support for the *école unique* entailed just such a risk, some syndicalist and Socialist educational experts avoided a reply by posing another question: was a new kind of culture possible, one not historically associated with the bourgeoisie? It cannot be said that they ever satisfactorily answered either question.

On the eve of the war, Albert Thierry, a young professor of working-class origin, had published a series of articles on education which mirrored the old syndicalist conviction that the working class could depend for salvation only upon itself.[35] The public system of higher education, Thierry charged, was "a suction device installed to extract new spiritual forces from the people and put them into the service of the bourgeoisie."[36] Only at the price of class betrayal could a proletarian obtain a higher education; it was therefore his duty, Thierry argued, to avoid the public system. Working-class children could retain their revolutionary ardor and at the same time cast off the shackles of ignorance only if the syndicalist movement set up its own educational system and created a new mode of culture, stripped of bourgeois prejudices.[37]

[34] Jules Michelet, *Le Peuple*, 2nd edn. (Paris, 1846), p. 35.

[35] On this attitude, peculiar to the French labor movement, see the incisive editorial comments of Jacques Julliard in *Clemenceau, briseur de grèves* (Paris, 1965), pp. 27-28. On Thierry, see Maurice Dommanget, *Albert Thierry* (Paris, 1950). Thierry purposely chose to teach in an *école primaire supérieure* instead of a lycée, in order, he thought, to be closer to his own people. He was killed in action in the First World War.

[36] Albert Thierry, *Réflexions sur l'éducation* (Paris, 1923), p. 118. This book is a posthumous collection of the articles that first appeared in *Vie ouvrière*, an organ of the revolutionary *tendance* of the CGT.

[37] *Ibid.*, p. 133.

Postwar syndicalist educational experts considered themselves the spiritual heirs of Thierry. Obvious difficulties, however, stood in the way of carrying out his suggestions. As Charles Andler pointed out, the working-class movement simply could not afford to construct an educational system parallel to the public system. And despite the claims of the working class to represent the universal aspirations of mankind, Andler could not see how a "proletarian culture" would be any less ridden with class prejudice than the dominant culture.[38]

Nonetheless, syndicalists such as Zoretti insisted on following Thierry's lead in an effort to work out a definition for a "proletarian culture." But the discussion was singularly vague. And there was a cleavage between the thought of working-class representatives and their action. For from the moment the CGT and the Socialist party endorsed educational reform in a bourgeois society, they implicitly rejected Thierry's rigorous *ouvrierisme* and left it to the Communists.

Zoretti had to admit that he was not quite sure how a proletarian culture could be defined. Clearly, the class struggle would become the subject matter of history. But a proletarian art or a proletarian literature "will be defined, will be created little by little, when the proletariat is master."[39] Indeed, a good deal of the speculation about "proletarian culture" was little more than an assertion that, once the revolution had come, a new culture would arise spontaneously from the ruins of bourgeois civilization. Georges Lefranc, a *normalien* closely associated with Zoretti, called for the liberation of culture from its "bourgeois domination" but could not define the content of a proletarian culture any more rigorously than had Zoretti. Its goal, "the harmonious formation of the personality," had to await a "total revolution of the mercantile values of the bourgeoisie."[40]

[38] Charles Andler, *L'Humanisme travailliste* (Paris, 1927), p. 23.

[39] Ludovic Zoretti, *Elite, sélection, culture* (Paris, 1935), pp. 183-96. This book is a collection of articles originally published from 1920 to 1933, as well as material added in 1934.

[40] G. and E. Lefranc, *Le Problème de la culture* (Paris, 1931), p. 4. Lefranc helped partly to fulfill Thierry's dream of a syndicalist educa-

Jean Guéhenno argued that those who sought to work out a specifically "proletarian" culture, in order to preserve intact the revolutionary ardor of the workers, had falsely posed the whole question of the relationship between education and social class.[41] There was only one kind of humanism, Guéhenno argued, neither bourgeois nor proletarian, but simply human. It was true, he believed, that the humanities had become merely a collection of formal disciplines with which one had to become familiar in order to acquire the proper credentials for leadership in bourgeois society.[42] The task of the Left should not be to engage in futile discussions on "proletarian culture," but to restore to the humanities their ancient spirit: "the Promethean spirit which does credit to man and to all men."[43]

In a more brutal fashion than had Guéhenno, Henri de Man likewise questioned the effort to work out a proletarian culture. This Belgian socialist made a career of exposing what he considered the delusions of contemporary socialism, until he succumbed to some delusions himself. De Man argued that the idea of "proletarian culture" was the invention of a handful of socialist intellectuals, desperately reacting against evidence that "the masses increasingly find satisfaction for their instinctive needs in bourgeois civilization."[44] Modes of culture were products of historical epochs, not of social classes; a cultivated socialist had more in common with a bourgeois contemporary of the same intellectual level than he had with Karl

---

tional establishment when he became director of the Institut supérieur ouvrier, established in 1932. He was also a founder of *Révolution constructive*, a planist *tendance* within the Socialist party that included other University syndicalists interested in educational reform.

[41] J. Guéhenno, "Culture et bourgeoisie: réponse à Julien Benda," *Les Nouvelles littéraires*, February 16, 1929; on this see also Williams, *Culture and Society*, p. 320.

[42] Jean Guéhenno, *Conversion à l'humaine* (Paris, 1931), p. 138.

[43] Guéhenno, *Les Nouvelles littéraires*, February 16, 1929.

[44] Henri de Man, *Au delà du marxisme*, 2nd edn. (Paris, 1929), p. 182.

Marx.[45] The acquisition of culture, de Man pointed out, required a personal autonomy and leisure time that were precisely contrary to the nature of working-class life and to the demands of the class struggle.[46] Certainly there was no more urgent task than to open access to the western cultural tradition to the working class; but this demanded a clear head: "It must be seen that the civilization to which the working class demands access is none other than bourgeois civilization."[47]

Despite their theorizing about "proletarian culture," in practical action working-class educational experts followed the course that de Man pointed out, that Thierry had warned against, and that Guéhenno puzzled over. It is hard to see how they could have done otherwise. Certainly their hopes for the *école unique* were not the hopes of the Radicals. But they were powerless to control the social effects of the expansion of educational opportunity; they could not impose a "proletarian culture" upon the public school system. They had to work with that which existed. Moreover, had they really had revolution and proletarian culture uppermost in mind, the syndicalists would not have built their educational program upon the report of the Comité d'étude et d'action pour l'école unique, which was not revolutionary and had nothing to do with proletarian culture.

IF THE development of a proletarian culture had to await the creation of a classless society, some syndicalists felt that the arrival of Utopia could be hurried along by means of a nationalization of the educational system.

The initiative for the nationalization scheme came from the primary school teachers' union, the Syndicat national des instituteurs. Since the establishment of the free, lay and compulsory primary school, school teachers had been figures of considerable prestige in small communities; the "hussars of the Republic," as Péguy called them, they were the personification of the Red against the Black of the village *curé*. And

[45] *Ibid.*, p. 186.   [46] *Ibid.*, p. 183.   [47] *Ibid.*, p. 202.

136

the trade unionists among them were thought to be especially Red. The most militant and sectarian defenders of *laïcité,* the members of the SNI felt a sort of mystical identification with the working class, manifested in an often simple-minded Marxism and a rigidly idealistic pacifism.[48]

The syndicalist school teachers resented the priority given to secondary education in the reform projects associated with the *école unique.* They felt that important problems of primary education were being slighted; they found it hard to become enthusiastic about a reform that seemed to have little to do with them and that, for all they knew, might threaten some of their own interests.[49] Unable to muster more than lukewarm enthusiasm for the reform itself, the school teachers instead placed their considerable zeal behind a scheme for the nationalization of the educational system and proclaimed that, without it, the *école unique* could not truly be built. The scheme, however, was quite vague; it is doubtful that the SNI really expected it to be carried into effect. Conceived partly as a threat against those the school teachers considered the adversaries of *laïcité,* nationalization was a distant goal at best.

Inspired by the CGT's program for the nationalization of industry, the idea of nationalizing the educational system had circulated for some time before the SNI gave it definite shape. The Compagnons had suggested a sort of nationalization in their proposals for a University corporation. At its congress of 1927, the Syndicat national des instituteurs adopted a resolution in favor of the principle of nationalization,[50] but had no plan to discuss until its congress at Rennes, in August 1928.

[48] On the SNI, see André Bianconi, "Le Syndicat national des instituteurs de 1920 à 1939." Unpublished thesis for the *doctorat de recherche*, Fondation nationale des sciences politiques, 1964.

[49] Interview of the author with André Delmas, former secretary-general of the SNI (October 27, 1965).

[50] *Le Populaire*, August 7, 1927. The *Bulletin national du syndicat national des instituteurs* is not available in the public libraries of Paris, for the period 1920-1929. In 1929, the SNI changed the title of its organ to *Ecole libératrice*, which is available at the Bibliothèque nationale.

Syndicalists as vigorously opposed a state monopoly of education as did Catholics; monopoly, syndicalists argued, made the educational system simply the tool of the party or class in control of the state. The nationalization scheme of the SNI was simple, despite the mass of detail that encumbered it. All the educational facilities of the nation were to be placed under the control of a tripartite corporation, independent of the state, composed of representatives of the state, of parents, and of teachers.[51] Presumably, the representatives of the state were to be administrators; it was unclear why teachers, as state employees, were not representatives of the state, too, nor was it certain that the "users" [*usagers*] of the system were actually to be parents; some syndicalists argued that "users" meant the trade unions that represented the productive forces in the state. But the SNI made clear that lay laws would prevail in the entire system; the confessional schools would come under the control of the corporation. According to L. Boulanger, the *rapporteur* for the plan, "there are only two essential conditions for operating a private school: tripartite control and absolute *laïcité* of personnel and instruction."[52]

Coming straight from a congress of the Ligue des droits de l'homme that had rejected a resolution in favor of a state monopoly of education, Ferdinand Buisson admonished the assembled delegates of the SNI. Their scheme, he warned, had grave implications, for it denied the confessional schools the right to direct their own affairs and to give religious instruction. That, of course, was exactly what the school teachers intended.[53]

The nationalization scheme provoked *Le Temps* to another of its violent denunciations of the SNI,[54] and it allowed the

[51] *Le Peuple*, August 7, 1928.

[52] *Revue de l'enseignement primaire*, October 10, 1928.

[53] According to Stephen Valot in *L'Oeuvre*, August 7, 1928, Boulanger replied to Buisson: "We desire freedom and all its consequences, but not the freedom to mutilate thought."

[54] *Le Temps*, August 8, 1928: "Ce syndicat dit national aspire, avec une audace non déguisée, non pas seulement à régenter, mais à mener la nation, et à l'horizon de ces imaginations échauffées monte la dictature des maîtres d'école."

school teachers to get in a blow against the enemies of *laïcité,* real or imagined, but it did not advance the cause of educational reform. It was an idea quite independent of the *école unique,* despite the insistence of the school teachers that reform could not truly be accomplished without a nationalization of the system. If the SNI had its way, the confessional schools, under a nationalized system, would suffer the same fate as under a state monopoly of education. For if they were unable to give religious instruction, the confessional schools would have no reason to exist.[55]

THE PROBLEM of educational reform, brought before a congress of the CGT in 1919, did not seriously figure in another congress until 1925. In the intervening years, the CGT had undergone a schism that created grave problems of tactics and organization and crowded less urgent issues off its agenda. In 1925, the CGT maintained the educational demands it had already adopted in Lyon in 1919, and in its "minimum program" of 1924.[56] In 1927, partly as a gesture of protest against the continued inactivity of the government, the CGT voted to maintain the problem of educational reform permanently on its agenda.[57]

[55] The Ligue de l'enseignement took up the question of nationalization in a long and confusing debate at its congress in Lille, in 1928. The League adopted the scheme of the SNI and at the same time proclaimed its respect for freedom of education. It is quite likely that the League, like the SNI, considered nationalization as much a weapon to wield against adversaries as a feasible program. Marceau Pivert fervently defended the nationalization thesis, calling freedom of education "a means for the rich to crush the poor." Edouard Herriot opposed the nationalization plan. If the University needed to be defended against subordination to religious doctrines, he said, it needed to be no less vigorously defended against subordination to political dogmas. "44ᵉ congrès, Ligue de l'enseignement, Lille. 14-17 juin 1928, compte-rendu," *Action laïque,* No. 629 (April-June 1928).

[56] *Confédération générale du travail, XVIIIᵉ congrès confédéral tenu à Paris du 26 au 27 août 1925. compte-rendu des débats* (Paris, 1925), p. 176.

[57] *Confédération générale du travail, XIXᵉ congrès confédéral tenu à Paris du 26 au 29 juillet 1927. compte-rendu des débats* (Paris, 1927).

But the first real advance over its position of 1919 came after the congress of 1929, when the Administrative Committee appointed a committee to draw up a detailed plan of reform. Francis Million, editor of *Le Peuple,* headed a joint committee of workers and teachers; most of the technical work fell upon the newly formed Fédération générale de l'enseignement, an offshoot of the Fédération de l'enseignement aux 2ᵉ et 3ᵉ degrés, or Zoretti Federation.[58]

In 1927 the Zoretti Federation had had only 500 members, professors in the lycées and universities. Organized at the beginning of 1923, it was vastly outnumbered by the Syndicat des professeurs de lycée, a conservative professional society the majority of whose members had little taste for trade unionism. Seeking better to coordinate the syndicalist movement within the University, representatives of the Zoretti Federation and the Syndicat national des instituteurs undertook a series of arduous and complicated negotiations that led to the formation of the Fédération générale de l'enseignement at the end of 1928.[59] The new federation might have appeared to be the SNI in disguise. Though thirteen organizations with a combined membership of 82,000 joined the new federation, over 76,000 of them were primary school teachers.[60] Nevertheless, the SNI apparently did not use its overwhelming numerical strength to impose its own point of view upon the FGE.

The work of the CGT's special committee on the *école unique* required over a year. Million wrote that the committee's first concern "should tend essentially to raise the intellectual level of the mass, rather than aiming particularly at pushing a very restricted élite to the summit."[61] If there was any speculation

[58] L. Boulanger, "La Commission confédérale de l'enseignement et l'éducation nationale," *Ecole libératrice*, November 9, 1929.

[59] See Ludovic Zoretti, "La Fédération générale de l'enseignement et l'éducation nationale," *L'Ecole publique française* (Paris, 1937), pp. 170-76; Paul Gerbod, "Associations et syndicalismes universitaires, 1828-1928," *Le Mouvement social* (April-June 1966), 3-45.

[60] *L'Université*, January 1930. There are great gaps in the collection of the FGE's organ at the Bibliothèque nationale.

[61] *Le Peuple*, May 28, 1930.

about proletarian culture, it did not appear in the published report of the committee. Work on the reform of the public system focused on secondary education, as it had done since the war. The committee did not strike out in any new directions. Instead, it adopted the Organic Statute of the Study Committee on the *école unique* as the basis for its own project, and indeed made few changes in it. Nor did the conflict of interest between reformers primarily concerned with raising the cultural level of the mass and reformers more concerned with the problem of intellectual élites disappear simply because the committee did its work under the auspices of the CGT.

According to Henri Boivin, lycée professor and *rapporteur* for the reform project, the thorniest problem of reform remained that of establishing links between the first and second degrees.[62] The committee of the CGT adopted the fairly rigorous method of selection recommended by the Study Committee, an apparent contradiction of its avowed preoccupation with mass education. The entrance examination seemed designed to siphon off the most able students for the secondary level without regard for what happened to the unselected. But the committee recommended a compulsory "complementary course," an extension of the primary school, for children unable or unwilling to go on to some form of secondary education.

The CGT committee made its most important contribution to the reform movement in its suggestion for a two-year common course at the beginning of the secondary level. A child of limited financial means could not afford to make mistakes in his choice of options; he had no family income to fall back upon if he failed a major examination and was required to drop out of school until he made it up. A working-class child, it was believed, needed to finish his formal education as rapidly as possible, in order not to place an unbearable financial strain on his parents.

The "orientation class" was designed to minimize errors

[62] H. Boivin, "La Réforme de l'enseignement envisagée au point de vue technique," *La Réforme de l'enseignement (école unique) et l'éducation ouvrière* (Paris, 1931), p. 13. The text of the CGT plan was published in this pamphlet.

in choice of options through careful observations of individual aptitudes and consultation between teachers and parents. The Committee intended the class to include not only a common program of general studies, but also the fundamentals of each of the three options. It was true that the Study Committee had suggested an orientation class of one year, but the syndicalists did not consider one year long enough for such a delicate task. They failed to agree, however, on what the content of the common program should be; conflicts of professional interest among committee members prevented a decision.[63] Nonetheless, the project proclaimed "the fundamental spiritual unity of public education," a rebuke to the social and intellectual compartmentalization of the prevailing system.[64] The orientation class was clearly a translation of the desire of reformers to raise the cultural level of the majority of students, not simply of an élite.

Behind the idea of orientation stood a conception of equality of opportunity that differed markedly from that behind the idea of selection. Selection implied that once external impediments to advancement were removed, all children would have an equal start in a competitive intellectual race, at the end of which the winners would be awarded the prize of admission to secondary education, and the losers would be ignored. Orientation, on the other hand, implied that the removal of external barriers to advancement was not enough to establish real equality of opportunity; it rejected the idea that school was a race for honors that required winners and losers. Indeed, the attempt to match each child to the sort of instruction that best suited his own abilities and interests suggested that there existed no universal criteria by which all children could be judged, regardless of the circumstances in which they found themselves. The concept of orientation opened the way for the development of an interventionist idea of equality of educational opportunity. Selection, congenial to the Radicals' view of equality, held that intelligence was fixed genetically. It simply needed to be found, measured and encouraged wher-

[63] *Ibid.*, pp. 15-16.   [64] *Ibid.*, p. 19.

ever it existed. This had been the position of the Compagnons in 1918. But the idea of orientation demanded that intelligence be regarded as itself acquired; this conception of equal educational opportunity called for a commitment actively to help families help their children. Selection and orientation rested uneasily together in the same document; few on the CGT committee perceived the conflict between the two. It was true that if only a few children were to go on to secondary education, no conflict existed: they could be first selected and then oriented. But this was not the intention of the devisers of the CGT project.[65]

More concerned to see a reform carried into effect than to insist upon doctrinal purity, after all the years of disappointment, the Committee moderated the demand of the SNI for a nationalization of the educational system. It suggested that a "National Office of Education," embodying the tripartite principle of representation, should be merely a consultative body, with no administrative authority.

At its congress of 1931, the CGT adopted the reform project of the special committee with no debate.[66] Zoretti claimed that the plan was a vindication of the ideas of Albert Thierry,[67] but the section of the plan that dealt with public education was more clearly a triumph for the Compagnons. Zoretti argued that two currents had existed in the reform movement since the war, sometimes apart, often mingling together: "a bourgeois reformers' current and a revolutionary workers' current."[68] But Zoretti was surely engaged in wishful thinking if

[65] On changes in the concept of equal opportunity see the remarks of Martin Trow in the mimeographed transcript of the "Conference on Quality and Equality in Education," Princeton University, December 2 to 4, 1964, p. 16.

[66] *Confédération générale du travail. XXIᵉ congrès confédéral tenu à Paris le 15 au 18 septembre 1931. compte-rendu sténographique* (Paris, 1931), pp. 457-58. The interest of the delegates was decidedly elsewhere. At the 1931 congress took place a heated debate over a proposition for reunification of the CGT with the CGTU, the Communist-dominated organization that had split from the CGT in 1922.

[67] Zoretti, *Elite, sélection, culture*, p. 38.

[68] *Ibid.*, p. 31.

he believed that the plan adopted by the CGT was an engine of social revolution. There was not a trace even of the verbalism of revolution in the project, not a mention of the word "worker." And it was not at all clear how the opportunity for a worker's child to exchange backbreaking manual labor for a more secure and less physically exhausting existence would instill in him a greater revolutionary ardor than he had possessed before. In a developed industrial society, so long as there are enough jobs to go around, education tends to be an integrative, not a disintegrative social force. Few, if any, of the opponents of the *école unique* perceived that educational reform might be one means of easing the French working class out of its isolation from the rest of society. The Manichean world-view of Marxist intellectuals such as Zoretti blinded them to this point, too. The division of French society into the "We" and the "They" described one dimension of reality, but it did not take into account de Man's observation that one of the deep-seated aspirations of the "We" was a share in the society of the "They." The plan of the CGT was obviously reformist and evolutionary in concept; it encouraged proletarians to work for their own disappearance—perhaps into the bourgeoisie, perhaps not.

THE Socialists always insisted that their conception of the *école unique* should not be confused with the conception of the Radicals. But the Socialist party did not adopt a reform program of its own until its congress of Nancy in 1929; the question of education did not figure importantly in any congress until then. It is true that individual Socialists participated in the Comité d'étude et d'action pour l'école unique; most of the University syndicalists who helped to draw up the CGT plan were Socialists as well. But the party neither demanded nor received credit for these efforts. In the 1920's Charles Andler, Socialist university professor, lamented that in the matter of educational reform his party seemed merely to be tagging along after the Radicals: "It has appeared once again that our socialism is only the prolongation of democracy, and not the profound revolution of minds and characters that it [once] promised to be."[69] In the absence of a party plan for educational reform, the task of defining the Socialist version of the *école unique* fell to individuals, not all of whom were in good repute with the majority of the party. According to the recollections of one Socialist,[70] the leadership of the party, in the person of Léon Blum, never displayed as much interest in the problem of educational reform as did the leadership of the Radical party, in the person of Edouard Herriot.

In large measure, the party derived its official ideas on education from the syndicalists.[71] Borrowing the program of the CGT was perhaps a sensible course of action; as an ostensibly working-class party, the point of view of the Socialist party roughly corresponded to the point of view of the CGT. But it is curious that the Socialists, engaged in a constant battle in the political arena to set themselves off from the Radicals, left the initiative in educational reform to a non-political arm of the working class.

At the end of 1927, Léon Blum, his eye on the coming elections, wrote in *Le Populaire*: "We Socialists must demand the *école unique* in the *social sense*. . . . For us, *école unique* signifies a national school with a view to the best possible utilization of social units."[72] In contrast to the Radicals, who considered the *école unique* primarily a ladder of individual social ascent, Blum conceived it as an instrument employed by and for the collectivity in the development and distribution of the nation's intellectual resources. But he did not elaborate upon the implications of this conception; he did not indicate, for

[69] Andler, *L'Humanisme travailliste*, p. 6.

[70] Interview of the author with Georges Lefranc (October 18, 1965).

[71] Zoretti was strangely silent within the Socialist party on the problem of reform; he directed all of his efforts toward the CGT. In 1935 he wrote that "On ne peut pas dire que le socialisme officiel ait eu une part décisive ou même une part importante dans l'évolution idéologique [of the reform movement] de ces 15 ans." *Elite, sélection, culture*, pp. 19-20.

[72] *Le Populaire*, November 25, 1927. The meaning of Blum's use of the term *unités sociales* is unclear. Presumably he meant individuals fulfilling a useful function in society.

example, whether he believed that the state should exercise a control over the vocational choices of its citizens.

But Blum clearly favored a state monopoly of the educational system. No authority other than the state, he argued, had the right to perform the task of selection. An unregulated confessional school system created social distinctions between the public and private schools that Socialists could not tolerate. Moreover, Blum did not believe that, in the matter of education, the liberty of the family could be reconciled with the rights and duties of the state: "Between the family idea on the one hand, and the national and social idea on the other, a choice must be made. We Socialists have made our choice."[73]

The party's "Program of Immediate Action," drawn up with a view to the elections of 1928, did not undertake to elaborate a specifically Socialist conception of the *école unique*. The program declared that the reform would lead to "decisive social consequences," and assailed the Radicals for not understanding this point, but it did not indicate what Socialists hoped those consequences might be. Indeed, only the party's partial adoption of the nationalization scheme of the sni clearly distinguished the Socialist program of educational reform from that of the Radicals. The party limited its demand for nationalization to primary education, perhaps largely to please its own considerable clientele of primary school teachers.[74]

Georges Lefranc has suggested that, if the Socialists had come to power in 1932, Marcel Déat would probably have become minister of public instruction.[75] In our day Déat's name evokes the sinister collaborationist days of Vichy France, but in the 1920's he was a rising young hope of the Socialist party. He was one of the few Socialists who bothered to do much thinking about educational reform within the context of socialism, and if Lefranc's suggestion is correct, Déat was

[73] *Ibid.*

[74] *Le Programme immédiat du parti socialiste, voté au congrès national extraordinaire de Paris, décembre 1927* (Paris, 1928), pp. 32-35.

[75] Georges Lefranc, *Histoire du front populaire; 1934-1938* (Paris, 1965), p. 297.

clearly considered among the party's leading educational experts, however unorthodox his brand of socialism may have been.

He was well equipped for such a position. Among the last of the *normaliens* to come under the spell of Lucien Herr, he had been a brilliant student of Célestin Bouglé, from whom he obtained a thorough familiarity with Emile Durkheim's sociology of education. A philosophy professor at the lycée in Reims from 1923 to 1925, he had close ties with the syndicalist movement within the University, having helped to found the Fédération de l'enseignement aux 2ᵉ et 3ᵉ degrés, and he was an active member of the Ligue de l'enseignement.[76]

Déat, though a follower of Henri de Man, rejected de Man's argument that the working class merely wanted its own share of the traditional culture. On the contrary, he insisted, the working class desired to create a new system of values. He did not, however, more than vaguely indicate the character of this new system: "Culture is not only knowledge, but the unlimited enrichment of the entire being—feeling and acting as well as thinking . . . a vision of the world."[77]

Aside from his excursions into the debate on proletarian culture, Déat was an articulate spokesman for a desire shared by reformers—perhaps humanists might be a better word—of quite diverse political sympathies. Liberal education, it was felt, had become merely a collection of disciplines narrowly tied to preparation for specialization in the liberal professions. The distinctive task of socialism, Déat argued, was to see that a general culture was dissociated from this connection, and made accessible to the masses as well as to a restricted élite. Déat, like the authors of the CGT reform plan, considered the

[76] On Déat, see Lefranc, *Le Mouvement socialiste*, pp. 288-92. Lefranc knew Déat well; Claude Varenne, *Le Destin de Marcel Déat* (Paris, 1948), especially chapter 1. See the forthcoming Stanford University doctoral dissertation of Emily Goodman on Déat.

[77] "Le Programme scolaire du parti," *La Vie socialiste*, November 21, 1931. *Vie socialiste* was the organ of the right wing *tendance* of the party, to which Déat was attached.

common basis of study at the beginning of the secondary level a practical means of carrying out this task.[78]

By suddenly opening new horizons to the culturally deprived, Déat argued, the *école unique* would be a "formidable fabricator of social explosives."[79] New intellectual élites, recruited from the masses, would furnish the leadership cadres for the revolution: "At the end of a rather short time everything will blow up."[80] Déat simply made a positive good out of the argument of conservatives that the *école unique* would create a dangerous horde of *déclassés*. Furthermore, once the principle that each individual had the right to ascend as high as his abilities permitted was firmly implanted in the educational system, then it would be impossible not to apply the principle to the entire society.[81]

Déat's constant juxtaposition of the words reform and revolution makes ambiguous the meaning he attached to either word. Moreover, it would be misleading to suggest that his somewhat idiosyncratic notion of the social consequences to which the *école unique* would lead had a wide following within the party. It is hard to imagine, for example, that the rationalist Blum found Déat's essentially irrational notion congenial.

But Déat's consideration of the problem of culture represented an official party line; perhaps he was most responsible for the Socialist party's adoption of the syndicalist scheme for nationalization of the educational system. A number of Socialists, including Léon Blum, were hostile to the idea of nationalization. They preferred to see the entire educational establishment under the direct control of the state, not under the authority of a semi-autonomous corporation, as the nationalization scheme implied. Unlike some syndicalists, Déat did not consider nationalization a necessary precondition of

---

[78] Marcel Déat, *L'Ecole unique et le problème de la culture* (Paris? 1931), passim; "La Réponse de Marcel Déat à notre enquête sur l'école unique," *La Voix*, April 6, 1930.

[79] *La Vie socialiste*, November 21, 1931.

[80] *Ibid.*   [81] *Ibid.*

educational reform. But he constantly urged on the party the view that, in a capitalist society, a state monopoly of education would be an instrument of bourgeois propaganda, a cradle for lulling the workers asleep.[82]

In 1929 the Socialist party devoted a large part of its congress in Nancy to the problems of "the school and *laïcité*" J. B. Sévérac, who belonged to the left wing of the party, informed the delegates that the congress needed above all to give the parliamentary group and party workers a precise outline of the Socialist attitude toward education,[83] a recognition that the party's position had been much less than precise. Despite Sévérac's instructions, however, debate focused upon broad questions of principle. Sharp confrontations occurred between *tendances* of the party over the issues of *laïcité* and the nationalization of the educational system.

However interesting this remarkably sophisticated debate,[84] the concern here is less to distinguish between diverse tendencies within the party than to determine the position of the party as a whole on educational reform. This purpose is best served by a brief examination of the lengthy resolution of the congress—a compromise—on reform and *laïcité*.

It seems curious, at first sight, that the resolution dwelt upon the problems of *laïcité* and nationalization at great length, almost to the exclusion of the problem of reform itself. These issues, though closely related to the *école unique*, were distinct from it. Relegated to a few brief paragraphs, the reform proposals merely reaffirmed the long-standing demands for an educational system free at all levels, the raising of the school-leaving age, an end to the isolation of technical education,

[82] See, for example, "La Nationalisation de l'enseignement," *La Vie socialiste*, December 10, 1927.

[83] *Parti socialiste S.F.I.O. XXVIᵉ congrès national tenu à Nancy le 9, 10, 11 et 12 juin 1929. compte-rendu sténographique* (Paris, 1929), pp. 208-9, hereafter cited as CRS.

[84] The debate on *laïcité* opposed a traditional free thinkers' tendency to a Christian socialist tendency defended by André Philip, and to still a third tendency represented by Déat.

the common training of teachers. In addition, the resolution incorporated the syndicalist idea of orientation.[85]

But the Socialists by no means considered the religious question an echo from the past; and they were more concerned with the framework of general ideas within which their reform proposals were contained than with the proposals themselves. Though they shared with the Radicals a conception of *laïcité* theoretically grounded in respect for freedom of conscience, guaranteed by the neutrality of the state in matters of belief, the Socialists parted company with the Radicals in the bases of their anticlericalism. Wary of the use of the anticlerical issue as a diversion from social problems, the Socialists rooted their anticlericalism in the conviction that the Church had always been the ally of the forces of capitalism against the working class. The battle for *laïcité* was therefore inseparable from the class struggle.[86] That the party should have felt it necessary to make a vigorous restatement of these principles in 1929 indicated that the religious question, if it no longer occupied the center of the political stage, was nonetheless far from moribund.

Education fitted quite logically into the center of Socialist concerns, for the whole point of socialism, as a movement and as an ideology, was human emancipation from servitude of any kind. Perhaps a ready-made theoretical apparatus made it seem unnecessary to Socialists to go beyond general statements of principle in their educational doctrine, which was only part of a total conception of the relationship between man and society. In the Nancy resolution, preoccupation with the question of *laïcité,* at the expense of the *école unique,* also seems to reveal a conviction that the essential educational mission of socialism, like the mission of the Church, was the propagation of the faith, in this case a faith in reason. For the principle of neutrality that was to prevail in the entire reformed educational establishment was one that no Catholic could admit, based upon "neither doctrine, nor

[85] CRS, p. 422. [86] *Ibid.,* p. 419.

dogma, but demonstrated truth and the exercise of reason."[87]

Perhaps the Socialists' vision of the *école unique* found its most succinct expression in a phrase that the resolution borrowed from Jaurès. The purpose of reform was to be "the coordination of one's own life in the general life."[88] The Socialists sought a coordination between individual abilities and the needs of society by means of the educational establishment. They intended no sort of regimentation, although liberals were convinced that they did. The humanistic Jaurèsian strain in the French socialist tradition, however, was too strong to permit Socialists to succumb to the temptations of regimentation. The party resolution proclaimed that "Socialism is not only an economic movement. It intends the highest kind of moral transformation, which permits to each human being the blooming of his personality, and which opens to him, in the collective interest, access to all the knowledge commensurate with his aptitudes.[89] Avoiding the old dilemma of reform and revolution, the resolution did not make clear whether Socialists considered this moral transformation a goal that might be realized within bourgeois society as part of an evolutionary progression toward socialism, or a task of the distant revolution.

Against the wishes of Blum and other delegates, the syndicalist scheme for the nationalization of the educational system was incorporated into the party's demands, and assumed an equal footing with the *école unique* itself: "Nationalization, *école unique*, extension of *laïcité*—such are the essential reforms that socialism proposes."[90] Finally, the resolution insisted that the immense task of building the *école unique* was a task that only socialism could perform, and reaffirmed the old revolutionary urge to harmonize "the word and the deed."[91]

As Zoretti pointed out, there existed two tendencies within the reform movement. He chose to call them a "bourgeois reformist" tendency and a "revolutionary workers'" tendency,

[87] *Ibid.*, p. 421. [88] *Ibid.*, p. 420. [89] *Ibid.*, p. 420.
[90] *Ibid.*, p. 422. [91] *Ibid.*, p. 423.

though he might more accurately have called them individualist and collectivist. Individualists and collectivists expected the same structural reform to do quite different things. The *école unique* was expected to be a ladder for individual social ascent and at the same time to furnish educated leaders to the working class; to set off a cultural revolution and to preserve intact the classical humanities; to make working-class children into members of the middle class, and in the name of the working class to wrest control of the lycée from the bourgeoisie; to effect a coordination between individual abilities and the needs of society and to allow free play to the demands of the intellectual marketplace.

The *école unique* could not bear this weight of ideology. For the enormous tasks it was called upon to perform, the bases of the *école unique* were modest indeed: a free school system, selection and orientation. On the other hand, the achievement of these goals was in itself an enormous task. In democratic society, political organizations of the left have always had to face the intractable problem of effecting a transition between the "word" and the "deed," between thought and action, while remaining within the bounds of legality. Under the Third Republic, the grand designs of educational reformers and the ideas that lay behind them had all to undergo the scrutiny of parliament if they were ever to become reality.

The Radicals might be suspected of some insincerity in their advocacy of the *école unique*; to them it was a political device, a piecemeal reform clothed in noble language. The same cannot be said of the architects of the CGT plan, who sacrificed a particularist working-class point of view to what they conceived to be the general interest, in order to work out a reform plan which, they believed, stood some chance of being acted upon by parliament. In their support for the *école unique,* the Socialists never escaped the appearance of being Radicals who really meant what they said.

Under the exigencies of practical politics, differences among the partisans of the *école unique* disappeared. Unable to resolve the dilemma Guéhenno had posed, working-class representatives put it aside. Contradictory points of view were subordinated to the egalitarian urge that informed all of them. The Study Committee on the *école unique,* upon whose work the CGT heavily depended, was the most important manifestation of this tendency. To be sure, fundamental differences remained over the meaning of equal opportunity, but fortunately it never became necessary to make them explicit. In the perspective of hindsight, the movement for educational enfranchisement was a kind of partial restoration of the nineteenth-century alliance between working class and lower middle class in the movement for universal suffrage.

Chapter vi. The Politics of the Possible: Free Secondary Education

> . . . les bourgeois d'alors se faisaient de la société une idée un peu hindoue, et la considéraient comme composée de castes fermées où chacun, dès sa naissance, se trouvait placé dans le rang qu'occupaient ses parents, et d'où rien, à moins des hasards d'une carrière exceptionnelle ou d'un mariage inespéré, ne pouvait vous tirer pour vous faire pénétrer dans une caste supérieure.
>
> —Marcel Proust

FREE secondary education, one major support upon which the *école unique* rested, was not the accomplishment of a triumphant majority of the Left. It was adopted through a series of parliamentary maneuvers, against the inclinations of the government in power. The lycée became free not as part of a legislative bill on educational reform, but as the consequence of a ministerial decree forced by economic necessity.

On July 23, 1926, Raymond Poincaré formed a government of national union, to achieve a political truce under which the continuing financial crisis could be resolved. Edouard Herriot became minister of public instruction in this party coalition, which extended only from the Right through the center, excluding the Socialists and Communists.[1] As part of his effort to save the franc, Poincaré undertook to tidy up the administration. Each minister was responsible for finding ways to pare

---

[1] Herriot, who had accepted a portfolio on behalf of the Radicals (there were three other Radicals in the cabinet), found himself in an equivocal position. He had been an architect of the Cartel des gauches; now he sat in a government that the Socialists opposed. Many Radicals yearned for the alliance with the Socialists, or at least a free hand, and opposed the government on purely political questions, despite their party's representation in it. The right, which supported Poincaré, did not distinguish between Radicals who supported the government and those who did not. Goguel, *Politique des partis*, pp. 239-41.

154

down his own department, and the work proceeded by decree.

In later years, Herriot claimed that Poincaré had said to him: "We must make economies, ferocious economies. . . . You're going to suppress the *collèges*."[2] A *collège* was a municipal secondary school to which the state accorded subsidies, named the teaching personnel and sent state scholarship holders. To a number of these *collèges* were annexed *écoles primaires supérieures*; in other localities, an *école primaire supérieure* was annexed to a lycée. But *écoles primaires supérieures* and secondary schools operated independently, even where they shared the same plant. And it will be remembered that the lycées and *collèges* charged tuition, but the *écoles primaires supérieures* were free.[3]

Instead of suppressing a number of *collèges* outright, as Poincaré had urged, Herriot undertook, in a decree of October 1, 1926, to consolidate the secondary course with the *école primaire supérieure* in the establishments that offered both. Henceforth, pupils of both branches would together take certain of the same courses from the same teachers: French, modern languages, mathematics, sciences and physical education.[4] Herriot later recalled that he had had a long-range plan in mind before he made this decision.[5] But it may well be that he became aware of the possibilities of the decree only after he had made it. On the face of it, the amalgamation of courses that the lycée and the *école primaire supérieure* shared in common should have pleased partisans of a certain conception of the *école unique*. But the decree also made quite noticeable an inequality that Herriot meant to exploit to the fullest: it placed together in the same classroom, taking the same courses from the same teachers, some students who paid tuition and some who did not.

Herriot intended his "economy measure" to make sure that

---

[2] "L'Ecole unique et la 3e République." *Conférence de M. Edouard Herriot sous la présidence de M. Paul Langevin, 6 décembre 1945* (Paris, n.d.).

[3] Richard, *L'Enseignement en France*, p. 48.

[4] J.O., *Lois et décrets*, October 2, 1926, p. 10909.

[5] *Jadis*, ii, 257.

part of the Radical program did not become lost in the ava-
lanche of decrees that poured forth from the Poincaré government. Edouard Daladier claimed that, since the decree had
been approved by the cabinet, the government of National
Union supported the *école unique*; this amounted to the assertion that the government was abandoning its own program to
take up that of the Radicals.[6] Jean Guiraud complained that
Herriot "is upsetting our educational system from top to bottom."[7] Charles Maurras called Herriot's action "insane,"[8] and
Le Temps appealed to parliament to halt the "demogogical
devaluation" of secondary education.[9] The Société d'éducation
called Herriot a dictator,[10] and a writer for *Etudes* remarked
that, despite the political truce, the *école unique* remained "the
great demagogical idea for which all the fanatical sects are
united in a coalition."[11]

If Herriot's decrees outraged some Catholics and rightists,
the Chamber scarcely took notice of them. Urged by Poincaré
to pass the budget as quickly as possible, the Chamber pushed
through the budget of public instruction for 1927 with little
debate. On the floor of the Chamber, Léon Bérard announced
that he intended to question Herriot on the implications of
the decree, and he demanded a full-scale debate on the *école
unique,* if only, he remarked ironically, to find out just what
it was.[12]

It was true that *école unique* had always been a vague and
confusing slogan. Herriot himself came to consider it a liabil-

[6] *L'Ere nouvelle*, October 8, 1926.

[7] *La Croix*, December 28, 1926.

[8] *L'Action française*, October 3, 1926.

[9] *Le Temps*, December 12, 1926.

[10] Louis Crousaz-Crétet, "Un Dictateur de l'instruction publique:
M. Herriot," *Bulletin de la société générale de l'éducation et de
l'enseignement*, LVIII (1927), 851-57. In 1927, at the annual convention
of the society, Colonel Keller declared: 'The adversary has changed
teams and changed games, but he's pursuing his work with a redoubled
activity," *ibid.*, 448.

[11] Maurice Vallet, "Le Laïcisme dans l'enseignement actuel; étapes
et progrès nouveaux," *Etudes*, 189 (1926), 278.

[12] *J.O.Ch.* (1926), p. 3643.

ity. He believed that he had found a way to keep some of his party's promises on educational reform, but the phrase of the Compagnons did not really describe his undertaking. The decree of October 1 had the potential to set in motion a step-by-step progression toward free secondary education, but that was all. No one had done more than Herriot, however, to suggest that *école unique* meant a vast democratic reform of the entire educational system. By 1927 he had probably admitted to himself that a vast reform was out of reach. In order to extract the maximum political credit from his action as minister, Herriot had two alternatives: he could either try to convince public opinion that *école unique* and free secondary education were synonymous terms, or he could try to quash the slogan *école unique,* and substitute "free lycée" in its place, in order to square the public debate with what he believed he could accomplish. But the second alternative might allow the Socialists to charge him with faintheartedness. Herriot did not choose between alternatives; he used them both at once.

He worked closely with Hippolyte Ducos, who, as *rapporteur* for the budget of public instruction, had a seat on the finance committee. If democratic idealism inspired the effort to open up the lycée to all who could benefit from it, a keen awareness of the possible was required to wring the necessary money out of the finance committee; and the awareness of Ducos, a former lycée professor from a Radical stronghold near Toulouse, was very keen indeed.

Ducos calculated that the state currently spent 202 million francs a year on secondary education—the lycées and *collèges* —and received 58 million francs in fees. Therefore, he argued, families paid in fees only one-fifth of what it cost the state to educate their offspring. This discrepancy meant, in effect, that for no reason except that their parents could afford the initial fee, privileged children held state scholarships for 80 per cent of the cost of their educations.[18] The cheapest way to begin to abolish this privilege, Herriot pointed out to the finance committee, was to get rid of the absurdity created by his decree of October 1, 1926, in which some pupils paid to attend the

[18] Zoretti had advanced this argument in 1918.

157

secondary establishments he had consolidated, and some did not. After some mild demurrers by André François-Poncet, the committee approved the request for 330,000 francs for this purpose.[14]

Herriot then made a concession of his own. At a hearing before the Senate committee on education, he declared: "Gentlemen, I suggest giving up the equivocal formula *'école unique'* in order to adopt the more concrete and realistic one of free lycée."[15] The proposition marked the end of a stage in his effort to make his promises conform to the possibilities of the decision—the decree of October 1—originally forced upon him by the financial crisis. Friends of the *école unique* wondered if it had expired altogether, like so many of the promises of the Cartel des gauches.[16] Adversaries did not believe that changing the label changed the contents: *école unique* or free lycée, one was as pernicious as the other.[17]

Partisans of Herriot's piecemeal tactics found an ally of sorts in Raymond Poincaré. A *laïque,* the son of a civil engineer, the brother of an inspector general of secondary education and himself a former minister of public instruction, Poincaré, like Jules Ferry before him, was an *homme de gouvernement,* a representative of that part of the bourgeoisie which had an acute, if often narrow sense of the public interest, enough confidence in its own ability and enough security of position to think that a free lycée might be a good idea.[18] Though doctrinaire in his own peculiar way, Poincaré had no time for party wrangles; his overriding concern was to preserve his majority, in order to nurse along the recovery of the franc. As minister of finance, he had given the initial approval to Herriot's request for funds. The credit of 330,000 francs was to eliminate tuition for the first three years of secondary study in fifty-three secondary establishments to

[14] *Le Temps,* October 9, 1927.

[15] *Progrès civique,* December 17, 1927.

[16] *Ibid.*

[17] *Le Temps,* December 12, 1927.

[18] The most recent biography of Poincaré is Pierre Miquel, *Poincaré* (Paris, 1961).

which an *école primaire supérieure* or a technical school had been attached by the decree of October 1, 1926.[19] Against an attempt to throw out article 59 of the finance law, authorizing the expenditure of these funds, Poincaré observed that the article made no commitment whatsoever to the *école unique,* or to anything in the future, for that matter. It was merely a limited measure taken to correct an existing abuse, nothing more. The disjunction was rejected. Article 59 was enacted into law.[20]

In the elections of April 1928, the *école unique* remained in the electoral programs of the two great parties of the Left, but there was little new that could be said.[21] It had been helpful as an ideological bond between Radicals and Socialists in the confrontation of Right and Left in the elections of 1924. But the election of 1928 was less an ideological clash than a sort of referendum on the policy of Raymond Poincaré. The reform movement was not a victim of the party truce, but it reflected the confusion caused by the truce. The *école unique* had helped to forge the Cartel des gauches, but at the end of 1927 Herriot was carrying out part of the reform in a government that the Socialists opposed and that his own party only lukewarmly supported.

The elections helped to clear up some of the confusion by giving Poincaré a fairly stable majority on the Right: he no longer required the support of the Radicals.[22] In addition, the

[19] *J.O.Ch.* (1927), p. 3232.

[20] *J.O.Ch.* (1927), p. 3879.

[21] The Socialists demanded the nationalization of the primary school. During the electoral campaign Blum charged that the Radicals had betrayed their own program, and particularly the *école unique*, in participating in the government of national union: ". . . quelles que soient les contrariétés d'essence et doctrine entre les deux partis, le programme radical est englobé dans le nôtre ou s'achemine vers le nôtre. . . . Est-ce l'union nationale ou le parti socialiste qui appuierait l'institution de l'école unique, même au sens étroit et fragmentaire où l'entendent les Radicaux?" *Le Populaire*, April 14, 1928.

[22] Charnay, *Les Scrutins politiques*, pp. 112-13.

concurrent stabilization of the franc put an end to the party truce, and allowed the game of politics to take up where it had left off. By the end of 1928, the partisans of the *école unique* at least found themselves together again in the opposition, and it had become apparent that the majority of the Right was not as solid as it had seemed immediately after the elections. Thus the elections did not advance the cause of reform, but neither did they harm it. Even had the Left won, it is unlikely that it would have abandoned the mechanism Herriot had stumbled upon for attaining free secondary education. The mechanism could be manipulated almost as well, if more slowly, from a minority position as it could from the government bench. Moreover, as a purely political device, the *école unique* could draw Socialists and Radicals together when they were in opposition, but it was too secondary an issue to keep them in agreement when they were in the majority. The cause of educational reform could therefore benefit more with the Left as a whole in opposition than when Radicals assumed power with the Socialists' equivocal "support."

Herriot stayed on as minister of public instruction in Poincaré's new government, despite efforts of the right to dislodge him. But the participation of Radicals in the government became increasingly awkward after the election of a majority clearly oriented to the right. For the first time, the Socialists had received a higher percentage of the vote than the Radicals. Many Radicals interpreted this as punishment for their collusion with parties of the Right, and, chafing under the restriction of the government of national union, militants sought freedom of action in the opposition. At the Radical congress of Angers, November 4-5, 1928, the Poincaré government was condemned for maneuvers favorable to the Church. The whole business was a piece of trumpery, but the Radical ministers bowed to party discipline and resigned from the government.[23] After two years as an uncomfortable ally of Poincaré, the Radical party found itself firmly in the opposition. But it also brought down the Radical minister who

---

[23] On this complicated and unedifying affair see Bonnefous, *Histoire politique*, IV, 275-89.

had done the most toward implementing one of its electoral promises. As leaders of the Société d'éducation observed in an attack on Herriot a few months before his fall, "He has had time to give a very precise orientation to the school policy of the national union government."[24]

Poincaré formed a new government, and managed to avoid tying himself firmly to the Right by including a few members of left-center splinter groups in his cabinet. Pierre Marraud, a senator of the *gauche démocratique,* became minister of public instruction. But the composition of the cabinet mattered less than the composition of the finance committee of the Chamber, for continued progress of the scheme Herriot and Ducos had devised. Though the Left constituted a minority in the Chamber, it managed to secure the presidencies of thirteen out of twenty committees for the parliamentary session of 1928. Louis-Jean Malvy, Radical-Socialist and bête noire of the nationalist Right, became president of the finance committee;[25] Hippolyte Ducos remained *rapporteur* of the budget of public instruction.

On September 27, 1928, he asked the finance committee to approve the extension of the measure of 1927 to cover all six years of secondary study in the same establishments, which he calculated should require an additional credit of 2,786,000 francs. The committee granted his request.[26] Once again the Chamber, in its haste to pass the entire budget by December 31, gave little time to general discussion of the budget for public instruction.[27]

[24] Antoine Lestra, J. de Valmon, Charles Bausson, "M. Herriot, dictateur de l'instruction publique," *Bulletin de la société générale d'éducation et d'enseignement,* LIX (1928), 599.

[25] Bonnefous, *Histoire politique,* IV, 258-59.

[26] *J.O.Doc.parl.* (1928), annex no. 613, p. 1764.

[27] Defending the credit of 2,786,000 francs, Ducos made clear that his party considered it not a stopgap measure, but one more step on the road to the *école unique. J.O.Ch.* (1928), pp. 3705-6. In the Senate, however, Marraud, minister of public instruction, assured his colleagues that it was *not* a step toward the *école unique. J.O. Sénat* (1928), p. 1521. In any case, parliament voted the money.

The measures undertaken toward free secondary education since 1926 had applied to a small number of provincial institutions—mostly municipal *collèges*—and those of a special kind: establishments that grouped together under one roof three sorts of education for adolescents. Parliament absent-mindedly voted the necessary funds, which did not amount to much. But when it became clear that the next step was a general measure that would affect the most prestigious Parisian lycées, such as Henri IV and Louis-le-Grand, as well as obscure backwoods *collèges,* the opposition stiffened. In 1929 and 1930 there took place the most extensive debate on the *école unique* that the Chamber ever held, and the greatest victory of the reform movement between the wars, though great only in comparison to past and future disappointments.

The finance committee continued to play a key role in the strategy of the partisans of free secondary education. To the consternation of the conservative majority in the Chamber, Malvy was reelected president of the committee for the parliamentary session of 1929. Because it had the authority to amend estimates of expenditure submitted to it by the ministries, a finance committee hostile to the government could be troublesome indeed: it could attempt to initiate reform against the wishes of the parliamentary majority.[28]

In the budget of 1930, Ducos intended to ask the finance committee only for enough funds to dispense with day school tuition for the sixth class, or first year of secondary studies. But at the same time he and his allies sought to force the Chamber to commit itself to the *principle* of free secondary education by means of the finance committee's wording of the article that prescribed how these funds were to be spent. The first line of this article read: "With a view to progressively achieving a completely free day school, in secondary establishments. . . ." Jean Locquin, Socialist member of the committee, suggested an amendment that would nail this statement of principle to a promise to carry it out: "The benefits of the

[28] On the power of the finance committee under the Third Republic, see W. L. Middleton, *The French Political System* (London, 1932), pp. 164-66.

measure dealt with in the first line of the present article will be extended, beginning January 1, 1931, to students of the fifth and following classes."[29]

Ducos made a lengthy defense of his request for funds before the finance committee in late August 1929. The party make-up of the committee worked to his advantage, and the request passed by one vote, 18 to 17; the division corresponded exactly to the division of the members between Left and Right.[30] It was apparent from the split in the committee that there would be a battle on the floor of the Chamber.

At least the Radical leadership thought it was apparent. But the government which Briand formed to succeed Poincaré, who had retired in utter exhaustion, lasted only until the end of October. President Doumergue, after demonstrating that the old Cartel was incapable of forming a government, called on André Tardieu.[31] Tardieu had never hidden his intense enjoyment of politics, nor disguised his brilliance, nor troubled to conceal the prickliness of his character under a veneer of camaraderie. Moreover, he had ideas. He was not well liked.[32] The majority elected in 1928 had lost its stability; defections on its right and left wings had brought down Briand. Tardieu sought to enlarge his majority to the left. He offered the Radicals eight cabinet posts and sent them a draft of a program incorporating a good share of their own proposals—including free secondary education.

The Radicals turned him down.[33] Ostensibly, they did so because they had little taste for Tardieu's majority of the Right; but they also had little taste for Tardieu himself. Radi-

[29] Interview of the author with M. Hippolyte Ducos (October 13, 1965). The text of the finance committee's article may be found in *J.O.Ch.* (1930), p. 1027.

[30] Letter of M. Hippolyte Ducos to the author (September 1, 1965).

[31] Bonnefous, *Histoire politique*, IV, pp. 369-71.

[32] On Tardieu, see the lively essay in Rudolph Binion, *Defeated Leaders: The Political Fate of Caillaux, Jouvenel and Tardieu* (New York, 1960), pp. 197-337.

[33] On this episode, see Binion, *Defeated Leaders*, pp. 291-92; Bonnefous, *Histoire politique*, 371-75.

cal proposals were, after all, Radical proposals. It was unheard of for a conservative minister to embrace them as his own. As far as free secondary education was concerned, the Radicals apparently preferred its defeat at the hands of a hostile majority, rather than allow Tardieu to take credit for easing it through as head of the government.

But before he had the chance, his government fell. The opposition challenged Henri Chéron, minister of finance, over the use of budgetary surpluses. In Tardieu's absence, Chéron made a minor issue a question of confidence; the left wing of the majority deserted the government. The Radical party, as the largest opposition group, had the responsibility of forming a new government. It was an impossible task. Camille Chautemps found that he could rely only on his own party, and some members of splinter groups of the left-center. In his ministerial declaration, he sought to conciliate both Left and Right. To the Right, he offered a tough line in foreign policy; among his pledges to the Left, he adopted the line of the majority of the finance committee on free secondary education. But Chautemps could not appease both extremes at once. His government was overthrown at its first appearance before the Chamber.[34]

It was Tardieu's turn to try again, and again he sought the support of the Radicals. Once more, he offered them a precise program incorporating a number of their own party measures; once more, they turned him down. Tardieu resorted to his old majority, but called on four members of the opposition who agreed to enter his government on their own responsibility, so as not to balance his cabinet too far to the right. On March 5, 1930, Tardieu presented his government to the Chamber, and in his speech declared: "in the course of the discussion of the budget, the government will, of course, ask you to vote the texts relative to free secondary education in the sixth class."[35]

Three months earlier, when harassed by the Left over some

---

[34] Bonnefous, *Histoire politique*, v, 14-15; *J.O.Ch.* (1930), p. 808.
[35] *J.O.Ch.* (1930), p. 848.

minor issue, Tardieu had abrasively replied, "Are you going to shoot at me at the very moment when I come before you bearing your children in my arms?"[36] One of those children was free secondary education. But Tardieu's solicitude for this particular child showed that he was not so concerned about the welfare of the children of the Left as he claimed to be. For Chautemps had accepted the principle of free secondary education; Tardieu merely declared his government's readiness to make the sixth class of the lycée free. He doubtless knew that a good share of his majority was not prepared to go even that far, and he made no further commitment.[37]

The finance committee's text on the abolition of tuition for the sixth class had become article 67 B of the finance law for 1930. The debate was scheduled for March 12, only a few days after Tardieu formed his second government. The stormy discussion extended far into the night. The opponents of free secondary education employed a series of parliamentary maneuvers in an effort to block passage of the measure. Party spokesmen followed one another to the tribune and repeated arguments for or against the *école unique* that had been constantly reiterated since the war, in the political press, in dozens of books and hundreds of articles and in previous debates in the Chamber. In the view of the Union républicaine démocratique, largest party of the Right, the *école unique* meant the ruin of French culture; the suppression of the rights of the family; a state monopoly of education.[38] The free lycée would merely be a free government handout to those quite able to pay. The triumvirate of educational experts of the Left—Ducos, Bracke and Herriot—undertook their by now familiar defense of the *école unique,* under a barrage of shouts and interruptions from the Right.[39]

[36] Quoted in Binion, *Defeated Leaders,* p. 295.

[37] According to M. Hippolyte Ducos, Tardieu flatly told Herriot that he did not believe the measure would pass. (Letter to the author, September 1, 1965.)

[38] *J.O.Ch.* (1930), p. 1032.

[39] *Ibid.,* pp. 1045-47; 1049.

The participants in this debate believed that far more was at stake than article 67 B. What seemed to be at stake was the quasi-monopoly of a social class over the levers of command and influence in the Third Republic. The structure of the educational system of the republic had always been the best counterweight to universal suffrage, the most substantial buttress of the "stalemate society."[40] The movement for the *école unique* was a claim on behalf of the many for educational enfranchisement, and among its more radical proponents an assault on that society. No matter how anodyne article 67 B may have been, it symbolized the claims of competence to speak with at least as much authority as wealth, social position, and family ties.

After more than eight hours of angry debate, Tardieu refused to accept the text of the finance committee on article 67 B. His government would make no commitment to the principle of free secondary education, he declared. Tardieu considered the free sixth class an experiment, nothing more. The finance committee sought to impose an educational reform upon the country by means of a finance law, an inadmissible procedure.[41] But the finance committee maintained the entire text against the government, and Blum and Herriot announced their parties' support of the committee.[42]

The Chamber voted first on the commitment to the principle of free secondary education—the crucial paragraph, in the eyes of the partisans of the *école unique*. It passed by the narrow margin of six votes, 292 to 286.[43] The government had been defeated, but Tardieu had not chosen to make the

[40] This is Stanley Hoffmann's term for what he calls the "Republican synthesis" of the Third Republic, in which French society was "the halfway house between the old rural society and industrialization," dominated by the bourgeoisie, which controlled its positions of power and shaped its values. See Hoffmann's brilliant essay, "Paradoxes of the French Political Community," in Hoffmann, *et al., In Search of France* (Cambridge, Mass., 1963), pp. 1-117.

[41] J.O.Ch. (1930), pp. 1060-62. [42] *Ibid.*, p. 1068. [43] *Ibid.*, pp. 1134-35.

vote a question of confidence. The second paragraph, that dispensed with tuition for the sixth class as an "experiment," had the approval of the government, and passed easily, 420 to 165.[44]

In the face of this show of force, Ducos concluded that the opposition had obtained all that it could. The first paragraph of article 67 B already seemed to ensure that the free sixth class was not merely a provisional measure, but the first in a series on the way to a free lycée. Ducos withdrew Locquin's amendment, which would have made sure these steps followed year by year.[45] The opposition won the commitment to the principle of free secondary education; Tardieu succeeded in limiting its application to the sixth class. The Chamber adjourned at one o'clock in the morning.

Herriot was jubilant. Under the headline "Victoire, une journée parlementaire historique!" he undertook to draw a lesson for the Left: "We have united for the protection of poor children. Let the result obtained encourage us to forget sterile group squabbles."[46] It was true that the crucial vote on the principle of free secondary education corresponded almost exactly to the nominal division between Right and Left in the Chamber. But the vote was less an indication of the unity of the Left than of the fickleness of the center.

In the Chamber elected in 1928, the line between the majority of the Right and the opposition of the Left ran not between the Radicals and the Gauche radicale but through the Gauche radicale, about a third of whose members usually voted with the Left, while the rest voted with the government.[47] Six members of the Gauche radicale who had voted confidence in Tardieu when he presented his government on March 5 de-

[44] *Ibid.*, pp. 1135-36. An amendment that sought to exclude from the benefit of this measure those who possessed taxable incomes of more than 50,000 francs per year was turned back, 291 to 289.

[45] *Ibid.*, p. 1062.

[46] *L'Ere nouvelle*, March 13, 1930.

[47] See Siegfried, *Tableau des partis*, p. 151.

serted him in the vote on article 67 B.[48] Looking perhaps to their electoral districts where, as André Siegfried once remarked, the center did not exist, they either voted with the opposition or abstained. Had Tardieu been able to hold the Gauche radicale in line, he could have prevented passage of the commitment to the principle of free secondary education. Herriot had little cause for jubilation over leftist unity. None of the issues that divided the Left was at stake in the vote; no deputy firmly on the Left could possibly have voted against free secondary education. But it required deputies who habitually worked both sides of the street to make it pass.

The press of the Right assailed Tardieu for not posing the question of confidence on the first paragraph of article 67 B.[49] Guiraud accused him of a "lack of nerve."[50] *Le Temps,* however, supported Tardieu's tactics. Perhaps he could have won a vote of confidence on the first paragraph. But the really important clause was the Locquin amendment, that Tardieu had successfully turned back. In spite of the statement of principle, the free sixth class remained an experiment.[51]

Article 67 B still had to get by the Senate, which took it up on April 11, 1930. Because the voting of the finance law had already extended past the beginning of the fiscal year, the Senate hurried its discussion, which was a shorter and less passionate version of the debate that had already taken place in the Chamber. Jean Philip, *rapporteur* of the budget of public instruction, rightly observed that both sides had exaggerated the intrinsic significance of the article, that merited "ni cet excès d'honneur ni cette indignité."[52] The Senate adopted

[48] This conclusion was reached by a comparison of the party lists published at the beginning of the parliamentary session, on January 24, 1930, with the division on the vote of confidence in Tardieu's government, March 5, 1930, and the division on the commitment to the principle of free secondary education, March 12, 1930.

[49] See, for example, *L'Echo de Paris,* March 13, 1930; *L'Action française,* March 13, 1930.

[50] *La Croix,* March 18, 1930.

[51] *Le Temps,* March 14, 1930.   [52] *J.O. Sénat* (1930), p. 1013.

article 67 B by a show of hands. The commitment to the principle of free secondary education had been won.

CONTRARY TO the hopes of *Le Temps,* and the opinion, feigned or real, of André Tardieu, the free sixth class was not merely an experiment. In 1931 the measure was extended to the fifth class; by 1933, it included all seven classes of the lycée. The great debate on the *école unique* that conservatives demanded, largely as a maneuver to block reform, never took place. In 1931, the free fifth class was nearly as adamantly opposed by the Right as the sixth had been in 1930; Edouard Herriot made the hyperbolic declaration that "Never, since I have been in parliament, have I seen the institutions of the Republic as jeopardized as they are today."[53] But the debate was largely a reenactment of the debate of 1930, and Jean Guiraud was closer to the mark when he bitterly observed: "Step by step we're moving toward completely free secondary education."[54]

The commitment to the principle of free secondary education had been voted at a time of apparent prosperity; the financial crisis had been resolved, there was even a surplus in the treasury. But in the fall of 1929, the stock market had collapsed in New York, and by 1932 depression covered France. As far as the Chamber was concerned, the stock of educational reform took a plunge, too. Jules Ferry had thought it essential to spend at least one-sixth of the national budget on education. Just prior to the war, however, the state devoted only 7 per cent of the budget to this purpose. By 1931, nearly half the budget went to servicing an enormous public debt, nearly one-quarter to national defense; expenditure on education had been reduced to 6.1 per cent, far from the goal Ferry had set.[55] Nonetheless, the Chamber did make good on its commitment, assisted by a favorable majority of the Left. The opponents of free secondary education continued to object, but as *Le Temps* lamented when all classes were made free in 1933, it

[53] *L'Ere nouvelle*, March 12, 1931.
[54] *La Croix*, March 3, 1931.
[55] Sauvy, *Histoire économique de la France*, I, 371.

was a "ritualistic debate."[56] And one political commentator observed: "This year, the opposition has not shown much animosity toward the project, and the debate has been particularly academic."[57]

Free secondary education and selection based on merit had been the interlocking supports on which the Compagnons had rested their reform proposals in 1918. Finally, in 1930, the first of these was on its way toward accomplishment. Although the Compagnons took some satisfaction in the vote of parliament, they warned their supporters: "There are other numerous and urgent tasks to be done; more than ever, we must be active and vigilant."[58]

Day school fees of course made up only a fraction of the real cost of secondary education.[59] But aside from party experts on education, most deputies doubtless considered free secondary education not one aspect of a sweeping plan for reform, but an isolated issue that could be forgotten, once they had voted upon it. It is questionable whether pressure groups behind the *école unique,* from the Compagnons to the CGT, really had much to do with making the lycée free; most deputies were probably unaware of the existence of their plans for reform. Educational reform in a democratic society is especially likely to be hindered by gaps in communication between those who believe they know what needs to be done, and those who are in a position actually to do it. And because the usual source of initiative for change is the political Left, ideological considerations that are not always entirely relevant to the issue

[56] *Le Temps,* April 13, 1933.

[57] *La Jeune République,* April 28, 1933.

[58] *L'Université nouvelle* (January-February 1930).

[59] It is impossible to arrive at a precise estimate of the charge for the *externat,* or day school tuition. Charges varied not only from establishment to establishment, but from class to class within each establishment. For example, in the lycée Buffon, in Paris, the charge for the *externat* in classes 6 through 3 was 549 francs a year, and 648 francs for classes 2 through the terminal class; at the lycée in Poitiers, however, the charge was 306 francs and 405 francs for the same classes. These figures are given in Richard, *L'Enseignement en France,* pp. 549-50.

at hand set up additional roadblocks between thought and action.

The Radicals had made free secondary education a party issue. And their opponents, with the possible exceptions of Poincaré and Tardieu, had been quite willing to allow them to do so. The Radicals had also captured the Socialists, for the Socialists could not possibly oppose free secondary education, no matter how much they differed with the Radicals over the objectives of educational reform. Perhaps the debate on the issue displayed a fragile sense of the national interest because the lycée was hardly considered to be a national establishment. Instead, both sides thought of it as the private preserve of a social class. One side sought to end the ascendancy of "the bourgeoisie" over the lycée, the other sought to preserve it, though no one bothered to find out to what extent a class that could be defined with some rigor as "the bourgeoisie" really controlled the lycée.

The religious question aside, it is difficult to understand the bitterness of the dispute over free secondary education unless it is seen as a confrontation over the possession of political power in a very broad sense. The builders of the educational system of the Third Republic had understood that, politically, a little knowledge was quite a safe thing, and had accordingly founded the primary school. So long as the bourgeoisie maintained its hegemony over the upper reaches of the educational establishment, it was able to maintain its authority over the entire society, and therefore to model the institutions of that society after its own image of what was right and just. The Revolution had proclaimed careers open to talent, but raw ability did not suffice; the right to command also required expertise. Without this expertise, and with no means of acquiring it, a citizen could not fairly claim the right to command. He had to content himself with a passive sort of political power—the right to elect his "betters": those who did seem to have the right to command because they possessed the expertise that he did not. By 1930, it had been made abundantly clear that one social class had a disproportionately large share of the places in the upper reaches of the educational system,

171

and an attempt was made to put an end to this state of affairs. But the tool designed for the task, free secondary education, or even the *école unique,* had not the strength to accomplish it.

Did abolishing the charge for the *externat* draw greater numbers of working-class and peasant children into the lycée, as the politicians claimed it would, as reformers intended it should? Did it lead to an increase in the number of children attending secondary school? Available evidence permits only the crudest sort of answer. In the 1920's, for example, no inquiries of which I am aware were made into the social origins of lycée students. There is some fragmentary evidence, however, which suggests that making secondary education free failed to have any immediate impact on class patterns within the lycée, although it may have contributed to a significant increase in the number of students attending.

There are only two pieces of sociological evidence at hand. In 1932 the Carnegie Foundation sponsored an inquiry into the social origins of candidates for the baccalaureate in the Academy of Paris.[60] In 1936, the Bureau universitaire de statistique undertook a study of the social origins of pupils entering the sixth class in all of metropolitan France.[61] The socio-professional categories established by the BUS differed considerably from those used in the Carnegie Inquiry; neither is precise.[62] One inquiry studied beginning students, the other

[60] *Commission française pour l'enquête Carnegie sur les examens et concours en France. Enquêtes sur le Baccalauréat. Recherches statistiques sur les origines scolaires et sociales des candidats au baccalauréat dans l'académie de Paris* (Paris, 1935). Hereafter cited as *Carnegie Inquiry.*

[61] This study remained in manuscript form until 1959, when it was published in an article by Christian Peyre, "L'Origine sociale des élèves d'enseignement secondaire en France," *Ecole et société* (Paris, 1959), pp. 6-34.

[62] The Carnegie Inquiry used thirteen socio-professional categories, the BUS inquiry ten. The category *fonctionnaire,* employed by both, included post office clerks and army generals, who could not be considered to belong to the same social group. The categories *agriculteurs* and *cultivateurs* do not distinguish between land owners and farm workers.

172

terminal students; one included all of France, the other was restricted to the Academy of Paris. Clearly, any conclusions drawn from a comparison of the two are extremely tenuous. With this warning in mind, one rough generalization can be made.

Presumably, the students who took the baccalaureate examination in 1932 entered the lycée in 1926, when the charge for the *externat* was still in force. According to the Carnegie Inquiry, only 2.7 per cent of the candidates were the children of workers; 1.27 per cent had rural backgrounds.[63] The inquiry of the BUS showed that in 1936 2.6 per cent of the students in the sixth class were workers' children; 1.7 per cent were of rural origin.[64] Between 1926 and 1936 there was apparently no significant increase in the number of working-class or peasant children who entered the lycée, despite the intervening abolition of tuition charges. And in 1930, workers and farmers constituted nearly half the active population.[65]

As the table below shows, when the sixth class became free in 1930, there was a considerable jump in the enrollment of lycées and *collèges*.[66] This is not, however, unequivocally a relationship of cause and effect. Enrollment in public schools follows the birth rate fairly closely. The average age of entry into the sixth class was eleven: children born, say, in 1919 would turn up in the sixth class in 1930. From 1918 to 1919, there was only a slight increase in the birth rate, that had plummeted during the war. Yet enrollment in the secondary

[63] See plate 18, *Carnegie Inquiry*. Of the subjects in this inquiry, 14.3 per cent were children of members of the liberal professions; 25.23 per cent the children of civil servants.

[64] Peyre, *Ecole et société*, p. 10. According to the BUS study, 10.5 per cent of the pupils in the sixth class were the children of members of the liberal professions; 28.5 per cent the children of civil servants.

[65] See the tables on the breakdown in the active population according to occupational categories given in Alfred Sauvy, *Histoire économique de la France entre les deux guerres; 1918-1931* (Paris, 1965), I, pp. 455-60.

[66] This table is based upon figures given in Louis Jaubert, *La Gratuité de l'enseignement secondaire* (Bordeaux, 1938), p. 69. The following remarks draw heavily upon this study.

classes rose considerably; perhaps the free sixth class caused the increase. The increase in enrollments in 1931 and 1932, however, might as easily be attributed to the sharp increase in the birth rate in 1920 and 1921 as to the attraction of the free lycée. Nevertheless, between 1930 and 1936, the total number of students enrolled in the lycées and *collèges* rose from 109,928 to 170,157, an increase of one-third in six years. And from about 1922, when those who entered the sixth class in 1933 were born, the birth rate continued its century-old downward trend. It is hard not to think that free secondary education accounted for at least part of the increase in enrollments in those years. But it is impossible to know how much.

Year	Number of births	School year	Number of students entered in sixth class	Percentage of entries in sixth class in relation to births	Total number of students in lycées and collèges	Total number of students in lycées, collèges and écoles primaires supérieures	Number of students in private collèges
1913	746,014	1924–1925	19,832	2.65	116,678	164,916	109,2
1914	593,769	1925–1926	19,604	3.30	118,777	166,360	111,5
1915	386,966	1926–1927	15,335	3.96	99,431	156,819	113,8
1916	313,013	1927–1928	12,013	3.83	92,287	147,792	118,9
1917	342,454	1928–1929	13,868	4.04	105,375	156,377	120,8
1918	399,456	1929–1930	16,047	4.01	104,016	163,065	128,8
1919	403,479	1930–1931	22,000	5.45	109,928	175,998	147,8
1920	833,518	1931–1932	30,048	3.60	123,021	194,757	145,9
1921	811,776	1932–1933	34,463	4.24	138,588	210,943	181,2
1922	759,702	1933–1934	31,905	4.19	146,917	217,942	194,0
1923	761,258	1934–1935	29,603	3.88	152,751	220,551	193,7
1924	753,529	1935–1936	28,961	3.84	160,361	225,747	224,3
1925	770,060	1936–1937	29,495	3.83	170,157	233,523	226,3
1926	767,475	1937–1938	29,397	3.83			

There is another set of intriguing statistics, however, that hints at change in the social composition of secondary educa-

174

tion. In 1933, the ministry of public instruction began an annual inquiry to determine whether children entering the sixth class of the lycée had previously attended the public primary school, the elementary classes of the lycée or a private school. In 1932, this inquiry into "school origins" showed that 9,414 children entering the sixth class had attended the elementary classes of the lycée; less than half that number, 4,803, had gone to the public primary school. Then between 1932 and 1938 took place the great increase in enrollments in secondary education. In 1938, the last school year of peacetime, 11,975 children who entered the sixth class had previously attended the elementary class, an increase of 2,561 over 1932. But 17,568 children who enrolled in 1938 had formerly attended the public primary school—an increase of 12,765 over 1932. In 1936, the number of public school enrollees for the first time exceeded the number from the elementary classes of the lycées and collèges; by 1938 they were in the great majority.[67]

But what do these figures mean? What kind of social change do they represent? The ministry of public instruction did not inquire into the social origins of the new entries into the sixth class. In times of severe economic depression a tendency arises to keep children in school longer, in order to keep them out of the labor market where they would compete for jobs with heads of families. Some of the influx from the public primary school might be attributed to the depression. This influx would seem to indicate a downward shift in the social composition of the lycée, a sort of "popularization" of its clientele, but there is no way precisely to find out the occupations to which the parents of these new children belonged. One can hazard the guess, however (and it is no more than a guess), that the lower middle class was the great immediate beneficiary of free secondary education. Poised midway between the bourgeoisie and the working class, ever fearful of falling into the latter, the small grocer, the baker, the office clerk possessed a higher level of aspiration than the worker; he regarded himself

[67] *Archives nationales* F[17] 13952. *Rapport des chefs d'établissements et statistiques sur l'âge moyen et l'origine des élèves admis en 6ᵉ 1933-1940.*

as a sort of apprentice to the bourgeoisie, and avidly hoped and planned for his son to become a member of it.[68] Education was an almost certain means of upward social mobility, and a family preoccupied with questions of social status would be quick to seize the advantages free secondary education afforded. Secondary education took up a lower proportion of middle-class budgets in the interwar period than it had before the First World War. In a sense, therefore, the opponents of the *école unique* may have been right. It appeared that those who somehow could afford to pay were the greatest beneficiaries of the abolition of charges.[69] This was not what reformers had in mind.

The table shows at least one thing clearly. Contrary to the fears of the defenders of the confessional school, the free lycée had no adverse effect on private secondary schools. Indeed, after 1931, enrollment in private schools increased more rapidly than in the public schools.

The scarcity of relevant statistical information, that mid-twentieth century deity, prevents any but a crude assessment of the impact of a hard-fought political victory upon the educational establishment. Friends of the *école unique* celebrated the victory at the time, but they, too, were dubious about its importance. Alice Jouenne wrote in *Le Peuple* at the beginning of the 1930 school year that the free *externat* was simply "the remittance of a pretty small sum to parents." It appeared to her that a good many children of the *petite bourgeoisie* were taking advantage of the free sixth class, but few workers' children.[70]

Obviously a free lycée was more attractive to parents of precarious financial means than one that charged tuition. But serious obstacles persisted to the entrance of greater numbers of working-class and peasant children into the lycée. A work-

[68] On this see Michel Crozier, "Le Rôle des employés et des petits fonctionnaires dans la structure sociale française contemporaine," *Transactions of the Third World Congress of Sociology* (1956), 311-19.

[69] Marguerite Perrot, *Le Mode de vie des familles bourgeoises 1873-1953* (Paris, 1961), p. 105.

[70] *Le Peuple*, October 16, 1930.

ing-class family that sent a son to the lycée would be faced with the prospect of giving up a perhaps badly needed wage earner, and might not be willing to assume the risk. A peasant who lived far from a secondary establishment had to see that his child was housed and fed, and might not have the means, despite the abolition of tuition charges. A child in the lycée had to be supported for seven years, and a lycée education was not an end in itself but a preparation for university education, which required additional resources. To send a child to the lycée was no casual decision; it required a consideration of the size of one's pocketbook for the next ten or a dozen years, and many families of limited means could scarcely have this prescience. In 1930 an average working-class family of four spent 60 per cent of its income on food; such a budget made education a luxury indeed.[71]

Doubtless psychological barriers persisted too. A lycée education had been the mark of the bourgeois, the man in fine clothes, the boss. The world in which one's children went to the lycée as a matter of course was a world removed from the common experience of a worker, and therefore strange and perhaps intimidating. A family might not easily commit its children to the unknown. But there is no way to measure the suspicion or even hostility that workers or peasants may have felt toward an educational establishment from which, as social groups, they had always been excluded. Leftist politicians claimed to speak for "the People"; trade union leaders believed that they spoke for "the People"; but to the historian, "the People" themselves seldom, if ever, speak of their private antipathies and hopes.[72]

[71] For the working-class budget see Sauvy, *Histoire économique de la France*, ii, 527.

[72] But see the new preface that Henry de Montherlant wrote in 1933 for his previously published essays, *La Relève du matin* (Paris, 1933). Montherlant, whose political sympathies were on the right, used an anecdote to show how his opinion had changed on problems about which he had written thirteen years earlier. He had had the occasion, he remarked, to visit a family in which the father had become incurably ill and was unable to work. The man's wife was "fat, dirty, pretentious

and smelly." The surroundings were miserable and dirty. As he was about to leave, Montherlant noticed on the table a text of Virgil: "Quel saississement! Pas un instant il ne m'était venu à l'esprit que ce garçon fût écolier autre part qu'à l'école primaire, ou dans une école professionnelle. Ainsi donc, dans ce décor sordide, au milieu de ces soucis sordides, dans le milieu où rien, au matériel et au moral, n'était et ne serait jamais autrement que sordide, quelqu'un—et qui donc! maintenait l'idéal d'une civilisation de l'esprit et d'une vie désintéressée! A ma question, le père répondit que son fils . . . avait bénéficié de la '6ᵉ gratuite' et faisait sa sixième, gratis, au lycée.

Si l'on nous parle de l'école unique, ou de la sixième gratuite, les objections se présentent en foule. . . . Bien des opinions, ainsi fondées, ne tiennent plus au contact de l'être vivant."

> Si l'école est, par excéllence, le point sensible de notre vie publique, c'est parce qu'en effet, elle met en cause l'attachement de l'homme à ses enfants, de la famille à ses intérêts les plus sacrés, de la nation à son avenir tout entier, de l'humanité à sa destinée terrestre, et même (et surtout) de chacun à ses fins suprêmes et éternelles.
>
> —MAURICE BLONDEL

> Il faut faire en sorte que le mérite de chacun lui permette d'accéder aux degrés supérieurs et d'arriver dans la société à des postes et à des responsabilités aussi adaptées que possible à ses talents et à sa compétence.
>
> —JOHN XXIII, *Pacem in Terris*

CATHOLICS such as General Castelnau, Colonel Keller and Jean Guiraud never wavered from their attitude of intransigent opposition to the *école unique*. Aging representatives of the tradition of religious defense, they identified the interests of the Church with the values of a conservative social order fashioned by centuries of Christianity; they never altered their conviction that behind the movement for the *école unique* stood arrayed the antireligious heirs of the Revolution, bent solely upon the destruction of that order and, consequently, upon the dechristianization of France.

But while these conservatives remained attached to an old tradition, French Catholicism was undergoing a transformation in its relationship to republican society.[1] In the 1920's, as the result partly of conscious effort, partly of fortuitous his-

---

[1] Any brief mention of this extraordinarily complex transformation must be oversimplified. The following paragraphs rely on the excellent synthesis of Mlle. Aline Coutrot in A. Coutrot and F. Dreyfus, *Les Forces religieuses dans la société française* (Paris, 1965), pp. 67-88; Latreille and Rémond, *Histoire du catholicisme en France*, III, 573-623; Dansette, *Histoire religieuse*, pp. 707-94; also Adrien Dansette, *Destin du catholicisme français; 1926-1956* (Paris, 1957), which is especially concerned with the Catholic Action movement; see also H. Stuart Hughes, *The Obstructed Path; French Social Thought in the Years of Desperation* (New York, 1967), ch. 3.

torical change, the movement of reconciliation between Church and republic, doomed to failure in the late nineteenth century by mutual incomprehension and mistrust, underwent a revival. The experience of the wartime Sacred Union had encouraged the integration of Catholics into republican society. The reestablishment of the French embassy at the Vatican, and the liquidation of disputes over the separation of church and state, enabled a cordial official relationship between Rome and Paris that in turn induced Catholics to relax their suspicions of the republic.

Initiatives toward reconciliation often came from Rome, one aspect of Pius XI's vigorous effort to rejuvenate the universal Church. The condemnation of the Action française, at the end of 1926, marked the dramatic beginning of what has been called the "second *ralliement*." For years a kind of "quasi-official political expression of French Catholicism,"[2] the hypernationalistic, authoritarian, antirepublican and pseudo-positivistic doctrine of Charles Maurras was in fact quite foreign to the precepts of Christian transcendentalism. Its condemnation made clear that the Church did not look with favor upon the continued collusion of French Catholics with the forces of the extreme Right. Most important, the condemnation greatly encouraged an indigenous renaissance of Catholic political and philosophical thought, the participants in which, whatever their differences, shared the desire to work out a new relationship between the Church and the modern world. The Catholic Action movement, which urged Catholics to live their worldly lives by the precepts of their faith, to Christianize secular institutions by their presence in them, implied that the isolationist attitude of religious defense was neither the best nor the only means of protecting the welfare of the Church.

This second *ralliement* created dissension between those who might be called the renewalists, who supported it, and the traditionalists, who opposed it. These were old divisions within

[2] Coutrot and Dreyfus, *Les Forces religieuses*, p. 57. On the *Action française* see Eugen Weber, *Action Française; Royalism and Reaction in Twentieth Century France* (Stanford, 1962).

French Catholicism, but after the First World War the renewalist tendency, encouraged from Rome, acquired a new legitimacy.

The school question remained the one outstanding divisive issue between Catholics and the republic; toward the end of the 1920's, the *école unique* became a divisive issue among Catholics as well. The renewalists undertook to examine the problem of educational reform from a new perspective. To be sure, the older attitudes toward the *école unique* persisted: the forces of tradition retained a much greater collective strength and a larger audience within Catholic ranks than did the forces of renewal.

TORN between his political sympathies and his fidelity to Rome, Jean Guiraud tried to minimize the importance of the condemnation of the Action française; he mentioned it in *La Croix* only four months after the event. The Vatican believed that *La Croix* had failed in its duty as a Catholic newspaper; consequently Guiraud's authority was considerably circumscribed. On the personal initiative of Pius XI, Father Léon Merklen was made co-editor at the end of 1927; by 1929, he had become editor-in-chief. Under Merklen's direction, the newspaper became an instrument for the expression of papal thought, firmly committed to the policy of *ralliement*.[3] Guiraud continued to pursue the same intransigent line he had maintained for years on the school question, but, reduced to a subordinate position on the staff, in conflict with the conciliatory policy of Merklen and out of step with Rome, he could no longer write even on his specialty with the authority he had once enjoyed.

By Guiraud's own admission, the Association catholique des chefs de famille was threatening to collapse. Even in the Catholic strongholds of the west, he confessed, its local chapters had disbanded or become moribund; in the diocese of Paris few Catholics showed much interest in questions of

[3] René Rémond, "L'Evolution du journal *La Croix* et son rôle auprès de l'opinion catholique, 1919-1939," *Bulletin de la société d'histoire moderne*, LVII, No. 7 (1958), 3-10.

education.[4] Not only were Catholic laymen indifferent to Guiraud's organization; in the hierarchy there was outright hostility toward it. One bishop, Guiraud reported, had written him that "Never, as long as I live, will an *association des chefs de famille* be set up in my diocese."[5]

In April 1929, Guiraud flatly stated that the campaign for *répartition proportionnelle scolaire* had come to a halt.[6] It is quite likely that most Catholics considered RPS, as one Catholic university professor described it, "an impossible demand, that is inopportune and contrary to the spirit of peace."[7] The election of 1924 had already shown that few Catholic candidates were prepared to burden themselves with such an extravagant and politically dangerous issue. Most Catholics were not prepared to act as if the confessional schools were threatened by the state when no such threat existed; and the somnolence of the ACCF indicated that few of them adhered to the provocative method of religious defense prescribed by Guiraud.

Defenders of the confessional school by no means relaxed their vigilance. Beginning in 1930, the ACCF and the Société d'éducation had to face a sort of competitor on their own ground. A new organization, the Association des parents d'élèves de l'école libre was founded for the defense of the confessional school; three years later the APEL claimed 52,000 subscribers to its periodical, *Ecole et liberté,* far more than the ACCF could boast.[8] Though the APEL, like the older organizations, continued both to demand state subsidies for confessional schools and to follow a conservative policy of religious defense, its pronouncements on the public school were not

[4] *Ecole et famille*, XI (April 1929).

[5] *Ecole et famille*, XI (February-March 1929).

[6] *Ecole et famille*, XI (April 1929).

[7] P. Camenen, *Pour la Paix scolaire* (Paris, 1932), p. 32.

[8] *Ecole et liberté*, November 15, 1933. The first three years of this periodical are missing from the collection of the Bibliothèque nationale. The point of view of the APEL, however, was often reported in *La Vie catholique*. It should be remembered that *La Vie catholique* took a much more conciliatory attitude toward educational reform than did any of the parents' organizations.

marked with the hostility and suspicion of a Guiraud or a Keller. Its divergence from the line of the ACCF and the Société d'éducation became quite apparent when, in early 1931, the leadership of the APEL announced that it had no intention of maintaining an attitude of systematic opposition to the *école unique*.[9]

Among members of the teaching clergy there appeared unmistakable signs of an easing of hostility toward the *école unique*. One of their associations, the Alliance des maisons d'éducation chrétienne, comprised the directors of more than 900 confessional secondary schools. In the course of a lengthy discussion on educational reform at a conference of the Alliance, in August 1930, one delegate observed that "it would be neither just nor wise to allow oneself to be imprisoned in the dilemma: *for* or *against* the *école unique*."[10] The confessional school directors had no objection either to selection by merit or to free secondary education, which, they conceded, contravened no Catholic doctrine. They were understandably concerned, however, about the effect these measures might have upon their own schools, and demanded "a legal statute which will permit confessional education to live in independence and with dignity."[11]

THE DECLINE of the Association catholique des chefs de famille indicated a growing disinclination on the part of Catholics to subscribe to Guiraud's intransigence. If other groups charged with the defense of the confessional school adopted a more flexible and less hostile attitude toward the *école unique,* they did not stray from the path of religious defense. They continued to be concerned almost exclusively with the impact that a reform of the public school system might have on the confessional school. They did not regard the *école unique* as an undertaking that required the active participation of Catholics.

[9] *La Vie catholique*, March 7, 1931.

[10] "Compte-rendu. 49ᵉ assemblée générale de l'alliance des maisons d'éducation chrétienne," *L'Enseignement chrétien*, L (1930), 47. Emphasis in original.

[11] *Ibid.*, 48.

But some Catholics did, and in the late 1920's their voices began to be heard. No label adequately describes these Catholics. Passionately engaged in the Catholic renewal, committed to the task of dissociating Catholicism from its ties with the conservative order, those who urged a conciliatory attitude toward the *école unique* as one consequence of this commitment have customarily been called "Catholics of the left." It should be pointed out that the term takes account neither of the diversity of opinion within this "left wing" of French Catholicism, nor of the important issues that divided it.[12] But because there exists no better descriptive term than "Catholics of the left," or "leftist Catholics," it is used here; with regard to their common attitude toward educational reform these Catholics might be called "participationists."

The Catholic press, as René Rémond has pointed out, has always been the most visible expression of diverse tendencies of thought within the Church, and their principal mode of organization. Under Pius XI a remarkable number of new Catholic publications appeared in France—some weekly, some monthly, some strictly Catholic, some non-confessional, some religious, some political. Their appearance destroyed the semi-monopoly that conservative and nationalist newspapers such as *L'Echo de Paris* had exercised over Catholic opinion.[13] In the pages of these new publications the views of the participationists on educational reform were first expressed.

Two of these journals—*Politique* and *La Vie intellectuelle* —showed from their inception a particular concern with problems of education. The one political, the other confessional, they also represented two distinct dimensions of the Catholic renewal. *Politique* was the theoretical organ of the Parti démocrate populaire, organized in 1924 to give expression to a Chris-

[12] Moreover, the division of Catholicism into tendencies of "Right" and "Left" should not be allowed to obscure the fact that there did not truly exist two homogeneous blocs of opinion within the Catholic community.

[13] René Rémond, *Les Catholiques, le communisme et les crises; 1929-1939* (Paris, 1960), p. 14.

tian democratic current equally hostile to socialism and to individualist liberalism. Timidities of leadership and the weight of traditionalist opinion hampered the Popular Democrats as a political force from the outset. Nonetheless, the PDP had in its ranks a vigorous band of young Catholic intellectuals, who used *Politique,* founded in 1927, for the elaboration of Christian democratic doctrine and its application to contemporary problems.[14]

La Vie intellectuelle, founded in 1928 by the Dominicans of the publishing house Cerf, shared with *Politique* the desire for a Catholic renaissance. At least since the time of Lamennais, in the first third of the nineteenth century, the Dominicans had been an often unsettling influence in French Catholicism. To be sure, as a confessional publication *La Vie intellectuelle* had to work within certain fixed limits; its editors never worked out a coherent political or social doctrine. Nonetheless, *La Vie intellectuelle,* along with *Sept,* another more audacious Dominican publication, played a most important role in the effort to reconcile Catholicism with modern society.[15]

Whatever their differences, the participationists all shared the premise that the traditionalists' attitude toward the *école unique* was not merely sterile, but inimical to the interests of the Church. Louis Delaisne wrote in *La Vie intellectuelle* that Catholics who maintained a purely negative attitude toward the *école unique,* and at the same time defended the traditional lycée, acted in a manner more bourgeois than Christian.

---

[14] A Christian democratic current had existed in French Catholicism for some time, but its political doctrine had been singularly imprecise and its sympathizers unorganized; in the nineteenth and early twentieth centuries it had made little headway against the dominant mood of Catholic conservatism. Charles Flory and Marcel Prélot, both former members of the *Association catholique de la jeunesse française,* founded *Politique.* See Marcel Prélot, "Histoire et doctrine du parti démocrate populaire," *Politique,* No. 19-20 (1962), 307-40.

[15] See Aline Coutrot, *Un Courant de la pensée catholique: l'hebdomadaire 'Sept'; mars 1934-août 1937* (Paris, 1961), especially pp. 24-32.

Despite the deplorable anti-Catholicism of some partisans of the *école unique,* Delaisne argued, it should be pointed out that the existing school system was an offense to Catholic notions of justice.[16]

André Giraud, an educational expert of the Popular Democrats, granted that the hostility of many Catholics toward the *école unique* might be partly explained by their old habit of regarding any tinkering with the public school system as a maneuver directed against themselves. But it was time, Giraud urged, to move beyond the isolation of the defensive attitude. Catholic interests could be safeguarded only if Catholics took part in the task of educational reform, and ensured that it was carried out in the proper spirit. Employing a major theme of the Catholic renewal, Giraud remarked: "If Catholicism wishes to live and to develop in France, it is above all necessary that Catholics . . . act in public life as French citizens, in a spirit of truth and sincerity."[17] Maurice Blondel, noted Catholic philosopher, observed in *Politique* that for Catholics to persevere in a hostile and obstructive attitude toward a sorely needed reform, for the sake of political interests that did not coincide with the interests of the Church, would be an error "whose consequences would be infinitely prejudicial and inevitably ruinous for the causes that one claims to defend."[18]

In the spirit of Giraud's suggestion, the Popular Democrats undertook a lengthy discussion of educational reform at their congress of 1930. Basing their deliberations upon a detailed study made by André Bastianelli, director of the party's research office,[19] the Popular Democrats approved a resolution

[16] Louis Delaisne, "L'Education de l'état et l'école unique," *La Vie intellectuelle,* II (1929), 41.

[17] André Giraud, "L'Ecole unique, problème social," *Politique,* II (1929), 23. See also Giraud's articles "L'Ecole unique et la démocratie," *Politique,* II (1929), 110-35; "Autour de la réforme scolaire," *Politique,* III (1929), 1023-35.

[18] Maurice Blondel, "Notes sur la réforme de l'enseignement et les projets de l'école unique," *Politique,* IV (1930), 786.

[19] André Bastianelli, "Pour une réforme générale de l'enseignement," *Politique,* IV (1930), 385-422.

on the *école unique* that unequivocally endorsed its basic principles of free secondary education and selection. Moreover, the resolution called for subsidies to parents who could not afford to lose a wage earner to the lycée. The Popular Democrats displayed their concern for the confessional schools by adopting an ingenious if scarcely practicable plan for submitting the nation's educational facilities, both public and confessional, to the control of an autonomous corporation, in which the confessional schools would benefit from state subsidies. The plan bore a great similarity to the nationalization scheme of the Syndicat national des instituteurs, though the school teachers had quite different ideas about the role of the confessional schools in the corporation.[20]

COLONEL KELLER denounced as "defeatism" the attitude of Catholics who sought to participate in the work of reform. Recent articles that had appeared in the Catholic press, he claimed, especially in *Politique* and *La Vie intellectuelle,* were taking Catholics straight down the road to atheism.[21]

The traditionalists considered the conciliatory attitude not merely an unwise tactic, but a betrayal of Catholic principles. To justify their own intransigence, they seized upon an encyclical on education, *Divini illius magistri*, issued in late 1929. As a universal document intended to remind Catholics of all countries of the immutable principles of the Church, the encyclical made no reference to special circumstances of Catholic education in any one country.

In part, *Divini illius magistri* recalled that religious and secular instruction were inseparable; according to canon law, Catholics were forbidden to attend any school from which religious instruction was excluded. Even in a nation divided by religious belief, the encyclical declared, it was the duty of the state, on the initiative of the Church, to grant subsidies to the confessional school. Traditionalists made much of the fact that the word "unique" was employed in the encyclical,

[20] *Le Petit Démocrate*, November 23, 1930.
[21] *Bulletin de la société générale de l'éducation et d'enseignement*, LXI (1930), 344.

though it was clear from the context of the statement that it intended to condemn any form of state educational monopoly, and not a specific reform project in France.[22]

Jean Guiraud declared that the encyclical had come at a most opportune time: "In an excessive desire for conciliation . . . a number of Catholics, and not the least influential among them, have so reduced their demands with regard to the school that our principles are gradually being effaced." When Catholics not only resigned themselves to the *école unique,* but even actively supported it, it was high time that the papacy called them to order. Guiraud claimed that the principles enunciated in *Divini illius magistri* were exactly those that the ACCF defended, and implied that the conciliators disregarded them.[23] Colonel Keller asserted that the encyclical forbade Catholics to support the *école unique.*[24]

The conciliators made a vigorous riposte to the efforts of the traditionalists to use the encyclical against them. Francisque Gay, the intellectual conscience of the Christian democrats, undertook to respond to the accusations of Guiraud and Keller. A talented journalist and publisher, in 1924 Gay had founded the influential weekly *La Vie catholique,* and its editorial position enthusiastically supported Pius XI's initiatives toward *ralliement.*[25] The confrontation between the traditionalist leaders and Gay, leader of the forces of renewal, was one between those who believed that French Catholicism had, whatever the cost, to dwell in isolation from a hostile and pernicious society, and those who sought to establish a dialogue between the Church and the modern world.

Addressing a Catholic gathering at Marseilles in August 1930, Gay charged that certain influential Catholic notables

[22] A French translation of the encyclical was published in *Documentation catholique,* XXIII (1930), cols. 400-10.

[23] *La Croix,* January 14, 1930.

[24] "L'Encyclique sur l'éducation chrétienne de la jeunesse et l'école unique," *Bulletin de la société générale de l'éducation et d'enseignement,* LXI (1930), 439.

[25] On Gay, see the biographical sketch in Rémond, *Les catholiques, le communisme,* p. 277.

had grossly misused the encyclical on education for partisan ends.[26] Shortly after Gay's address, an article appeared in *Ecole et famille* which reasserted that Gay and his allies had recommended an attitude toward school reform condemned by the encyclical.[27] Outraged by this grave charge, Gay printed a lengthy and strongly worded "response to the unjust insinuations of M. Jean Guiraud" in *La Vie catholique*.[28]

Gay declared that he had had Guiraud, Keller, the Société d'éducation and the Fédération nationale catholique in mind when he made his statement the previous August. But he had especially thought of Guiraud, and his "insidious commentaries" on the papal encyclical. Guiraud had no right, Gay asserted, to set himself up as the sole qualified interpreter of a document that was the patrimony of all Catholics. As a layman, he had no authority to insinuate that the encyclical implied that membership in the ACCF was the only efficacious means of defending the confessional school; other means existed, and the choice of means was a decision for each bishop in his own diocese. Neither did the encyclical recommend supporting any campaign for *répartition proportionnelle scolaire,* as Guiraud suggested. Nor did he have a right to confuse his own political views with the interests of the Church, as he had done when he accused Catholic deputies who had voted in favor of the free sixth class of violating the encyclical.

The fundamental issue between Gay and Guiraud was the old distinction in the interpretation of church doctrine between thesis and hypothesis. The thesis is "the principle, immutable in its rigor, to which the teaching of the Church remains inflexibly attached"; the hypothesis is "the concession imposed or advised in conduct by circumstances." Church doctrine was one thing; the demands of real life were another.[29] *Divini illius magistri* had been a statement of the thesis— the immutable principles of the Church. Nonetheless, traditionalists such as Guiraud had implied that the encyclical

[26] *La Vie catholique*, August 9, 1930.

[27] *Ecole et famille*, XII (September 1930).

[28] *La Vie catholique*, November 22, 1930.

[29] Dansette, *Histoire religieuse*, pp. 313-14.

was an absolute guide to practical conduct even in a nation divided by belief; and they believed that they had always acted accordingly.

But Gay argued that the politics of the school, like any political action that involved the Church, had to be considered in the light of the hypothesis, or the lesser evil; the welfare of the confessional schools depended upon a transaction between Catholics and a society in which the unity of faith had long been broken. In these circumstances, intransigent verbalism accomplished nothing. Instead, Catholics should work to obtain those safeguards for the confessional school which they could reasonably expect to achieve. And against Guiraud's policy of systematic opposition to the *école unique,* Gay advised a policy of prudence and conciliation: "You [Guiraud] appear to many Catholics to be a singularly compromising defender of many causes which are dear to us. It is above all in your defense of the confessional school that many of us fear certain excesses of your polemics."[30]

Soon after his denunciation of Guiraud appeared, Gay reported that he had received hundreds of letters supporting the stand he had taken—more letters, in fact, than he had received on any issue since the foundation of *La Vie catholique.*[31]

The Abbé Desgranges added his influential voice to the criticism of the traditionalists. Elected to the Chamber in 1928 and possessed of a keen political sense, he was firmly committed to the practical application of the policy of *ralliement.* Though Desgranges himself had little sympathy for the *école unique,* he spoke out against the pretensions of Keller and the Société d'éducation to represent all Catholics on the matter: "The absolute and violent character of this leadership would be marvelously understood on the part of oppositionist Catholics, preoccupied with overthrowing the Republic. But for those who are trying to improve our institutions and our legislation . . . attitudes and language cannot be the same."[32] Referring to the encyclical on education, Desgranges observed

[30] *La Vie catholique,* November 22, 1930.
[31] *La Vie catholique,* January 3, 1931.
[32] *La Vie catholique,* January 10, 1931.

190

that the Church never enunciated immutable principles without regard for circumstances of time and place. The Church, as he succinctly put it, never overlooked the facts; and in France, the public school was a fact.[33]

Father Léon Merklen, whom Pius XI himself had chosen to impose a new orientation upon *La Croix,* usually left comment on matters of education to Guiraud. But in an editorial published in late 1931, Merklen revealed that his sympathies lay with the opponents of the traditionalists. In a scarcely veiled reference to the encyclical, Merklen observed that the demands of abstract principle did not always neatly coincide with the demands of practical action. A rigorously defensive attitude toward the problem of education did not suffice; it had to be complemented by a certain prudence.[34]

It was quite true that the initiative for educational reform came from groups hostile to the Church; the anticlerical past of the Radicals, especially, made their motives for supporting the *école unique* suspect; the nationalization scheme of the sni, the Ligue de l'enseignement and the Socialists, however harmless it might actually have been, had alarming implications, for it denied the confessional schools the right to give religious instruction. Free public secondary education seemed to pose problems for confessional secondary schools, which could not afford to dispense with tuition charges. Catholics of the left ignored none of the risks of cooperation with those who had shown little regard for Catholic sensibilities in the past, nor did they forget that "only the Christian school is capable of giving a child an education that fully conforms to his human and natural destiny."[35] In part, they urged Catholics to participate in the task of building the *école unique* because of the threats it might pose to Catholic interests, not despite them.

In late October 1930, Cardinal Liénart, bishop of Lille,

[33] *Ibid.*

[34] *La Croix*, October 15, 1931.

[35] ***, "La Controverse autour de l'école," *La Vie intellectuelle*, iv (1931), 9.

warned Catholics against the folly of unreasonable attacks upon the state educational system. Soon after he had arrived in Lille in 1928, the then Mgr. Liénart had sided with Catholic trade unionists in a bitter strike against Catholic textile producers; the Vatican had supported him, and a few months after the strike ended Pius XI made Liénart a cardinal, an act interpreted as a sign of extraordinary papal confidence. At the time, Liénart was the youngest cardinal in France.[36] A courageous, forceful and yet benign leader of the *ralliement,* he appealed to his audience at a diocesan conference in Lille to face some facts: "One should not go into battle just to be beaten. We are in the midst of a profound reform of education in France. As it has existed up until now, the organization of the school system has not given us entire satisfaction. So much the better! We will profit from the present situation in order to have our own word to say about it."[37]

Inspired by Liénart's appeal, a number of young Catholic intellectuals began to meet together regularly to discuss the problem of educational reform. In May 1931, they published an article entitled "Les Projets de réforme de l'enseignement devant la conscience catholique" in the *Nouvelle revue des jeunes,* a journal that had close ties with *La Vie intellectuelle.* Insisting that their article was merely "a document tossed into the debate" and not a manifesto, they clearly expected it to create controversy. Bound together only by the demands of their own consciences, they had undertaken their study in order to "find out under what guarantees Catholics concerned about participating in the civic life of this country could contribute their support or even their aid."[38] Nine of the twenty-

[36] On this episode see Rémond, *Les catholiques, le communisme*, pp. 21-39.

[37] *La Vie catholique*, November 22, 1930.

[38] "Les Projets de réforme de l'enseignement devant la conscience catholique," *La Nouvelle revue des jeunes*, III (1931), 424. Hereafter cited as Lille Document, NRJ. According to Pierre-Henri Simon, who served as secretary for the study group, its members had two purposes clearly in mind: to show Catholic opinion that a democratic reform was possible without a monopoly of education; to dissociate the defense

five signers of this document were faculty members of the Catholic faculty of Lille, including the vice-rector of the university and the dean of the faculty of sciences. Doubtless the best known member of the Lille circle, as well as the eldest, was the Dominican theologian and a member of the Institut, A. D. Sertillanges, who must have lent an air of orthodoxy and respectability to what seemed a daring statement. Lay members of the group included the Catholic social worker and essayist Robert Garric; Maurice Lacroix, lycée professor, political journalist and trade union activist; and Pierre-Henri Simon, later to become a noted literary critic, novelist and member of the Académie française.

The appeal for Catholic cooperation in the task of reform implied both a conception of Christian civic action in a de-christianized society and a view of the best means of assuring the progress of Catholicism that were quite in opposition to the traditionalist thesis. The signers of the Document argued that in order to be truly faithful to the Christian spirit one had to make a sincere effort to understand the ideas of his adversaries. Moreover, the history of the past fifty years had often shown that what had been done without the aid of Catholics had often been done against them. The traditionalists' opposition to the *école unique* drew Catholicism into the old error of appearing to be opposed to progress.[39]

These young Catholics pointed out that the essential supports upon which the *école unique* depended—free secondary education and selection—in themselves contained nothing contrary to Catholic doctrine. The Church recruited its clergy by opening its seminaries to working-class and peasant boys.

---

of the Church from the defense of bourgeois conservatism. The group had other interests to which it later devoted its attention, but the first problem approached was the school question; it continued to meet until about 1935. Cardinal Liénart played no direct role in the group, but according to Simon, his diocese provided a "favorable atmosphere" for such an undertaking. Simon considered the Document "un premier signe du virage de gauche du catholicisme" (interview with the author, October 25, 1965).

[39] Lille Document, NRJ, 427.

Why should not secular society similarly draw upon these same untapped intellectual resources for the common good?[40]

It was true, the authors of the Document went on, that free public secondary education held certain risks for the confessional schools, but it should not be forgotten that the Church herself had once been the champion of free education. Moreover, the arguments of traditionalists against the free lycée had too often been supported by "inexact or inefficacious considerations that are, in any case, foreign to the demands of Catholic doctrine."[41]

Certainly selection posed difficult problems, but as conceived by reformers it could hardly be called a threat to the rights of families; what about the rights of parents who saw their children denied secondary education simply because they could not afford it? At any rate, if Catholics were concerned about social justice, a fair and methodical selection was obviously more just than selection based upon the size of one's pocketbook. Moreover, selection was not a great novelty: few families were heard to complain that their rights had been violated if their sons failed to pass the entrance examination for the Ecole polytechnique.[42]

But the Lille group by no means gave its unreserved adherence to the principles of the *école unique*; the signers of the Document were no less concerned than traditionalists to protect Catholic interests. They charged with hypocrisy those partisans of the reform who proclaimed their belief in freedom of education but showed no concern for the repercussions the *école unique* might have on that freedom. Adapting an old suggestion of the Compagnons, the Lille group recommended subsidies to private schools to the degree that they carried out an educational function of the state; for religious instruction, the confessional schools should continue to depend upon private funds.[43]

Annoyed by the charge that the *école unique* merely concealed a plan for a state monopoly of education, the Lille group

[40] *Ibid.*

[41] *Ibid.*, 427.   [42] *Ibid.*, 432.   [43] *Ibid.*, 434.

pointed out that any monopoly or nationalization scheme had scarcely the slightest chance of being enacted. Nor was it prudent for Catholics to charge that free secondary education would impose a crushing financial burden upon the state, and in the next breath demand *répartition proportionnelle scolaire,* which would almost certainly impose an even greater burden. Committed to the struggle to dissociate Catholicism from its rightist political affiliations, the Lille group concluded: "It would seem to us not only unwise, but even very dangerous to bind the Catholic cause to the attitude of violent opposition taken [toward the *école unique*] in certain circles."[44]

Those circles violently opposed the Document. General Castelnau, who personified the alliance between Catholicism and the traditional social order, remarked that "in order for one to collaborate, there must be at least two parties. Now up through today, the defenders of confessional education have been unable to discover this indispensable and precious partner."[45] The crusty old general, aware that he commanded a wider Catholic audience than these young unknowns from Lille did, dismissed them with a shrug: "No need to get upset about it—they don't carry much weight."[46]

Colonel Keller declared that he could scarcely believe the naïveté of the Lille group: "Where is there a probability, a possibility, the slightest chance of an understanding, of a sincere and profitable agreement? The era of resistance is unfortunately not yet closed."[47] At the heart of the traditionalist attitude lay the conviction that Catholics had to set aside whatever divided them in order to unite in the defense of religious interests threatened by a common adversary; but

[44] *Ibid.,* 443.

[45] *Credo,* July 1931. Blaming what he called their "impetuous generosity" upon their youth, Castelnau called the signers of the Document "armchair strategists," who had not experienced the bitter prewar struggle to maintain freedom of education.

[46] *Ibid.*

[47] "Collaborations unilatérales," *Bulletin de la société générale d'éducation,* LXII (1931), 561.

traditionalist leaders had always taken it upon themselves to identify both the interests and the adversary. Jean Guiraud accused the Lille group of *"breaking the united front of Catholics,* so necessary against the united front that Masonry maintains among all our adversaries."[48]

The contest between the traditionalists and the participationists, between two conceptions of Catholic action in modern society, between two attitudes toward historical change, was an unequal one. Castelnau and Guiraud had access to the daily press, and Castelnau headed the largest Catholic organization in France. The young signers of the Document had neither a public platform such as *L'Echo de Paris,* nor the opposition's strength of organization. Besides, their intention had not been polemical; they had no desire to set Catholics against one another. Yves de La Brière, noted columnist for *Etudes,* sought to play a conciliatory role in the controversy, but his heart was in Castelnau's camp.[49]

Nonetheless, there was a good deal of sympathy within Catholic ranks for the stand the Lille group had taken. *La Vie catholique* published the text of the Document; Francisque Gay assailed Castelnau for the tone of his criticism.[50] Jacques Maritain, eminent leader of the Catholic intellectual renaissance, wrote that he shared the attitudes of the Lille group, though he wondered if it had not been a trifle too eager to participate in the work of reform without sufficient guarantees for the rights of Catholics.[51] J. Calvet, editor of *L'Enseigne-*

---

[48] *Ecole et famille,* XIII (July-August 1931). Emphasis in original.

[49] Yves de La Brière, "Pour l'Union catholique dans la revendication du droit des parents à choisir l'école et les maîtres," *Etudes* 208 (1931), 17-26. La Brière claimed to see not the slightest difference between Castelnau's position and the position of the signers of the Document. But he remarked: "Aujourd'hui les promoteurs officiels de la gratuité ne cherchent nullement à détruire l'enseignement libre. Mais ils veulent simplement créer un état de choses dans lequel l'accès à l'enseignement libre sera rendu matériellement impracticable à l'immense majorité de familles" (p. 23).

[50] *La Vie catholique,* July 18, 1931.

[51] In a letter published in *La Nouvelle Revue des jeunes,* III (1931), 616-17.

ment chrétien, declared that the Document shared the spirit of the report on the *école unique* that the directors of the Catholic secondary schools had approved in 1930.[52] In a lengthy discussion of the controversy, the editors of *Vie intellectuelle* fairly presented the traditionalist argument, but their sympathies lay with the Lille group. Their commentary merits quoting at some length, for it incisively described the burden of history that the Lille group sought to lift from Catholicism: "For a century, religious interests have often had defenders only among the leisure classes, bound by the fidelity of their convictions to past regimes. For them, the ideal order is incarnate in a personal power respectful, in the same degree, of religion and the privileges of landed, industrial or capitalist property. The maintenance of manual workers in a state of intellectual and material inferiority appeared to them required by a necessary inequality of conditions. They felt that they were rallying around themselves the last square of the guardians of order and leading them into a perhaps desperate, but heroic, combat against anarchy."[53]

It would be quite misleading to suggest that the Lille Document had any impact at all upon the attitudes of most Catholics toward educational reform; it created a short-lived disagreement among Catholic leaders and then was forgotten. But the controversy, few though its participants may have been, concerned the entire Catholic community, for it opposed two quite different ideas of the relationship between French Catholicism and republican society. Because it was as much a conflict between generations as between points of view, the Lille group's position can be seen as the articulation of a growing tendency on the part of a younger generation of Catholics to regard the public school system, republican institution *par excellence,* as part of its own patrimony.

THE Lille Document not only called upon Catholics to abandon an attitude of hostility toward the *école unique*; the theme

[52] *L'Enseignement chrétien*, LI (1931), 469.

[53] ***, "La Controverse autour de l'école," *La Vie intellectuelle*, IV (1931), 23.

of cooperation also implied that Catholics should contribute their Christian point of view to the debate on reform. Catholics of the Left urged their coreligionists to extend their concerns beyond the relationship between the public school and the confessional school and to conceive education as a problem of the national community.

Pierre-Henri Simon made the most forceful statement of this point of view, as the title of his book, *L'Ecole et la nation,* suggests. A *normalien,* he had taken leave of the University to become a professor of literature in the Catholic faculty of Lille. His own experience in both traditionally hostile camps convinced him that the public and confessional schools shared too many values in their common task not to engage in a kind of dialogue. Simon served as secretary of the study group that published the Lille Document; his reflections on education were in part an elaboration of the collective viewpoint of the group.[54] One of the most prolific writers among the participationists,[55] Simon based his dispassionate yet deeply committed treatment of educational reform upon the framework of ideas and attitudes that informed the Catholic renewal. Essentially, Simon's work was a variation on the theme of recon-

[54] *L'Ecole et la nation; aspects de l'éducation nationale* (Paris, 1934), pp. 9-10.

[55] Simon was a contributor to *La Vie intellectuelle, Sept, Politique* and *Esprit,* among the most important forums for the expression of the diverse tendencies of the Catholic renewal. The most radical in its demand for a break with the past was *Esprit,* founded in 1932 by Emmanuel Mounier, who pushed to its logical consequences the refusal to compromise the Church with any temporal concern and rejected the attachment of Catholicism to any political party. Moved by the desire to be "totally Catholic and sincerely revolutionary," Mounier engaged *Esprit* in all the great debates of the 1930's and made of it a kind of meeting ground for believers and non-believers who shared his concern for the human condition. Of Simon's book on the school question, a reviewer for *Esprit* remarked: "L'amitié qui désormais lie les amis d'*Esprit* à M. P.-Henri Simon, nous autorise à reconnaître dans '*L'Ecole et la nation*' toute notre doctrine en matière de l'enseignement, en même temps que notre plan d'action. C'est un ouvrage que . . . nous faisons nôtre." *Esprit,* II (1934), 572.

ciliation between Catholics and the republic: "A Christian in a century when the [major] political problem is to put triumphant democracy in the service of justice, born a Catholic in a republican country, I believed that my voice, if I should raise it, could only speak in favor of concord between these two incontestable powers, the Church and the Republic."[56]

It was evident, Simon argued, that in a community divided in belief, only a pluralist approach to educational reform offered a means of resolving a problem of the national interest —or the common good—without violating particular rights or interests. Pluralism required common areas of agreement to be carried to their furthest limits; at the same time, each "spiritual family" had to be allowed the freedom to cultivate the beliefs that set it off from the others.[57] The whole point of Simon's effort was to explore those areas in which agreement could be reached without the sacrifice of the principles of any group.

No reconciliation could be effected on the basis of philosophical principles. It was true that both Church and state possessed a profound urge to seek a kind of unity of consciences rooted in a common belief. Doubtless many partisans of the *école unique* considered the reform a means of suppressing divisions of belief by imposing a sort of rationalist, positivistic faith upon the entire nation. As a Catholic, Simon could not deny that a unity of belief was desirable, but a unity based upon principles quite opposed to those of a non-believer. Because Catholics and Marxists could never agree upon matters of principle, fundamental philosophical questions had to be set aside: "agreement can obviously be reached only on a sort of middle level, on an order not of philosophical consent, but of pure intellectual discipline."[58]

Simon was acutely aware that the ramifications of the prob-

[56] *L'Ecole et la nation*, pp. 284-85.

[57] *Ibid.*, pp. 8-9. See also Pierre-Henri Simon, *Les Catholiques, la politique, et l'argent* (Paris, 1936), p. 211.

[58] *L'Ecole et la nation*, pp. 211-12. See also Pierre-Henri Simon, "Le Problème de l'unité dans la réforme de l'enseignement," *La Nouvelle Revue des jeunes*, IV (1932), 575.

lem of culture, questions of belief aside, were matters of considerable dispute even among partisans of the *école unique*. He defended a position quite similar to that of the supremely rationalistic Guéhenno and the maverick Socialist de Man. Both bourgeois and Marxist, he argued, committed the same error: each wished to impose class notions on the idea of culture: "the first sees in the . . . lycée the Bastille of his reign; the second launches the *école unique* as a conspiracy against the bourgeoisie."[59] These mutually hostile attitudes could be overcome only if it were recognized that culture was not the appurtenance of any social class but a discipline of the mind.[60]

On the other hand, as de Man and Guéhenno had done, Simon pointed out that the possibility of becoming a truly learned individual was bound to a style of existence that could only be described as bourgeois. For this very reason, a truly democratic reform could not justifiably be restricted to the development of a kind of mandarinate which would ignore the less able.[61] Catholics of Simon's persuasion were no less concerned than reformers such as Zoretti with raising the cultural level of the mass. For the Church's mission of preaching the gospel to every human being had as a corollary a concern for mass education; the idea that mass education simply turned out workers to fit into the industrial order as cogs in a machine was abhorrent to Catholic ideas of human dignity.[62]

The conflict between the rights of the family and the rights of the state had been among the bitterest points of contention

[59] "L'Ecole unique et nous," *Esprit*, I (1933), 794; see also "Culture et bourgeoisie: autour de l'école unique: l'aspect social du problème," *La Vie intellectuelle*, IV (April 1932), 84-87. Simon, however, came to the defense of the bourgeoisie, or at least those civil servants and members of the liberal professions who offered a valuable service to the nation.

[60] *Ibid.*, 88.

[61] *L'Ecole et la nation*, pp. 102-3.

[62] On this see also the deliberations of the *Semaines sociales de France*: *Nice, XXVIᵉ session, 1934*: "Ordre social et éducation," especially the remarks of Mgr. de Solages, rector of the Catholic Institute of Toulouse, pp. 199-207.

in the debate on the *école unique*. Doubtless public education always contains an inherent risk of conflict between these two authorities. But in the dispute over the *école unique,* the defense of the rights of the family had often been a subterfuge for the defense of class privilege, the defense of the rights of the state—an open-ended assertion, questionable in a democratic society, of the state's coercive power.

Seeking the middle ground of conciliation, Simon observed that in the sight of the Church a child was a possession neither of the family nor of the state; instead, these institutions existed mutually to assure the best conditions for his development. Certainly the rights of families and the rights of the state were quite distinct, but they were too easily viewed as opposed.[63]

Simon dwelt upon the problem of selection to show how these rights could be reconciled. Clearly, parents would betray their duty if they did not encourage their children to seek vocations that would make them useful members of the community; and the collectivity would fail in its duty if it did not help each child to develop his aptitudes to the maximum.[64] Of all those attentive to the problem of reform, Simon was almost alone in pointing out that the whole question of the *école unique* had been regrettably obfuscated and complicated by constant references to abstractions such as "The Family" and "The State": "Let us look at these things concretely: the Family, the State. Now when I am presented with a new pupil, the Family is this polite and amiable gentleman who approaches me cap in hand, and I am the state. Now what are we then—two jealous authorities who are competing over the same conquest . . . or two equally helpful powers—I was going to say paternal—who wish the well-being of the same child?"[65]

If Simon's pluralist outlook required Catholics to surrender their particularism in order to participate, with sufficient guarantees for their own rights, in an undertaking in the national interest, the same premise required the national community to show some solicitude for the confessional schools. Moreover,

[63] Pierre-Henri Simon, "L'Ecole unique et nous," *Esprit,* 1 (1933), 801.

[64] *Ibid.*   [65] *Ibid.*

if education were considered a problem of the nation as a living community, and not simply a problem of the state as a juridical abstraction, a consideration of the problem was incomplete unless private institutions were taken into account as well.[66]

A freedom could not truly be said to exist, Simon argued, unless there also existed guarantees that it could be enjoyed. Of course the state had every right to set educational standards for the confessional schools. But insofar as they assumed an educational function usually performed by the state, and for the benefit of the national community, there was no reason that the confessional schools should be refused aid simply because they also offered religious instruction.[67]

Simon's effort to show how, from a Catholic point of view, the educational establishment might cease to be a subject of discord and become, instead, an instrument of reconciliation, had no counterpart in the secular Left. Pluralism had never been a mode of political thought that the French Left found very congenial. But it is hard to think of a more reasonable way of protecting minority rights in a divided nation, or a more tolerant method of resolving inevitable conflicts among contending interest groups, than that suggested by a pluralist argument. The Leftist partisans of the *école unique,* who prided themselves on their progressivism and their tolerance, were, with regard to the school question, less progressive, less tolerant and much less inventive than the Catholics for whom Simon spoke.

OUTSIDE the narrow circle of Catholic activists who participated in the debate on educational reform, there extended, beyond the reach of the historian, the uncharted sea of the dispositions and feelings of rank and file Catholics. The attitudes of intellectuals are often a singularly unreliable guide to the collective state of mind of any group as large and extremely diverse as the French Catholic community; and generalizations about states of mind can seldom be more than conjecture. But that

[66] *Ecole et la nation*, pp. 12, 37.
[67] *Ibid.*, pp. 242-45.

which is neither quantifiable nor subject to detailed proof is
not necessarily unimportant.

Perhaps merely the unfortunate choice of the equivocal
phrase *école unique* to designate the reform had done most to
arouse the initial suspicions of Catholics. By any other name,
the reform might have created fewer difficulties. But *école
unique* seemed to imply that the confessional schools were to
be abolished in favor of one single state school system. By the
late 1920's, however, it must have become reasonably clear
that the imposition of a state monopoly of education was a
problem quite distinct, in the minds of most reformers, from
the proposals associated with the *école unique*. Besides, none
of the groups that found it necessary to threaten the confessional schools with some variation of monopoly had the re-
motest chance of actually carrying out its threats. After the
ignominious collapse of the anticlerical offensive of the Cartel
des gauches, no Leftist government was apt to employ the reform of the educational establishment as a weapon against
Catholics. In fact, none did.

By the early 1930's, the general proposals associated with
the *école unique* had been public knowledge for so long that
they had become commonplaces. As commonplaces it is doubtful that they truly disturbed a very large sector of Catholic
opinion. While the participationists urged upon Catholics a
cooperative attitude toward the *école unique,* and the traditionalists urged vigilant hostility, it is quite likely that the attitude of the majority of Catholics increasingly became one of
indifference. But indifference is a kind of acceptance; it is
only when people feel that their beliefs or their interests are
seriously threatened that they become sufficiently aroused to
protest.

Educational reform had been talked about for years; it had
been only a limited practical success. Free public secondary
education had no easily discernible adverse effect upon the
status of the confessional secondary schools; enrollment in
them increased. The reform apparently made the state educational establishment no more attractive to devout Catholics than
it had ever been. The majority of Catholics continued to vote

for the parties of the Right; the parties of the Right opposed the *école unique*. In their choice of political representatives, then, most Catholics showed little active sympathy for the broad social and political ideals associated with the *école unique*. But the repeated laments of a Guiraud or a Keller that Catholics were resigning themselves to the reform indicated that most of them did not consider it a threat to religious interests.

Catholics of the Left were determined that the traditionalist leaders should no longer appear to be the sole interpreters of the interests of the Church, either in the sight of non-believers or of Catholics. Between the world wars, their influence did not extend beyond a narrow sector of Catholic opinion. With regard to the *école unique,* the participationist tendency was an affair of intellectuals, but it cast a ray of light upon a formidably difficult question darkened by decades of misunderstanding between Catholics and republicans. Each side had had good reason to suspect the other. Reconciliation between those who hold conflicting conceptions of human destiny is far from easy. The participationists understood that a reconciliation over the problem of the school depended upon the establishment of a dialogue; if their appeal found no immediate response, the very fact that they made it was a hopeful sign that a dialogue might soon become possible.

Chapter VIII. The Popular Front and the Resurgence of Reform

> Le malheur veut que, dans les périodes de calme, où l'on pourrait travailler avec sérénité aux adaptations nécessaires, l'opinion soit généralement hostile aux réformes, qui risquent de troubler sa quiétude. Quand la tempête est venue, et qu'elle secoue les fondements de l'état, on déplore soudain une trop longue apathie. On remet tout en cause, le bon et le mauvais. . . . Si la passion politique s'en mêle, si elle joue son rôle dans les domaines où elle n'a que faire—les pires égarements en résultent.
>
> —JEAN ZAY

IN March 1930, when the Chamber of Deputies voted on the principle of free secondary education, the prospects of France seemed bright and serene. The franc was stable; the economy boomed. The war-devastated areas had been rebuilt and the Germans were faithfully paying reparations. The Locarno pact had induced an era of good feeling in international relations which seemed to guarantee that the French could enjoy their prosperity unmolested. But at the end of 1930 there appeared slight but nonetheless disturbing indications that France might not escape the deepening world economic crisis.[1]

By 1932, France, too, was in the grip of the depression; by 1933, Germany was in the grip of the Nazis. Republican institutions came under attack from right-wing leagues that made up in noise and vicious threats what they lacked in numbers. On the evening of February 6, 1934, members of the leagues, professing outrage at a dismal financial scandal, mounted a demonstration in the Place de la Concorde that led to bloodshed; if it was not a planned insurrection against the republic, it looked like one.

Politics descended into the street. The events of February 6 triggered an effort of the Left to organize against enemies do-

---

[1] See Sauvy, *Histoire économique*, pp. 101-104.

mestic and foreign. But despite the feverish sense of urgency that the night of rioting gave public life, the formation of the Popular Front required months of arduous negotiation, of false starts, hesitations, and recrimination among Radicals, Socialists and Communists. Finally, in January 1936, these strange bedfellows patched together a quilt beneath which they all could huddle in the coming elections, at the cost of leaving out material any partner found uncomfortable.[2]

In the fall of 1934, Ludovic Zoretti had written: "One wonders if there is any chance of interesting public opinion by speaking of the school. Attention is elsewhere. The house is burning. The firemen are bustling about. The school keeps its place in this collapse, but the Comité des forges and fascism occupy a much greater place."[3] Indeed, educational reform seemed to have little to do with the politics of the mass demonstration, the defiance of the clenched fist salute, the despair of unemployment, the darkening international horizon. Building the *école unique* seemed a task for safer times, a job that had to be set aside in order to meet the emergencies that the republic confronted.

But safer times had come and gone; the *école unique* had not been built. The Popular Front was not just an electoral alliance, formed by some to meet an emergency, joined by others to save their political skins. It was also the expression of a mood, an exalted hope that at last there was going to be a kind of New Deal for those who had never received much of a deal at all.[4] The program of the Popular Front, mild though it may

[2] The Socialists and the CGT gave up the most; they wanted a precise plan of sweeping economic and social renovation. The Communists, most interested in combatting fascism as a defense of the Soviet Union, had no desire to alarm the middle classes whose support they sought, and preferred a program of generalities; the Radicals, as representatives of the middle classes, had no desire to be alarmed. On the formation of the Popular Front, see James Joll, "The Making of the Popular Front," in Joll, ed., *The Decline of the Third Republic* (London, 1960). The most recent, and in many ways the best, general account of the Popular Front era is Georges Lefranc, *Histoire du front populaire* (Paris, 1965).

[3] Zoretti, *Elite, sélection, culture*, p. 7.

[4] The mood of the Popular Front is vividly conveyed in excerpts

have appeared, was a catalogue of economic and social demands that had gone unfulfilled since 1919 and before. Among its sincerer partisans, the *école unique* had always been a sort of new deal in education; as a largely unmet demand, educational reform fitted quite naturally into the program of the Popular Front.

The section of the program devoted to education made no sweeping demands; it must have appeared timid indeed to anyone unaware of the disappointments reformers had suffered over the past eighteen years. Under the main heading "Defense of Freedom," the program called for "Measures safeguarding the development of public education, not only by providing the necessary credits, but also by reforms such as raising the age for compulsory education to fourteen and, in secondary education, selection as the indispensable complement to free tuition [*gratuité*]."[5]

Many years before, the Compagnons had demanded "selection as the indispensable complement to free tuition." The raising of the school-leaving age had long been a goal of reformers. Despite the timidity of the electoral program, the reform plan drawn up under the Popular Front government proved to be the most ambitious official undertaking of any since the reforms of Jules Ferry in the 1880's. In the hopes it aroused, the controversy it created, and the disappointment in which it ended, the reform effort was characteristic of the Popular Front experiment. An epilogue to the interwar reform movement, the Zay plan was also a prologue to educational reform undertaken after the Second World War.

The electoral campaign of 1936 took place in an emotional

---

from the press, with editorial commentary, in Louis Bodin and Jean Touchard, *1936: Le Front populaire* (Paris, 1961). See also Georges Lefranc, *Juin 36; l'explosion sociale* (Paris, 1966). The program of the Popular Front can be found in David Thomson, *Democracy in France*, 4th edn. (New York and London, 1964), pp. 317-22.

[5] This is a somewhat altered version of the translation found in Thomson, *Democracy in France*, p. 319. Thomson's translation of *gratuité* as "grants" obscures the significance of the demand as a fulfillment of the *école unique* proposals.

207

atmosphere that recalled the passions of the Dreyfus Affair. Rational discussion of issues counted for little. No great shift of votes from Right to Left took place, but the economic and political crisis brought important changes in the balance of forces within the Leftist camp. The Socialist party became the largest in the Chamber. The Radicals lost fewer seats than they might have, had they not joined the Popular Front. But the most striking success belonged to the Communists, who received twice as many votes as in 1932, and six times as many seats in the Chamber. Victory brought uncertainty. To Socialist, Communist and Radical politicians the Popular Front was primarily an electoral alliance. But an alliance for what? The Communists considered it a means of checking the fascist threat and thereby aiding the Soviet Union; the Socialists expected from it an opportunity to undertake a precise reform program; the Radicals wanted to avoid an electoral isolation that might have been fatal to them—in any case, they had not suddenly become converts to even the reformism of the Socialists.[6] Launched as a kind of lifeboat in which the republic could be steered to safety, the Popular Front threatened to capsize as each member of the crew sought to row off in a different direction.

But May and June 1936 seemed a "springtime filled with an immense hope." In the exalted atmosphere of the great spontaneous strikes that rolled across France, educational reform appeared a sedate business indeed. As had happened to French politicians in the past, Maurice Thorez, Léon Blum and Léon Jouhaux found themselves obliged to follow the working class, because they were its leaders.[7] But the same *joie de vivre* that Simone Weil detected in the strikers infused educational reformers, too; Suzanne Collette, a Socialist school teacher, wrote in *Le Populaire*: "It has already become banal to express the immense hope of all those who expect from a Popular Front government an end to deadening stagnation

---

[6] This paragraph relies on Georges Dupeux, *Le Front populaire et les élections de 1936* (Paris, 1959), especially pp. 138-39, 173-77.

[7] On the occupation of the factories, see Lefranc, *Front populaire*, pp. 142-49.

and the elaboration of a new world. Nowhere, perhaps, is this expectation better founded than in the University."[8] It had to be admitted that popular enthusiasm did not support educational reform as fully as other tasks the government had to confront, but at least in the CGT project there already existed a plan for reform.[9]

Léon Blum became the first Socialist prime minister in French history. The Communists played the Socialists' old game; despite Blum's appeals, they refused to share responsibility in the government, and offered instead their "support." Blum put together a cabinet of Socialists and Radicals. He might have been wiser had he not risked compromising his reform program by including Radicals in his government. But when he made Jean Zay minister of national education, Blum had one Radical upon whom he could depend to be as energetic a reformer as any member of his cabinet.

Jean Zay was the youngest minister in the history of the Third Republic, and he brought to a post that had more often been held by such sobersides as Jules Ferry a young man's optimism, wit and enthusiasm. Zay had inherited the journalist's trade from his father, for whom he worked on the *Progrès du Loiret*. After a brilliant career as a student, he undertook the practice of law in Orléans in 1928. In 1932, at the age of twenty-eight, he won a seat in the Chamber. He brought to Paris considerable experience in local politics, some regret, perhaps, for the literary ambitions he had given up, a passionate interest in international relations and an acute sense of duty, for which he eventually paid with his life.[10]

[8] *Le Populaire*, May 28, 1936.

[9] *Le Populaire*, May 21, 1936.

[10] On Zay, see Maurice Chavardès, *Un Ministre éducateur: Jean Zay* (Paris, 1965). This slim volume is less a biography of Zay than a brief survey of Zay's accomplishments as minister of education. On Zay's personality, see the remarks of Jean Cassou in the preface to Zay's memoirs, *Souvenirs et solitude* (Paris, 1945), pp. vii-viii. Zay wrote his memoirs in the cell to which the Vichy government confined him on the trumped-up charge of desertion. He was murdered by the *Milice*, the collaborationist Vichy police, while being transferred from one prison to another in June 1944.

Zay was one of the Radical party's Young Turks. The Young Turks had neither an organization nor an ideology that set them off from the rest of the party, but they did have in common a state of mind: a spirit of revolt against conservative Radical graybeards and a keen interest in the renovation of the party and the modernization of France. Zay, for one, had vigorously supported the formation of the Popular Front. Perhaps the leadership of the party effectively reined in the Young Turks by giving them responsible jobs at an early age.[11] But if conservative Radicals considered Zay a troublemaker in the Chamber, they could not count on him to sit docilely at the rue de Grenelle, humbly grateful to have been handed a ministerial portfolio. Zay outlasted the Popular Front experiment; he was minister of education from 1936 until the outbreak of the war, when he chose to assume his responsibilities as a reserve officer. Under Zay's tenure the ministry of education, so often among the most frequent victims of the dizzying waltz of ministers, had a sustained and purposeful direction that it had seldom had in the past.

In his three years in office, Zay poked into almost every corner of his vast ministry. The plan for a reform of the educational system consumed only a part of his energy. Many of the tasks undertaken by his administration fall outside the scope of this study, but the most important of them deserve mention as an indication of its reforming zeal. Under Zay's direction, the Museum of Modern Art was established in Paris; a reform of the national theaters was undertaken; the Centre national de la recherche scientifique, a coordinating

[11] This is Larmour's suggestion in his *French Radical Party*, pp. 40-41. On the Young Turks, see also Alexander Werth, "Le Mouvement 'jeune-turc,' un phénomène radical de l'entre deux-guerres," *Cahiers de la république*, No. 2 (1956), 100-6. Georges Lefranc suggests that Blum first intended Zay to become an undersecretary of state attached to Blum's own office. Paul Rivet, professor at the *Muséum de Paris* and instrumental in the formation of the Popular Front, was perhaps to have become minister of national education, but Blum changed his mind and named Zay to the post. Lefranc, *Front populaire*, p. 155, n. 2; *Mouvement socialiste*, p. 329, n. 1.

organization for research in subjects ranging from archeology to zoology, was founded; a plan was drawn up for a national school of administration, in order to place the education of high civil servants under public control. Zay lent his support to the development of popular theater, undertook an investigation of the educational possibilities of films and radio, obtained an increase in the number of secondary school scholarships, made physical education obligatory and stepped up the school building program.[12] It is true that Zay had a brilliant team of assistants, but as minister, the responsibility for overseeing all of these tasks belonged to him.

Within the University, there was some resentment at his appointment. He was an outsider—a lawyer; what did he know about education?[13] Zay may have overcome the reservations of syndicalists at least, when he named his aides. As his adviser for secondary education, he chose Pierre Boivin, syndicalist and Socialist militant and the son of Henri Boivin, who had had a hand in drawing up the project of the CGT.[14] Zay clearly intended to seek the expert advice of the men most closely associated in the past with the movement for democratic reform. And in early July 1936, he announced that he intended to undertake a broad reform of the University.[15]

In the meantime, perhaps one long-standing demand of educational reformers benefited directly from the popular effervescence of the summer of 1936. In early June, seeking to resolve a crisis that seemed almost on the brink of civil war, Blum brought management and labor together to work out the Matignon agreement, which introduced the principle of

[12] On all this see Chavardès, *Un Ministre éducateur*, passim.

[13] Information obtained by the author from an associate of Zay who wished to remain anonymous, 1965.

[14] Boivin died in August 1937, at the age of only 31. A graduate of the Ecole normale, he was a boyhood friend of Zay, with whom he grew up in Orléans. He had been an unsuccessful Socialist candidate for the Chamber in the elections of 1932. Raymond Bouyer, an assistant secretary of the CGT, remarked of Boivin that he was "one of these intellectuals with whom workers are proud to be friends." See the introduction to Pierre Boivin, *Choix d'écrits* (Paris, 1938), p. viii.

[15] *Le Populaire*, July 9, 1936.

collective bargaining into labor-management relations and granted to workers wage increases that averaged around 12 per cent.[16] In the following weeks, a series of social reforms were rapidly passed through a parliament alarmed by the sit-down strikes. On August 7, 1936, the school-leaving age was raised to fourteen with surprisingly little debate. Nor did the press give much space to a measure that had lain dormant in parliament since 1922.[17] Public attention was riveted upon Spain, where civil war had broken out three weeks earlier.

But Zay did not have his reform project ready until March 1937. If May and June 1936 had been a springtime of immense hope, spring 1937 was a time of creeping disillusionment. The Popular Front government teetered on the brink of collapse. In February 1937, Léon Blum had found it necessary to announce a "pause" in the work of social reform. No vigorous economic measures had been taken to support the social reforms of the summer of 1936; at the Treasury, the government deficit rose at a dismaying rate. Inflation cut into labor's gains from wage increases. Industrial production did not rise much; unemployment did not fall. On March 2, 1937, with the prospects of the government as dreary as the Parisian winter, Zay presented his project to the Cabinet.[18]

The previous December, Louis Mérat, secretary of the Fédération générale de l'enseignement, had asserted that Zay had promised the plan of the CGT would serve as the basis for the government's reform project.[19] It is not certain that Mérat rightly understood Zay; nonetheless, the government's project owed a great deal to the plan of the CGT.

[16] See Lefranc, *Histoire du front populaire*, pp. 160-67.

[17] In *Le Populaire* for August 8, 1936, an editorialist remarked that the raising of the school-leaving age was "un bel exemple de la difficulté des réformes dans le beau régime économique et politique que les droites—et ce nom s'applique à des formations très étendues—continuent à vouloir conserver, même quand la raison ou la nécessité les amène à concéder sur quelques points."

[18] On the "pause," see the detailed discussion in Lefranc, *Front populaire*, pp. 205-31.

[19] *Information universitaire*, February 6, 1937.

In his introduction to the project, Zay declared: "The time appears to have come to give primary, secondary and higher education the coordinating statute [*statut d'ensemble*] that they have awaited for many years and for which numerous measures and experiments have prepared the way."[20] In a few brief articles, the project recapitulated the aims that democratic reformers had sought to achieve over the past twenty years, since the Compagnons' challenging manifesto of 1918.[21]

All children were to begin their education on an equal footing by means of a unification of the base of the school system. But the project disappointed the more radical reformers once again: it did not abolish outright the elementary classes of the lycée, but transformed them into public schools with the same teachers and programs as the primary school.

Zay met the intractable problem of linking the primary school to the secondary level by means of a compromise between the two dominant points of view within the reform movement. The more radical solution, advanced by the early Compagnons and Zoretti, and taken up by the primary school teachers, had been to postpone entry into the secondary level until the age of fourteen. But this meant the amputation of two years from the lycée, an operation to which many lycée professors reacted as if they had been asked to sacrifice their own legs. The loudest cries of indignation came from the professors of Latin, some of whom argued that Latin not begun at the age of eleven or twelve might just as well not be begun at all. Besides, anything the school teachers supported looked suspicious to them. The other solution had been to divide the examination for the *certificat des études primaires* into two parts: the first part, taken at the age of eleven, was to be an entrance examination for the secondary level; the second part, at age fourteen, was to remain an examination for the primary

[20] The Zay project is reprinted in Decaunes, *Réformes et projets de réforme*, pp. 255-58; and Chavardès, *Un Ministre éducateur*, pp. 121-24.

[21] The Compagnons had disbanded in 1933. Maurice Weber, who almost singlehandedly kept the organization going in later years, found himself too burdened with teaching duties to continue the task. (Maurice Weber, letter to the author, September 1, 1965.)

213

school diploma. This proposal, put forth by the Comité d'étude, preserved the first two years of the traditional lycée; it received the support of a good many lycée professors. But it also seemed to diminish the prestige of the CEP and therefore offended the school teachers. Zay proposed that a single examination for the *certificat des études primaires,* taken at the age of twelve, should be at once the final sanction for primary studies and the compulsory entrance examination for the secondary level; those most likely to go on to the secondary level, however, could take the examination at the age of eleven.

Despite frequent objections that the reform movement had never paid sufficient heed to problems of primary education, Zay's project focused upon secondary education, as had the attention of reformers since the war. For it had been agreed from the outset that the primary school, whatever its faults, was at least not undemocratic. The axis of Zay's whole project was the long-postponed and extremely delicate problem of orientation.

For some time the more radical reformers had insisted that the notion of selection of only the most intellectually able children for secondary education—which implied the abandonment of the rest—should be replaced by the notion of orientation: the direction of *every* child toward the kind of schooling that best suited his ability. The CGT plan had recommended two years of common study for all students at the beginning of the secondary level. Zay's project reduced the orientation class to one year, as the more conservative Comité d'étude had suggested.

Classical, modern and technical options branched out from this common trunk of the orientation class. Special courses were to be established to ease passage from one branch to another, in order to correct initial errors in orientation, and to permit late entries from the complementary course—an extension of the primary school. The project divided secondary study into two cycles. The technical section stopped at the end of the first cycle of four years; the modern and classical sections continued for three more years and culminated in the much criticized but still apparently indispensable baccalaureate examination.[22] Finally, students could remain in the secondary level only if they continued to demonstrate sufficient aptitude for it in yearly examinations.

Zay had been thirteen years old when the Compagnons first gathered at Compiègne. At the end of the preamble to the project, he restated the conviction that had drawn them together to plan the New University: "Does not social justice demand that, whatever the point of departure, each may go in his chosen direction as far and as high as his abilities permit him?"[23] After the years of party resolutions and grandiose promises, small victories and larger failures, private discussion and bitter public debate, there had finally appeared a vast reform project of official inspiration. The Zay project at least showed that under the Third Republic there were still lines of communication open between thought and action, between the private sector of expert opinion and the government, between the seekers of change and those in a position to effect change.

The Zay project would have required many years to put into effect, even in the best of times. In 1937, Zay must have realized chances were slim that parliament would vote upon the reform. Besides, the project shared a common failing of the Popular Front experiment: it sought ambitious ends without having at hand the financial means to carry them out. Moreover, the reform was made public in the most inauspicious circumstances. Popular apathy and resignation had replaced the euphoria of 1936. In June 1937, the Radical-dominated Senate overturned the Blum government when Blum sought the authority to legislate by decree.[24] Governments headed by Radi-

[22] At the end of the first cycle of four years, an examination and diploma were to be established so that students who did not go on to the second cycle could present to prospective employers proof of having attended the secondary level. The technical section, moreover, was to be a four-year course, to the displeasure of those who sought to make this section more than a trade school for the acquisition of narrowly practical skills.

[23] Decaunes, *Réformes et projets de réformes*, p. 256.

[24] On this episode see Georges Dupeux, "L'Echec du premier gouvernement Blum," *Revue d'histoire moderne et contemporaine*, x (1963), 35-44.

cals substituted drift for action. Zay remained in power while his own party helped to sabotage the experiment to which he had contributed so much of his energy.

But he did not seek an excuse for inaction in the wreckage of the Popular Front, nor resign himself to the fence-sitting of the government leadership. He did not propose to wait and see whether the Chamber might undertake discussion of his reform project. Instead, he set out to achieve as much of it as he could under his own authority.

IN TAKING action, Zay sought constantly to reassure public opinion, to explain each step he took, to conciliate opponents of the reform. But despite his obvious good faith, he was hampered by aroused ideological passions and the force of tradition.

One indication of Zay's effort at compromise was that when the project first appeared, it delighted no one; nor did it outrage anyone, except those prepared to be outraged by any sort of reform. Public reaction to the project was doubtless tempered by long familiarity with the outlines of the *école unique*. The idea no longer seemed quite so revolutionary as it had in the past. *Le Temps,* long among the most outspoken adversaries of the *école unique,* and no friend of the Popular Front, declared that the project "contains views worthy of being approved by enlightened minds. In fact, liberals can subscribe to it." The reorganization of secondary education did not seem to imply the "primarization" that *Le Temps'* editorialists had always decried. The orientation class evoked only a qualified approval, though *Le Temps* conceded that it seemed to take the rights of parents into account.[25]

On the opposite side of the political fence, the leadership of the teachers' trade unions rejoiced that its views had clearly been considered in the drafting of the reform. André Delmas, secretary-general of the Syndicat national des instituteurs and a leader in the formation of the Popular Front, declared: "Because of what it contains, the text to which M. Jean Zay has attached his name will arouse no great criticism in our cir-

[25] *Le Temps,* March 4, 1937.

cles."[26] The Fédération générale de l'enseignement had serious criticisms of detail, but it could not object to the general outlines of the Zay plan without denying its own paternity.[27]

To be sure, in some quarters the bitter ideological quarrels of the 1930's had pushed suspicion quite beyond reason. Some partisans of the *école unique* wondered if the Zay project was truly democratic, simply because it had received the approbation of some conservatives.[28] Ludovic Zoretti flatly stated that "the project gives nothing, absolutely nothing, to the working class that it does not already have."[29] But the irrepressible Marceau Pivert declared that the project was a revolutionary undertaking, so long as it was resolutely carried out within the context of the class struggle.[30] Of course Zay had no such intention. Still, it is curious that after all the years of agitating for reform, Zoretti responded with a sterile sort of Leftism to a project that reasonably conformed to his own aims.

The Communist party, in abandoning its own brand of rigorous Leftism to embrace the republic and all its good works, had changed its attitude of unremitting hostility toward the *école unique*. Until 1936, the reform was simply another bourgeois snare, designed to deprive the working class of its leaders. This view of the matter suited the party's political position at a time when it had a greater impact upon politics as a frighten-

[26] *L'Ecole libératrice*, March 6, 1937.

[27] See "La Réforme de l'enseignement: rapport présenté au conseil national de la F.G.E.," *Ecole libératrice*, February 2, 1937.

[28] Louis Mérat, secretary of the FGE, expressed this opinion of some of his associates in an article in *Essais et combats*, No. 12 (April 1937), 2-6.

[29] *Le Populaire*, March 19, 1937. Perhaps Pierre Boivin, whose leftist credentials were unquestioned, but who had had a taste of the practical difficulties of reform, had the point of view represented by Zoretti in mind when he wrote that access to culture should not be narrowly subordinated to the immediate needs of the class struggle: "Sur le plan de la pensée, il [the working class] ne revendique je ne sais quelle culture ouvrière que personne n'a jamais pu sérieusement définir, il revendique la culture humaine. Car il y a, qu'on le veuille ou non, des vérités valables pour tous, des valeurs indépendantes des régimes," *Le Peuple*, April 12, 1937.   [30] *Le Populaire*, May 3, 1937.

ing specter than as a substantial presence; purposely isolating itself from the rest of the nation, declining in membership, plagued with organizational difficulties, the party had a tiny parliamentary representation.[31] But despite their hostility toward the *école unique* and their hatred of its partisans, the Communist deputies had voted in favor of the commitment to the principle of free secondary education.

By 1936 the party had completed its tactical about-face in order to confront the threat of fascism at home and abroad; the class war had been set aside in favor of an alliance with the middle classes, a hand had been extended to all who might grasp it. As Maurice Thorez, party leader, succinctly put it: "We Communists . . . have reconciled the tricolor flag of our fathers and the red flag of our hopes."[32]

After the elections of 1936, Georges Cogniot, *normalien,* lycée professor and newly elected Communist deputy from the eleventh *arrondissement* of Paris, became *rapporteur* for the budget of national education—one sign of the party's greatly increased parliamentary strength. With considerable finesse, Cogniot managed to weave the new party line into a realistic appraisal of the Zay project.[33]

It was, he said, a splendid example of the alliance of workers and middle classes that Communists sought to preserve against the fascist threat. Though the project contained nothing at all of a distinctly Socialist character, it was nonetheless democratic and progressive and therefore merited the support of Communists: "We demand nothing which is not realizable at the present time, in complete harmony with the other parties of the Popular Front."

Despite his approval of the outlines of the project, Cogniot did have criticisms. Taking up a position on the left wing of

[31] See Jacques Fauvet, *Histoire du parti communiste français,* 2 vols. (Paris, 1964-65), I, passim; Annie Kriegel, "Le parti communiste français sous la troisième République, 1920-1939; évolution de ses effectifs, *Revue française de science politique,* xvi (February 1966), 5-36.

[32] Quoted in Fauvet, *Histoire du parti communiste,* I, 184.

[33] Georges Cogniot, "Réforme de l'enseignement et réforme de la fiscalité," *Cahiers du bolchévisme* (July 1937), 541-49.

the reform movement, the Communist Party advocated not just one year of orientation, but the extension of common classes to include all children from the ages of twelve to fifteen. Furthermore, Cogniot observed, the project made no real provision for children too poor to afford secondary education, despite the fact that it was free. Finally, he underscored what many partisans of the *école unique* had never been prepared to admit, however obvious it had become: without enormous amounts of money, the project was doomed.

It was doubtless true that at the outset, the Zay plan met an unexpectedly favorable welcome from quite diverse points of the political compass because it presented the most difficult and controversial problems in vague and general terms. As Henri Boivin, the father of Zay's adviser on secondary education, pointed out, "At bottom, the whole meaning of the reform is determined by this question of orientation."[34] Indeed, Zay himself considered the orientation class the key to the project. Because it was the aspect of the project that most visibly affected the status quo, and because Zay devoted his immediate attention to it, the orientation class was taken as symbol of the social and political implications of the entire reform, and controversy centered upon it.

In January 1936, General Castelnau had announced that if the Popular Front won the elections, "we will see the installation of a monopoly of education and a war against religion, as in the hell of the Soviet Union."[35] But anticlericalism played little part in the electoral campaign of 1936, despite the exacerbation of antagonism between Right and Left. For the first time in the history of the Third Republic, a leftist victory was not followed by a resurgence of the religious quarrel.[36]

[34] Henri Boivin, "Sur le projet ministériel de réforme," *Revue universitaire*, XLVI (1937), 3.

[35] *La France catholique*, January 1, 1936.

[36] See René Rémond, "Les Catholiques et le front populaire," *Archives de sociologie des religions*, V (1960), 63-69. See also the observations of a contemporary Catholic, "D'Une prudence qui est aussi une justice," *La Vie intellectuelle*, VIII (1936), 6-9.

Because the government of the Popular Front, unlike that of the Cartel des gauches, undertook no provocative religious policy, there was no deliberate official confusion between anticlericalism and educational reform. Since 1801, at least, quarrels between the major tendencies of Catholic opinion had never been more intense than they became under the Popular Front.[37] These internal disputes, however, had little effect on the relationship between Catholics and the government. The hierarchy made no pronouncements that concerned the Zay project. In the absence of any threat to religious interests, the problem of educational reform increasingly came to be simply one more of the issues that divided Catholics in their attitudes toward the secular city.

Catholics of the Right, alarmed by the Popular Front experiment, outraged by the ferocious anticlericalism of the republican forces in the Spanish civil war, and violently anti-Communist, employed the same charges they had hurled for years against educational reform, and imputed to Zay designs that he did not have.

Indeed, a fear of Communism obsessed rightist Catholics. The Fédération nationale catholique charged that the Zay project, if undertaken, would mean the installation of a kind of soviet regime in France.[38] Despite Zay's assurances that parents would be entirely free to reject the advice of the teachers of the orientation classes, the FNC insisted that parents would be forced to submit to the arbitrary will of the state.[39] The Société d'éducation called the orientation class a "conscription of youth";[40] the Association des parents d'élèves de l'école libre, though it lacked the clearly rightist political ties of the Société d'éducation, nonetheless shared its traditionalist attitude of religious defense. In the orientation class, the APEL detected a plan for the "mobilization by the totalitarian state, in a future

[37] See Rémond, *Les Catholiques*, especially pp. 125-254.

[38] *La France catholique*, March 20, 1937.

[39] *Ibid.*

[40] L'Enseignement libre et le front populaire," *Bulletin de la société générale d'éducation et d'enseignement*, LXVII (1936), 617-21.

soviet, of the human material fabricated by mothers and fathers."[41]

As he had done since the war, Jean Guiraud accused of betrayal of the faith any Catholic who had good words to say about reform.[42] Soon after the appearance of the Zay project, however, an incident occurred that indicated Guiraud's increasing isolation from the position of the hierarchy, at least, if not from the main body of Catholic lay opinion.

In March 1937, Guiraud alleged in *La Croix* that Zay had just announced the government's intention to suppress the confessional schools.[43] The Abbé Desgranges, fearful that Guiraud's article might have an unhappy effect on cordial relations between Blum and the Archbishop of Paris, undertook to assure the government that the article in no way reflected the opinion of the hierarchy.[44]

The government, in turn, responded to Desgranges' assurances. In a speech in Saint-Etienne, Zay made unmistakably clear that he had no intention of lending his support to any movement for a state monopoly of education: "I have never

[41] *Ecole et liberté*, April, 1938. But see the conciliatory attitude toward the reform of Philippe de las Cases, president of the APEL, in *Sept*, March 19, 1937. De las Cases did not question the principle of the reform, but merely had doubts whether the reform project contained sufficient guarantees for the confessional schools; he was disturbed, too, by the vagueness of some aspects of the reform project. Moreover, not all the local chapters of the APEL shared the intransigent attitude of some of the national leadership. In the liberal atmosphere of the diocese of Lille, for example, the APEL declared itself in favor of the orientation class, so long as the rights of families were respected. *La Vie catholique*, December 4, 1937.

[42] *Ecole et famille*, XVII (1937), 126-31.

[43] *La Croix*, March 12, 1937.

[44] Abbé Jean Desgranges, *Journal d'un prêtre-député; 1936-1940* (Paris, 1960), p. 96. Desgranges remarked that Guiraud got his information out of a right-wing weekly at Nantes without bothering to verify it: "Comment un professeur d'histoire peut-il manquer à ce point de loyauté ou d'esprit critique! . . . C'est avec cette légèreté coupable qu'on lance un brandon de discorde, au moment ou l'épiscopat fait un effort de concorde. . . ."

221

thought of putting freedom of education in peril in any way whatsoever. Any monopoly, in such a sphere, would be related to a totalitarian conception of the state, which is entirely absent from my mind."[45]

Responsible leaders in the hierarchy and the government did not consider monopoly of education a live issue, or at the least a question that should be allowed to trouble relations between church and state. But traditionalists such as Guiraud continued to insist upon fitting political adversaries into a sort of Manichean scheme of the Red against the Black that bore less and less relation to reality. Doubtless many anticlericals shared Guiraud's conception of the world, but they did not have a hand in the making of government policy.

Pierre-Henri Simon probably had Guiraud's position in mind when he warned Catholics against a defensive attitude that was "morally vicious and tactically unsound."[46] The Zay project, Simon argued, in no way interfered with the fundamental principles that a Catholic must necessarily hold.[47] The influence that Catholics of the left such as Simon exerted upon Catholic opinion cannot be measured. But if most Catholics had little active sympathy for the Zay reform, simply because their political sympathies remained with the Right, it is extremely unlikely that the majority shared the antipathy of a Guiraud or a Castelnau. The attitude of religious defense exerted less authority over Catholics as it became less certain that religion needed to be defended against political adversaries; the prophecy that reform meant a monopoly of education had become less and less credible as the years had gone by and no effort had been made to impose a monopoly. Despite General Castelnau's undeniable services to the Church, it was difficult to distinguish his defense of the rights of the family against the Zay project from the defense of social privilege.

[45] *L'Ere nouvelle*, April 5, 1937.

[46] *Sept*, July 10, 1936.

[47] Pierre-Henri Simon, "Vers une nouvelle réforme scolaire," *La Vie intellectuelle*, IX (1937), 420-34; see also the remarks of the Popular Democrats' educational expert, André Bastianelli, "Le Projet de réforme de l'enseignement public," *Politique*, X (1937), 259-63.

Though Catholics of the left had definite reservations about the orientation class, the key to the project, they did not object to it on the ground that it interfered with the rights of parents. Instead, they merely shared the uncertainty of some non-Catholic reformers over the nature and purpose of the class. Simon, for example, felt that the class might too closely resemble a crowded railroad station, in which passengers headed for different destinations constantly got in one another's way.[48] Other left Catholics supported the project. Jacques Lefrancq, who wrote on education for *Esprit,* enthusiastically supported the idea of the orientation class, charged that its opponents were merely defending selfish interests, and showed a subtle understanding of its purpose and potentiality.[49] And Daniel-Rops considered the orientation class an encouraging effort more closely to associate parents with the task of educating their children.[50]

Whatever the real extent of the inroads that the conciliatory position of Catholics of the left had made against the traditionalist position of religious defense, enough voices had been raised so that no man of good faith could claim that the Church stood unalterably opposed to democratic educational reform, just as no man of good faith could claim that the victory of the Popular Front had been a defeat for Catholicism.

SOME FAITHFUL leftist partisans of the *école unique* were by no means convinced that the orientation class was a sound idea. Bracke, the old Socialist champion of Latin, feared that the Zay project imposed the orientation class upon children too young to profit from it: "who will dare to say that an eleven-year-old urchin can and must be directed here or there?"[51] Although in large part the CGT plan inspired the orientation class, the Zay project did not precisely indicate what its nature

[48] Simon, *La Vie intellectuelle,* IX (1937), 424.

[49] Jacques Lefrancq, "Du massacre des innocents à l'orientation pédagogique," *Esprit,* VI (1937-38), 229-63; 386-420; 731-39. For the position of *Esprit,* see above, pp. 196-97, n. 55.

[50] *Sept,* March 19, 1937.

[51] *Le Populaire,* March 6, 1937.

and content should be; some trade unionists feared that traditionalists might employ the orientation class to maintain the prestige of the classical section, by skimming off the best students for the study of Latin and using the technical and modern sections as reservoirs for the less able.[52]

On the other hand, defenders of traditional secondary education and, along with it, of the traditional social order, professed to see in the project one more alarming example of the subordination of the Popular Front government to the CGT. One retired lycée professor charged that to put technical students and classical students side by side in the same class would be the ruination of classical studies: "For the CGT, it is a question of demolishing classical studies, that Bastille of the bourgeois spirit, although from Jaurès to Blum, all the leaders of socialism have drawn from their humanist culture a force which has promoted their party to the place we see it today."[53] An unsigned editorial in the *Revue des deux mondes,* the musty exponent of bourgeois respectability, charged that the orientation class would be "particularly dangerous, like the majority of the measures which are stacked up in the arsenal of recent social laws," one more example of "the tyranny of the state on the orders of the CGT."[54]

The charge that the ministry of education took its orders from the CGT came from the same people who had opposed free secondary education. The more tenacious defenders of privilege appeared unable to meet even the most gradualist efforts at social change with any more than a defensive reaction. The orientation class was of a piece with the forty-hour week, the paid vacation, collective bargaining—not an effort

[52] Mérat, secretary of the FGE, remarked, "C'est en somme vouloir introduire l'esprit de la réforme Bérard." *Essais et combats,* No. 12 (April 1937), 4. On this point see also Pierre Uri, *La Réforme de l'enseignement* (Paris, 1938), p. 89.

[53] Léon Blum, "Le Projet d'école unique," *Revue de Paris,* XLIV (1937), 185. This Blum should not, of course, be confused with the Socialist party leader.

[54] "La Classe d'orientation," *RDM,* CVII, 8e période (April 1937). The editorial appeared on the inside of an unnumbered front cover.

to enhance the quality of hitherto dreary lives, but a particularly dangerous social experiment.

It was true that the orientation class was a new and untried idea. Zay sought to keep public opinion informed of his intentions, in order to allay the suspicion that innovation always arouses. No better platform for this purpose could be found than among those who had voiced suspicion. In an interview accorded to *Le Temps* in April 1937, Zay announced that experimental orientation classes would be established in the fall, in centers that offered conditions as varied as possible. Only after parliament had voted upon the reform project would the methods tested in these centers be applied progressively, class after class, to the entire secondary level.[55]

In the meantime, Zay went about the task of reform by decree. In May 1937 he placed the elementary classes of the lycée under the same administrative direction as the primary school, in order to ensure that both were conducted in the same spirit and with the same methods. He then put the *école primaire supérieure* under the control of the director of secondary education, in order to prepare for consolidating the *école primaire supérieure* with the modern section of the reformed secondary level. A decree of May 21, 1937, prescribed certain courses for the sixth class of the lycée and for the first year of the *école primaire supérieure* and the technical school. Zay intended this measure, which at first involved only the academic subjects French, history, geography and mathematics, to make easier transfers from one school to another and to make way for the introduction of the orientation class.[56]

In June 1937, the Chamber's committee on education, presided over by Hippolyte Ducos, approved the experimental orientation class—how enthusiastically it is impossible to say.[57] Earlier, however, the committee had demanded that Zay cease issuing decrees on the reform until it had fully examined his

[55] *Le Temps*, April 22, 1937.

[56] These measures were taken in decrees and ministerial circulars of August 5, 1937; May 21, 1937; August 30, 1937; April 11, 1938; May 22, 1938.

[57] *Information universitaire*, June 12, 1937.

project,[58] and Zay later charged that the education committee deliberately postponed a discussion of the project in order to delay its appearance before the Chamber.[59]

It is not clear who the instigators of these obstructionist tactics were. But well-known and influential members of his own party, who did not share his enthusiasm for the Popular Front, considered Zay a demagogue.[60] His project, unlike the campaign for free secondary education, was not truly a Radical party measure. Aiming no doubt to keep the reform above party strife, Zay took vigorous action outside of the parliament. Hence it is likely that some deputies, with their notoriously inflated notions of the powers of the Chamber, felt that Zay had overstepped his ministerial prerogative and was treading upon their authority.[61] *Le Temps* professed to be scandalized that Zay was undertaking reform by means of "experiments" before parliament had deliberated upon the project: "Pardon us, but orientation, direction, and obligation, a trinity dear to Marxism, does not distract us from the consequences of these experiments for the intellectual and cultural future of the country."[62]

Undeterred by such reproaches, Zay went ahead with his experiment with the orientation class, an experiment to be interrupted shortly after it had begun by the outbreak of war. In a circular addressed to the academic rectors in May 1937, Zay directed preparations to be made for the establishment of the orientation classes.[63] In the weeks that followed, circulars on the organization of the experimental classes poured forth from the ministry. The recent great influx of students into the lycée had crowded classrooms with as many as fifty students; each experimental orientation class was to receive no more

[58] *Le Temps*, March 14, 1937.

[59] *Souvenirs et solitude*, p. 130.

[60] One of these fellow members, who asked to be left anonymous, expressed this opinion of Zay in an interview with the author in 1965.

[61] Zay himself felt this to be the case; it was an often repeated theme in his memoirs.

[62] *Le Temps*, August 8, 1937.

[63] *Horaires et programmes de l'enseignement secondaire* (Paris, 1938), pp. 135ff.

than twenty-five. Henceforth, the *certificat des études primaires* would suffice as the entrance requirement for secondary study. The curriculum, the same as that established for the first year of all secondary establishments, devoted ten hours a week to literary subjects—French, Latin, or modern languages, geography, history; seven hours to science, two hours to drawing, five to manual training, and two and one-half to physical education. Work in the classroom and individual study were to be alternated in such a way that homework would not be necessary.[64]

Reformers intended the orientation classes to make his studies suit the individual nature of each child as closely as possible; at the same time, the community would benefit from the effort to match each child's interests and ability with the course of study that best suited him. As Zay put it, "the whole problem of education is to reconcile these two conditions, to unite the individual and the social without sacrificing one to the other."[65] It was true that these two conditions seemed to pose the ancient problem of reconciling the rights of the family and the duties of the state. But Zay constantly emphasized that the orientation class in no way infringed upon the rights of parents, who were perfectly free to reject the advice teachers gave them on the aptitudes of their children.[66]

For the first time in the history of French education, primary school teachers and lycée professors would work side by side in a common task. But the disdain and suspicion with which each group regarded the other could not be expected to disappear overnight. Albert Châtelet, director of secondary education, felt constrained to warn the teachers that "they would fail at their task if they considered themselves recruiting agents for the kinds of education they represent."[67]

[64] *Ibid.*

[65] Zay, in the preface to Ministère de l'éducation nationale. Direction de l'enseignement du second degré, *Les Classes d'orientation. Rapports et documents. Notes* (Paris, 1937).

[66] See, for example, idem, "C'est à la famille de choisir, c'est à l'école de l'éclairer et de lui venir en aide."

[67] *Les Classes d'orientation*, p. 145.

Considerable uncertainty prevailed over the most effective means of achieving the ends intended for the orientation class. There had been a good deal more discussion about what reformers expected the class to do than about how they expected to do it.

The Zay experiment established three kinds of orientation class: one based on a modern language, without Latin; one class that offered Latin but not a modern language; one that offered neither Latin nor a modern language. Pupils were to spend the first three months of the school year together in one class; at the end of this "observation period," each child's teachers would deliberate on whether he should be advised to follow the classical, modern or technical option, differentiated by the emphasis given to Latin, a modern language or technical education. These options were intended to be tentative; pupils were to remain together for the rest of their subjects. The ministry emphasized that every child in the experiment should be able to continue his studies without delay in any existing secondary establishment.[68]

In the late summer of 1937 the volunteers who had been selected to teach the orientation classes underwent a week of special training in Paris. Most of the session concerned quite practical matters; indeed, officials in the ministry of education preferred to avoid speculation on such problems as the use of techniques of experimental psychology in the orientation classes. Gustave Monod, inspector-general of public instruction, made clear that "we prefer to put our confidence in common sense, in experience, in the teachers' feelings for their children."[69]

In October 1937 Zay oversaw the opening of some 120 orientation classes in forty-five experimental centers.[70] Zay adroitly answered the charge he had exceeded his authority by pointing out that parliament could eventually vote upon a far better re-

[68] *Horaires et programmes de l'enseignement secondaire 1937*, p. 137.
[69] *Les Classes d'orientation*, p. 60.
[70] P. Couissin, "La Session du conseil supérieur de l'instruction publique," *Revue universitaire*, XLVII, part 2 (October 1938), 227.

form project with the results of these experiments in hand.[71] In each center meetings were organized shortly after the opening of the school year to explain to parents the purpose of the class, and to assure them they need not fear for their own rights.[72]

It was remarkable that an educational establishment supposedly as inflexible as that of the Third Republic proved so open to experimentation. In the case of the orientation class the advantages of an energetic centralized direction were evident. To be sure, setting up the experiment within the confines of the old system considerably blunted its effectiveness. But Zay chose to act in the face of inevitable difficulties. By choosing to act first upon the most important part of the reform, he collected against himself a phalanx of long-standing opposition to the *école unique*. Nor did he escape severe criticism from his nominal allies.

But the experiment with the orientation class also had its fervent partisans, many of whom returned from the Second World War to assume key positions in the ministry of education and to continue their efforts at reform. Gustave Monod, for one, became director of secondary education. As a leading participant in the Zay experiment, Monod made clear that the orientation class had behind it not only a liberal concern for individual fulfillment, but a concern for the maintenance of social stability as well. Most partisans of the *école unique* had been extremely reluctant to admit that the success of certain children required the failure of others. Just as the Radicals chose to ignore evidence that a pattern of upward social mobility required a pattern of downward mobility as well, the partisans of the notion of selection had not much concerned themselves with the fate of the unselected. Nor, for that matter, had many pondered the implications of having on hand a surplus of intellectuals. Conservatives had instinctively meant

[71] Jean Zay, interviews with *Le Temps*, October 18, 1937; October 28, 1937. Zay remarked to his interviewer that he had so much confidence in the orientation class that he had established one in Orléans, his own electoral circonscription.

[72] *Horaires et programmes de l'enseignement secondaire 1938*, p. 178.

229

something of this sort when they protested that the *école unique* would inflame the ambitions of some children quite beyond their abilities at the same time that it created a mass of unemployed and unemployable intellectuals. Monod argued that the orientation class would fulfill what one sociologist has called the "cooling-out function" of education.[73] To give a child the educational experience for which his abilities seemed to suit him was a humane and sophisticated form of making one content with his station in life. A dull-witted child had gently to be disabused of the notion that he might become a physicist, just as a bright child, so the argument ran, might have to be encouraged to raise his sights.

The great rise in secondary school enrollments in the 1930's, concurrent with a severe economic depression, had created an unstable and potentially troublesome situation. There were too many children enrolled in the lycée, Monod argued—more than a prosperous labor market could absorb, let alone a depressed one. Moreover, far too many lycée students entered the classical section. It will be recalled that from 1930 to 1937 there was a 63 per cent increase in the enrollment of all kinds of secondary establishments: attendance in the lycée had jumped by 73 per cent. And of these lycée students, 76 per cent chose to enter the classical section, 82 per cent of them in Paris. There existed neither the classrooms nor the personnel needed to handle all the applicants. In 1937, 6,000 students were turned away from the lycée for lack of space.[74] The danger of turning out large numbers of unemployable intellectuals seemed real. Monod argued that the orientation class would allay this pos-

[73] Burton R. Clark, "The 'Cooling-out' Function in Higher Education," *American Journal of Sociology*, LXV (May 1960), 569-76. This article is reprinted in A. H. Halsey, Jean Floud, C. Arnold Anderson, eds. *Education, Economy and Society; a Reader in the Sociology of Education* (New York, 1961), pp. 513-23. See also Chalmers Johnson, *Revolutionary Change* (Boston, 1966), p. 26.

[74] Gustave Monod, "Les Enseignements du second degré; le projet de loi Jean Zay," *L'Information pédagogique*, II, No. 3 (May-June 1938), 97-99.

sibility by assuring a better distribution of children among the varieties of secondary education.[75]

Even the most enthusiastic partisans of the class had few illusions about the Zay experiment; they knew it could only approximate what they had in mind. As Roger Gal, a participant in the experiment, put it: "If our experiments were imperfect or unsuccessful, it is because they are, and can still only be, caricatures of orientation."[76] In the haste required to set up the experimental centers for the opening of school in 1937, the ministry inevitably committed some blunders. A circular had laid down that each class should contain no more than 25 children; but many teachers complained of experimental classes of 39, 49, and even more pupils.[77] Not all the centers had at their disposal a lycée, an *école primaire supérieure* and a technical school. Without all three options, the centers found themselves deprived of one of their main functions: the sorting out of their clientele for one branch of secondary education or another.[78]

But imperfections in the experiment forced reformers to think about some of the assumptions that underlay their plans. The absence of the full range of options in an orientation center impelled them to wonder whether there really existed three different sorts of minds and characters that corresponded to the three varieties of secondary education. Of course no experiment had ever indicated that such was the case. The classical and modern sections did not constitute two distinct options at all, but two somewhat different varieties of the same style of education: students in both sections received the same kinds of

[75] *Ibid.*, 101-3.

[76] "Expériences d'orientation scolaire," *Esprit* (November 1938), 269.

[77] Hélène Guénot, "Réunion des professeurs de classes d'orientation," *Revue de l'enseignement secondaire des jeunes filles*, xi (May 1938), 180.

[78] "Compte-rendu de la réunion des professeurs de classes d'orientation, 17 décembre 1938," *Revue de l'enseignement secondaire des jeunes filles*, xii (January 1939), 78.

instruction in the same ways, and prepared for the same examinations.[79]

Because students entered the varieties of traditional secondary education at different ages, in many centers there was a four-year age difference between the oldest and the youngest children. Teachers faced an almost insurmountable obstacle in devising lessons that children of such diverse educational backgrounds could do in common.[80] Most of the experimenters regretted the observation period was meant to last only three months, not at all long enough to become well-acquainted with 25 children. In 33 of the orientation centers, the option among the classical, modern and technical sections was introduced at the end of three months, a month later in 10; in three centers the option did not function.[81]

When asked whether the methods of the orientation class slowed down the acquisition of knowledge, 10 of 44 centers replied that they had; 22 that they had not; 6 did not reply. Ten centers responded that children might have learned somewhat less, but what they *had* learned had been learned better. Most important, 36 centers replied that the orientation class had indeed made easier the discernment of children's aptitudes.[82]

In Roger Gal's class, for example, 30 children had at the outset desired to enter the classical section of the lycée; during the observation period it had become apparent that 13 should be dissuaded from doing so, and the parents of 10 accepted this advice. Contrary to the fears of the ministry of education, most parents understood the purpose of the orientation class and in most cases accepted the advice of teachers. On the other hand, parents tended to suspect questionnaires sent them on the health or character of their children and answered them evasively. One somewhat unforeseen benefit of the orientation

[79] *Ibid.*, 79.

[80] Gal, "Expériences d'orientation scolaire," 269-70.

[81] Gilbert Sore, "Les Orienteurs nous parlent des classes d'orientation," *Esprit* (February 1939), 718.

[82] Lelay, "Sur l'expérience des classes d'orientation," *Pour l'ère nouvelle*, XVII (December 1938), 301.

class was the way in which it seemed to facilitate the learning of new material: children in one experimental class learned as much Latin in six months as their colleagues in an ordinary class learned in a year; and in a technical section, the professor in one year not only finished his own program, but two-thirds of that of the next.[83]

But the Zay experiment served the broader social aims of the reformers less well than the pedagogical ones. One aim of the orientation class was to make available to working-class and peasant children the information and advice about formal education that middle-class children received at home from their parents. Nor had the old dream that the school might become the means of reconciliation between social classes been abandoned. The first year of the experiment only confirmed the impression reformers had held for some time: for many working-class families the lycée was a strange place that should be avoided. Parents who had been advised their children would doubtless do quite well at the lycée still preferred to send them to the *école primaire supérieure* because it was shorter, cheaper, more familiar, and in most cases closer to home. Nor did there appear to be much fraternization among children who, in the absence of the orientation class, would have entered a lycée, an *école primaire supérieure*, a technical school. Gal noted that children tended to remake the old distinctions themselves by seeking out their old comrades at informal gatherings.[84]

In the summer of 1937 Gustave Monod had admonished those in charge of orientation to favor their "common sense" over the use of the uncertain techniques of child psychology.[85] As the year wore on, however, his advice seemed symptomatic of the vagueness and uncertainty that prevailed among the experimenters over the aims and methods of the class. No one knew what methods or standards were to be used to deter-

[83] Gal, "Expériences d'orientation scolaire," 276.

[84] *Ibid.*, 271; see also Henri Boivin, "Les Leçons d'une expérience d'orientation dans une école primaire publique de banlieue," *Education* (June 1938), 89-91.

[85] See above, p. 228.

mine whether a child should enter one section of secondary education or another; a study of that sort had never been made. What did one really mean by "abstract" intelligence as against "concrete" intelligence? Were these not simply kinder, but neither more precise nor more helpful synonyms for "bright" and "dull"? Lelay, *rapporteur* on the question of orientation for the Conseil supérieur de l'éducation nationale, complained that no one had ever clearly defined the goals the experiment expected to reach; the teachers had not been properly prepared for their work. Almost to a man they complained that the "observation booklet" drawn up for their use was much too complicated. Consequently, they made up their own booklets. Unfortunately, none was like the next. And the imprecision of the notations entered in them rendered them almost useless. The carefully noted observation that Jean had "a good memory" was not very helpful. Madame Louis Cazamian, wife of a former president of the Compagnons, wondered whether even the elementary conditions for the success of an experiment had been met.[86]

A sort of principle of inertia appeared to be at work. Teachers quickly discovered that if an orientation class was located in a lycée it proved almost impossible to send a child from there to an *école primaire supérieure* or a technical school. Most parents refused to accept the suggestion that their children would benefit from the move from a school with high prestige to one with little or none at all. Nor were there indications that able children migrated from an orientation center established in an *école primaire supérieure* to the lycée. The lack of movement between institutions may simply have revealed the reluctance of parents to uproot their children once they felt at home in one school. And the anomaly persisted that one could enter the lycée without undergoing an entrance examination, but in order to enter the less rigorous *école primaire supérieure* a child had to submit to an examination.[87]

---

[86] "Sur la classe d'orientation," *Pour l'ère nouvelle*, xvi (April 1938), 119.

[87] "Compte-rendu de la réunion des professeurs de classes d'orientation, 17 décembre 1938," *Revue de l'enseignement secondaire des jeunes filles*, xii (January 1939), 81.

Despite all these difficulties, the *rapporteur* to the *conseil supérieur* believed that the experiment had "opened new horizons to French education."[88] No one could deny that the accurate determination of a child's abilities was an enormously difficult task. However clumsy and inaccurate the methods employed in the orientation class, they were better than none at all; the odds that a child might be helped to find an interesting and satisfying way to spend his life were not overwhelming, but they were better than they had been under the old system where the better informed, the better educated and the wealthier one's parents, the better his chances. The great enthusiasm of many of the participants in the experiment compensated in large measure for its deficiencies of method. At the Lycée Chaptal, more teachers volunteered to take part in the second year of the experiment than there were places to accommodate them.[89] One professor remarked "I had never before known a class so well, and I had never had such confidence in one elsewhere."[90] By a substantial majority the Conseil supérieur voted to continue the experiment into the 1938–1939 school year.

ALWAYS quick to call attention to the reactionary maneuvers of political opponents, teachers were blind to their own deep-seated professional conservatism. Because the orientation class stood on the frontier between primary and secondary education, it gave rise to sharp conflicts between school teachers and lycée professors. Lycée professors suspected that the school teachers had designs on their preserve; the teachers believed the professors were plotting to deprive them of their best students. There was just enough truth in such assertions to keep militants in each camp busy rousing their own side to vigilance against the encroachments of the other. Ostensibly, pedagogical differences accounted for the hostility between lycée professors and school teachers. But these were com-

[88] Lelay, "Sur l'expérience des classes d'orientation," p. 303.

[89] "Les Orienteurs nous parlent des classes d'orientation," *Esprit* (April 1, 1939), 78. Observation of the principal, M. Le Verrier.

[90] Mlle. Geraud-Jardel, "Les Orienteurs nous parlent des classes d'orientation," *Esprit* (February 1939), 713.

pounded by matters of pay, of prestige, of conditions of work. A school teacher might be inclined to believe he and his fellows worked long hours in isolated villages for ridiculously low pay, in order to drill information into the heads of unresponsive farm boys, while his colleague, the lycée professor, put in his time imparting largely useless knowledge to spoiled adolescents—rubbing elbows with the rich, living on a respectable salary in a big city, and reserving a special contempt for primary school teachers.

Little wonder, then, that the Zay experiment aroused the suspicion of both camps. It was not that teachers opposed educational reform; many vigorously supported it—so long as it did not affect their own interests. Their opposition constituted one of the most effective barriers to reform, for their opinions rang with the authority of the expert. And opposition is often all the more effective for being couched in disinterested language that seems remote from politics. At no time between the wars was the teaching profession's hostility toward reform made more plain than in this struggle between primary school teachers and lycée professors over the Zay experiment.

The Société des agrégés led the opposition of lycée professors to the orientation class. The *agrégation* was not a degree, but a competitive examination for appointment to a permanent position as a lycée professor. It entitled one to nothing else. But such was the rigor of the examination that, once passed, it marked a man off as a lifelong member of an élite, whether he ever set foot inside a lycée or not. The agrégés were in a slight minority in the lycée—in 1937 there were some 1,415 agrégés out of 3,189 professors—but they always seemed to have friends in high places. They firmly believed they personified the French tradition of secondary education.[91]

At first, the Société des agrégés had given the Zay project a guarded approval, but only because they felt they had nothing to fear from it. In early February 1937, Gaston-Martin, president of the Society, made clear that the agrégés opposed any consolidation of the *école primaire supérieure,* the lycée and the technical school. Each had different ends and meth-

[91] *L'Agrégation*, January 1, 1938.

ods, he said; the genius of the lycée had always been its disinterestedness, which was somehow intimately related to the duration of the course of study. To enclose the lycée within the shorter limits of the more practical sorts of secondary education would seriously hamper it in its mission. Of course the agrégés desired a reform, Gaston-Martin asserted; they were nonetheless convinced that "any reorganization that would lead, even without intending it, to a devaluation of the traditional secondary education, would immediately express itself in a general diminution of all our education."[92]

The Society seemed momentarily reassured when the project appeared; indeed, the Zay plan had disappointed many of the more radical reformers when it left the structure of secondary education intact. But when the experimental orientation class began in the fall of 1937, the Society took alarm. It was a fundamental article of faith with the lycée professors that the accomplishment of their task required no less than seven years. They seemed unable satisfactorily to explain why this was true, but they defended against all assailants the trinity of duration, methods, content: "we consider these elements indispensable to its efficiency and its ends."[93] They charged that the orientation class amputated an entire year from the lycée. The Société des agrégés had not only set itself up as the defender of the traditional lycée, but as the interpreter of French democracy, and it tended to confuse the two tasks to the point of self-parody: "We claim to be the sole authentic defenders of a democratic conception of national education, which we refuse to allow to be demagogically sabotaged."[94]

By the spring of 1938 the agrégés had got round to a wholesale condemnation of the Zay experiment. At their annual meeting the *rapporteur* on the question of orientation submitted a resolution that called the experiment at once "excessive and insufficient." In place of the orientation class, the agrégés called for a return to the rigorous methods of annual selection that had been discredited in most of the reform movement for

[92] *L'Agrégation*, February 15, 1937.
[93] *L'Agrégation*, February 1, 1938.
[94] *Ibid.*

years.[95] Convinced that the Zay experiment was being made at their expense, the professors preferred to have the most intellectually able pupils handed on to them from primary school with a minimum of fuss at as early an age as possible.

The school teachers, on the other hand, naturally wished to hold on to their best students for as long as they could. This conflict, as one observer remarked, gave rise to disputes between professors who considered the orientation class a "spoliation to the profit of the primary school," and the school teachers, who wanted complete control of the class in order that "authority be concentrated in the hands of a single teacher, who is not specialized in the fashion of the professors of the secondary schools."[96]

The school teachers, it will be remembered, had always had a certain lack of enthusiasm for the reform movement. Its preoccupation with secondary education, they believed, left it blind to the needs of the majority of children. "Our aim," the Syndicat national des instituteurs reminded its members "is to educate the great worker and peasant mass."[97] The sni feared that the orientation class might be simply a device for winnowing out an intellectual élite, at the expense of everyone else.[98] The lowering of the examination age for the *certificat des études primaires* gave rise to these fears. To the school teachers, this simply meant the loss of their best pupils at an earlier age than before. It also seemed to mean the primary school being forced to subordinate itself to the lycée, all in the comparatively narrow interest of forming an élite.[99]

Even if lycée professors and school teachers resigned themselves to the orientation class, they had conflicting notions of what it should be. A good many lycée professors believed that if the class were allowed to exist at all, it should be merely another sixth class, the threshold of the lycée, in which the

[95] *L'Agrégation*, March 15, 1938.

[96] J. Lefrancq "Du Massacre des innocents à l'orientation pédagogique," *Esprit* (November 1937), 244.

[97] *L'Ecole libératrice*, March 13, 1937.

[98] *L'Ecole libératrice*, October 30, 1937.

[99] *L'Ecole libératrice*, January 15, 1938.

238

classical humanities remained predominant. As one Latin professor haughtily observed, "unless I am mistaken, the sixth class has always been considered a class of secondary education ... and not a primary class."[100] Spokesmen for the SNI, on the other hand, shared the view that the orientation class should be separate and distinct from the lycée, in order, they claimed, to permit the more rational guidance of children toward one kind of secondary education or another.

Still, this conception of the class made leaders of the SNI uneasy about the recruitment of new school teachers. Formerly, the path to becoming a school teacher had led from the primary school through the *école primaire supérieure* to the departmental *école normale*. But the orientation class broke this line of continuity. Now children who in former times would have entered the *école primaire supérieure* might abandon it in favor of the lycée. The orientation class might actually discriminate against poor children, the SNI charged, by making it more complicated for one to become a school teacher—the one sure means of limited social mobility.[101]

Whatever position the organized spokesmen of the teaching profession took on reform, the rank and file members were not solidly drawn up against it; both school teachers and lycée professors were divided among themselves over the merits of the orientation class and the worth of the Zay experiment. That the staunchest defenders of the class had participated in the experiment spoke well in its favor; few had illusions about its miracle-working capacities, but most were firmly convinced of its positive value. One administrator noted that skeptics had serious doubts about the reliability of the three-month orientation period, but no one involved seems to have questioned the principle of the class itself. The same observer also detected a sort of exalted enthusiasm for the experiment.[102] The scoffers, on the other hand, tended to be people who had had no

[100] *Revue de la Franco-ancienne* (April 1939).

[101] *L'Ecole libératrice*, November 19, 1938.

[102] P. Couissin, "La Session du conseil supérieur de l'instruction publique," p. 231.

contact with the orientation class, but thought it a bad idea, and were unlikely to be converted.

And as the Zay experiment continued into its second year, it provoked more and more attacks. In the face of the inaction of parliament, even nominal friends of the *école unique* felt increasingly uneasy about the fragmentary character of the reforms Zay had carried out. The grand plan for reform seemed once again to have been set aside in favor of tinkering with the old system. The leadership of the Ligue de l'enseignement feared that Zay's improvisations were causing teachers to lose their enthusiasm for the reform. Perhaps it might be better, the League suggested, to concentrate on getting the reform project passed through parliament as quickly as possible.[103] Faced with action on the *école unique* after having demanded it for twenty years, the leadership of the league apparently decided that it preferred inaction. André Delmas, secretary-general of the SNI, wondered if parliament might take up the Zay project by 1950; in the meantime the reforms already carried out needed certain urgent readjustments.[104]

A former Compagnon, who called himself Akademos, wrote in his column in a professional weekly that the orientation class, "with its pseudo-scientific pretensions, terrifies experienced teachers and frightens the friends of liberty."[105]

The Fédération des parents d'élèves de lycées et collèges, which had been so unenthusiastic about free secondary education, sent a delegation to Zay to protest against the orientation class; the parents feared that their interests were being "sacrificed to the general interest."[106] A physicians' organization, the Fédération corporative des médecins de la région parisienne, claimed medical data showed that the subjection of eleven-year-olds to the orientation class was a "physiological impossibility." The doctors demanded that parliament put an end to Zay's experiment.[107]

[103] *Action laïque,* No. 678 (December 1937).
[104] *L'Ecole libératrice,* April 1, 1939.
[105] *L'Information universitaire,* March 5, 1938.
[106] *Le Temps,* January 6, 1938.
[107] *Le Temps,* January 16, 1938.

The leadership of the Fédération générale de l'enseignement felt, no doubt unreasonably, that the orientation class had not done the job it was intended to do: the advice teachers gave to parents on the aptitudes of their children corresponded too closely to what parents wanted to hear.[108] Ludovic Zoretti, eternally dissatisfied, insisted that the Zay plan merely camouflaged in radical language an attachment to the status quo.[109]

In the year of the Anschluss and the Munich agreement, Léon Blum briefly returned to power in an effort to revive the Popular Front; but he, and almost everyone else, knew that the Popular Front was dead.[110] At the congress of the Ligue de l'enseignement Henri Belliot, secretary-general, asserted that the grave international crisis had not distracted the attention of the delegates from problems of education.[111] If their attention had not been distracted from the problems, however, their opportunities to act on them had been largely eliminated. As the nation's leaders sought a means of staving off war with Germany—some honorably, and some not—democratic educational reform became among the least urgent of tasks. As the Radical-dominated government and the CGT between them struggled over the maintenance of the forty-hour week, it seemed there was little energy available for any sort of undertaking in the national interest, whether warlike or peaceful.

Besides, there was no money to be had for the project. Despite Zay's energetic advocacy of reform, he had scarcely said a word about what his reform might cost.[112] When Paul Reynaud, a vigorous exponent of laissez-faire economics, became minister of finance in Edouard Daladier's government in November 1938, he put an ax to the forty-hour week, the great symbol of social reforms accomplished by the Popular Front.[113]

[108] *Le Peuple*, May 28, 1938.
[109] Ludovic Zoretti, *La Réforme de l'enseignement* (Paris, 1937), p. 7.
[110] See Lefranc, *Front Populaire*, pp. 271-76.
[111] *Action laïque*, No. 684 (June 1938).
[112] Henri Belliot claimed that throughout 1937, at least, Zay had *never* made a public statement about the cost of the reform. *Action laïque*, No. 689 (January 1938). Doubtless Zay knew there was nothing encouraging he could honestly say, and preferred to remain silent.
[113] Goguel, *Politique des partis*, pp. 531-32.

Reynaud's classical austerity program was eventually an economic success, but if its accomplishment required the government to jettison the most conspicuous reforms of the Popular Front, then clearly no money could be found for Zay's project.

Even before the disastrous general strike against the boldness of Reynaud and the timidity of Munich, Mérat, secretary of the FGE, sadly noted that "the reform of education has suffered the fate of the great social reforms halted and deformed by the inadequacies and hesitations of the Popular Front governments. . . . Even the notion of orientation has singularly shrunk. . . . It is no longer the directing idea of the reform, but only betrays a concern for the most rapid choice between rival educational establishments."[114] In December, the futility of expecting parliament seriously to consider Zay's project became abundantly clear when the Chamber passed the education budget for 1939 with little discussion; it had apparently not been thought necessary even to have a written budget report. On the floor of the Chamber, Georges Cogniot remarked: "It has now been eighteen months since the project for the reform of education filled the columns of the press. It must be observed that there is not yet any trace of this reform project in the budget for 1939."[115]

At the Easter recess of 1939, when the majority of teachers' associations held their annual meetings, the opponents of the orientation class launched a concerted attack. The Société des agrégés demanded that "the experiment with the orientation classes should be interrupted and the organization of these classes abandoned."[116] The Syndicat national des lycées et collèges deplored the "oblique and fragmentary manner" in which reform was being carried out, and took a swipe at the school teachers when it charged the orientation class was an attempt to transform secondary education, "its spirit, its programs, its methods, its personnel, in the direction of a conformity to a level that is not its own."[117] The Syndicat des

[114] *Information universitaire*, November 15, 1938.
[115] *J.O.Ch.* (1938), pp. 1820-21.
[116] *L'Agrégation*, May 1, 1939.
[117] *Le Temps*, April 9, 1939.

lycées insisted that it had in mind only the disinterested preservation of the unique French tradition of secondary education.[118] But Hélène Guénot, herself a lycée professor and a leader in the Zay experiment, struck closer to the mark when she charged that these vocal opponents of the reform were simply traditionalists "who are suspicious of methods that are impossible to judge if one does not practice them."[119] The demand of the conservative teachers' associations for a pause in the experiment outraged the experimenters. Teachers in over half the orientation centers signed petitions of protest against the SNES and the Société des agrégés; they had, the teachers charged, formed categorical opinions on the results of the experiment before it had even ended.[120]

But in the tense and gloomy atmosphere of 1939, reform had lost its momentum. The elan of 1936 was gone. The Conseil supérieur seemed to have lost its enthusiasm even for debate.

When Zay had appeared before its regular session in February 1939, he apologized for the Chamber's inaction and professed an optimism that perhaps he did not truly feel: "The hour seems to have come at last to open the debate at the tribune of parliament." Within the Council, opinion on the reform was divided and not easily classifiable. On one point, however, the representatives of these diverse tendencies agreed: Zay had to put a stop to experiments and provisional measures, on the ground that the Council had no legal authority to assume responsibility for a reform in "successive fragments." Only if parliament passed a general law on the reform would the Council agree to oversee its application.[121]

But parliament never discussed the Zay project. The Conseil supérieur approved the maintenance of the orientation classes in the centers that Zay had established, but in 1939 he undertook no new initiatives based upon the project. In May, he addressed the congress of the Ligue de l'enseignement. He was

[118] L'Information universitaire, April 8, 1939.
[119] L'Information universitaire, April 1, 1939.
[120] L'Information universitaire, May 20, 1939.
[121] Couissin, "La Session du conseil supérieur de l'instruction publique," Revue universitaire, XLVIII, part 1 (1939), 248.

acutely aware that time for educational reform had run out. French energies, he remarked, had now to be concentrated upon national defense. Moved to eloquence by the gravity of the international crisis, he chose not to apportion blame for the failure of his own hopes, but to affirm his belief that the University, whatever its imperfections, had never failed in its essential mission: "Besides the steel armor forged by our colleagues at the ministry of national defense, there is another armor that has never been pierced at any time in the history of France—the one that, across the centuries, her scholars, professors and school teachers have forged for her."[122] Among the last of his official speeches, it proved to be tragically prophetic: "France is at this moment a beacon, a torch, a light that contrary winds sometimes beat down; but everyone feels that if it were extinguished, a dark night would fall upon the world, one of those nights in which men would gropingly feel their way through the horror and terror in the anxiety of not being found in time."[123]

At the end of the cabinet meeting of September 3, 1939, the day of the declaration of a state of war with Germany, Jean Zay handed a letter to the premier, Edouard Daladier: "Mr. President: the law on the organization of the nation in time of war provides that members of the government, who are responsible for the direction of the war, remain at their posts. At the age of thirty-five, I do not intend to benefit from this arrangement and desire to share the destiny of the youth for whom I have worked in the government for more than three years. I therefore ask you to permit me, in case of hostilities, to share the usual lot of my age group."[124]

His request was granted. Zay entered the army and departed for the front. The movement for the *école unique,* launched at the close of one war, had come to an end with the beginning of another; less than a year later, the Third Republic had come to an end as well.

[122] *Action laïque*, No. 694 (July 1939).
[123] *Ibid.*
[124] *L'Information universitaire*, September 1939.

Conclusion

> Le résultat des luttes politiques est de troubler, de
> falsifier dans les esprits la notion de l'ordre d'importance
> des *questions* et de l'ordre d'urgence.
>
> Ce qui est vital est masqué par ce qui est de simple
> bien-être. Ce qui est d'avenir par l'immédiat. Ce qui est
> très nécessaire par ce qui est très sensible. Ce qui est pro-
> fond et lent par ce qui est excitant.
>
> —Paul Valéry

EVEN HAD the war not put an end to the Third Republic, parliament would still have been slow to act
upon the Zay project. Conceived under the auspices
of a government of the Left, the culmination of a
leftist reform movement, the reform was audacious for the
prevailing state of public opinion. The obstructionism of the
Chamber's committee on education and public protests against
the orientation classes suggest that Zay might have experienced
considerable difficulty in guiding his project unscathed past
parliamentary snipers. Its scope made it an easy target, and its
structure was such that to have altered any major part would
have destroyed the intent of the whole. Had Zay surrendered
the orientation class, for example, the remaking of secondary
education would have been reduced merely to a rearrange-
ment.

The fate of the reform project aside, Zay's tenure in office
was far from barren of accomplishment. The Popular Front's
contributions to educational reform were executive acts, except for the extension of compulsory schooling to the age of
fourteen. The groundwork laid for the integration of the
écoles primaires supérieures into secondary education, the
transformation of the elementary classes of the lycée into primary schools and the experiment with the orientation classes
were all carried out by ministerial decree. These were aims of
the movement for the *école unique,* but in terms of what it set
out to accomplish, the movement was in large part a failure.

245

Zay's executive action, for which he received a great deal of criticism, served to highlight the dilemma in which reformers found themselves at a time when parliament reigned supreme.

Reformers based their strategy for change upon the acquisition of a stable parliamentary majority that proved impossible to obtain. In 1924 and 1936, voters returned to the Chamber reformist majorities that fell apart within the space of a few months. Radicals and Socialists appeared to be natural allies for educational reform, but an alliance was always at the mercy of other considerations of principle and tactics. No other possible combination of political supporters for educational reform existed. In part, the failure of the reform movement was only one more lamentable consequence of the perpetual division of the French Left. In part, it was an effect of the shortsightedness imposed upon parliament by recurrent economic and political crises. Their attention riveted upon the present, deputies had no time for a consideration of the nation's future.

But the reform movement did not fail to reach its objectives simply because of the inefficacy of the political parties and parliamentary institutions of the Third Republic. Of all public institutions, an educational system is among the least amenable to change. Entrusted with the transmission of knowledge and values from one generation to the next, an educational system tends to look to the past, to consider its main responsibility to be preservation, not innovation. Structural arrangements designed to preserve inherited culture tend to become identified with the culture itself. Under the Third Republic, long-established educational traditions shackled change as much as, if not more than, political opposition and lack of money.

Teachers, although generally politically liberal, were professionally conservative. Primary school teachers and lycée professors agreed on the need for reform, but each group was inclined to think that it was the preserve of the other that most needed reforming. The lycée may have been the preserve of the bourgeoisie, but it was also in charge of the maintenance of high intellectual standards. Even reformers had misgivings about whether the reforms they proposed might not threaten those standards. Many parents doubtless felt that the kind of education they had received was adequate for their children as well; they were not inclined to look with favor upon experiments conducted with their offspring. Reformers too readily assumed that peasants and workers had an intense desire to send their children on to secondary education from the primary school, and were prevented from doing so only by inequalities in the system.

But structural reform was an inadequate means of drawing able working-class and peasant children into higher education. Most reformers tended either to overlook or to misunderstand the relationship between social background and educational achievement. For one thing, their work was severely handicapped by a lack of the proper sorts of information. As has been shown, they based their plans for reform on generalizations about education and social class that mirrored their ideological convictions, and these generalizations were supported by very little hard empirical evidence. No one knew in any more than a vague way, for example, how class patterns in a *collège* differed from those in a lycée and what accounted for the difference. Only after the Second World War did serious and sustained inquiry into the relation between social class and education begin. To be sure, in many instances scientific inquiry impressively confirmed the perceptions of prewar reformers. A study undertaken in 1953 showed that for the overwhelming majority of children—nine out of ten, to be precise—the pursuit of studies beyond the school-leaving age was decided at the age of eleven or twelve, as reformers had always claimed. And the imbalance in opportunity between social classes was made quite plain: in 1953 the children of agricultural workers had one chance in ten of entering the secondary level, compared with the eight or nine chances in ten of children of urban middle-class backgrounds.[1]

---

[1] Alain Girard, "Enquête nationale sur l'orientation et la sélection des enfants d'âge scolaire," *Population*, ix (October-December 1954), 615-18. Other important studies of the *Institut national d'études démographiques* include Alain Girard, "L'Orientation et la sélection des enfants d'âge scolaire dans le département de la Seine," *Population*, viii (Octo-

But what most prewar reformers had failed to perceive was that in their chances for success in school, middle-class children had an advantage over working-class and peasant children from earliest childhood, not from the beginning of formal instruction. It has only been since about 1945, as a noted English sociologist has pointed out, that social class has been regarded as a "profound influence on the educability of children," not simply as a bar to opportunity.[2]

The precise nature of the effects of social class on educability remains a controversial question. Nevertheless, at the risk of considerable oversimplification, the crux of the problem can be briefly put. Provided with books at an early age, stimulated by family conversations, taken to museums, plays and concerts, impressed by the high value placed upon formal education in the circles in which his family moves and assured of financial support, a lawyer's son, for example, takes it for granted he will enter a university. But in working-class families, formal instruction is likely to be considered strictly a part of childhood, that should not be allowed to slow up one's entry into the labor market. Because of his parents' low level of education, a working-class child receives little or no intellectual stimulation outside the classroom in which he spends only a fraction of his time. Academic learning is alien to his experience. He therefore has much less chance of reaching the upper levels of the French educational establishment than a middle-

---

ber-December 1953), 649-72; Alain Girard and Henri Bastide, "Orientation et sélection scolaires: une enquête sur les enfants à la sortie de l'école primaire," *Population*, x (1955), 605-24; Alain Girard and Roland Pressat, "Deux Etudes sur la démocratisation de l'enseignement," *Population*, xvii (January-March 1962), 9-29; Alain Girard, Henri Bastide and Guy Pourcher, "Enquête nationale sur l'entrée en 6e et la démocratisation de l'enseignement," *Population*, xviii (January-March 1963), 9-48; Alfred Sauvy and Alain Girard, "Les diverses Classes sociales devant l'enseignement; mise au point général des résultats," *Population*, xx (March-April 1965), 205-32.

[2] Jean Floud, "Social Class Factors in Educational Achievement," in A. H. Halsey, ed., *Ability and Economic Opportunity* (Paris, 1961), p. 94.

class child, even if all structural restraints to his advancement are removed.

Indeed, it has been argued that when the school system treats all children as if they were equal, it reinforces inequalities of environment. Literature, music, painting are part of an ethnologically defined middle-class culture. Literary subjects of the secondary school curriculum are patterned after the high culture to which middle-class children are exposed at an early age. But these are not a part of working-class or peasant culture. Success in literary studies is closely related to the ability to manipulate a "school language"—the formal and highly abstract language of academic discourse. But this is the mother tongue only of children of cultivated backgrounds; to children of most peasant and working-class families, it might as well be a foreign language that must painfully be learned. The language spoken in the family, according to this view, constitutes the most formidable cultural barrier to success in school. Culture is an inheritance as surely as is wealth: "each family transmits to its children by indirect rather than direct means a certain cultural capital, and a certain ethos, a system of implicit and deeply internalized values that play a part in defining, among other things, attitudes toward educational institutions."[3]

An able working-class or peasant child was encased in the limitations of his own environment like a turtle in its shell. But this was only dimly perceived in the interwar period. Especially in the 1920's, the movement for the *école unique*

[3] Pierre Bourdieu, "La Transmission de l'héritage culturel," in 'Darras' [Colloque d'Arras] *Le Partage des Bénéfices; expansions et inégalités en France* (Paris, 1966), p. 388; Bourdieu, a sociologist, is the leading French exponent of this view, which he has advanced in numerous articles and books. His most provocative statement of the relationship between success in formal education and social conditioning is P. Bourdieu and J. C. Passeron, *Les Héritiers; les étudiants et la culture* (Paris, 1964). Alain Girard, *La Réussite sociale en France: ses caractères, ses lois, ses effets* (Paris, 1961). Another important contribution to this discussion is Viviane Isambert-Jamati, "La Rigidité d'une institution: structure scolaire et systèmes de valeurs," *Revue française de sociologie*, VII (July-September 1966), 302-24.

emphasized mechanisms that could do no more than provide a formal, legalistic equality of educational opportunity. So long as middle-class children had a decided edge over working-class and peasant children in their chances for success in school, some remained "more equal than others," regardless of the structure of the system. Indeed, such measures as free secondary education and selection based on merit may have legitimized social inequality by lending credence to the idea that success in school depended upon natural gifts that had nothing to do with social conditioning.[4] But the partisans of the orientation class of the Popular Front did not make this assumption. In fact, as has been shown, the idea of orientation assumed the public school was an instrument to overcome inequalities of environment by treating each child as unlike any other. The period between the wars was the crucial period of transition between treating social class as a bar to opportunity and treating it primarily as an influence on the educability of children.

Certainly the removal of structural defects that militated against equality was the first order of business in educational reform. But through unfamiliarity with the social, as distinct from the institutional, causes of inequality in education, partisans as well as opponents of the *école unique* were misled into thinking that the reform would have social consequences that it could not have. One cost of the isolation of the worker from French society was that many well-intentioned intellectuals simply did not know much about him. The ideological constructions imposed upon the *école unique* by its diverse partisans were not only contradictory; they were based upon a narrow view of the problems of reform. It may be that left political parties were (and still are) reluctant to face the sociological causes of inequality in education because these causes seem difficult to counteract by legislative action.

Preoccupied with structural reform, most reformers gave little thought to the content of instruction. At the turn of the century, this was doubtless the proper strategy. Themselves

[4] Bourdieu, "La Transmission de l'héritage culturel," pp. 405-406.

trained in an intellectual tradition centuries old, reformers seldom doubted its continued viability. But in the twentieth century more people must be educated for a longer period of time to perform an increasing variety of tasks, and to live in a world in which the only certainty is change. Ailing since before the end of the nineteenth century, "the older high bourgeois culture, which assumed that an autonomous intelligence could apprehend and act upon the world as a totality, has disappeared. . . . The new conception of higher culture is in practice a specialized one that reflects, consolidates and legitimates the intellectual division of labor."[5] It now seems clear democratization requires not only broadening the social bases of recruitment to the educational system, but making what is taught there consonant with the social and political changes that have accompanied the cultural revolution. To be sure, this is an immensely difficult task. Too often the literary humanism that had revitalized schools and universities at the end of the Middle Ages became in its turn a bulwark of conservatism, as educational establishments fought a bitter rearguard action against the encroachment of the scientific revolution; in this they were not entirely unsuccessful. Preoccupied with demanding who should be educated, many of the Third Republic's reformers had not sufficiently pondered whether the education they sought to make available to more people truly met the needs of the society that sponsored it.

Furthermore, most of them assumed a high rate of social mobility to be an inherently good thing. Few but the working-class leaders ever devoted much thought to the severe psychological and social problems to which mobility can give rise. The dilemma Jean Guéhenno's proletarian origin and bourgeois education created for him has never been resolved. Perhaps a sort of instinctive social Darwinism convinced reform-

[5] Norman Birnbaum, "The Crisis of the European Universities and the Crisis of European Culture," typescript. I am indebted to Professor Birnbaum for allowing me to read his essay before its appearance in a forthcoming book on "The Crisis in the Universities," edited by Stanley Diamond and to be published by Random House.

ers the fittest would survive. But to extend this line of reasoning, one would have to conclude the "fittest" were merely those best inured against the rigors of a highly competitive system.

Doubtless reformers could have made plainer that despite the democratic rhetoric of the twentieth century reform movement, the equalization of educational opportunity meant the establishment of equal circumstances in which everyone could become unequal. For in contemporary society status has increasingly become a function of occupation, and one's place in the social hierarchy determined by his level of education. Far from helping to build the classless society of Socialist (or even Radical) dreams, an exclusive preoccupation with the promotion of intellectual merit might simply sharpen antagonisms based on the capacity of men's brains and the preferment intelligence brings. In the course of the nineteenth century the old landed aristocracy gradually gave way to the industrial and commercial bourgeoisie, but the newly rich remained eager to ape aristocratic manners and determined to maintain their offspring in the place they had seized. To a certain degree they were successful. But the inheritance of intelligence remains an uncertain matter indeed; each generation creates its own "meritocracy." A few years ago Michael Young, whose brilliant satire made the term current, pointed to some implications of the principle of equal educational opportunity that reformers had never sufficiently taken into account. Looking back on the twentieth century from the vantage point of the year 2033, Young's narrator observed:

"The perennial disagreements of old sprang from the inevitable conflict between classes when each contained a cross section of ability. The basic injustice was that intelligent members of the lower classes were not given their due, and in their attack on social disorder, which had for the time being to be waged without forfeiting the support of their classmates of all grades of intelligence, they seized on any and every available principle to justify their protests. When the basic injustice was remedied, and the intelligent from every class were given their full

252

opportunities, those who would have been enemies of the established order became its strongest defenders."[6]

Defense of the established order had never been what most educational reformers had in mind. Preoccupied with the predicament of the poor and bright child, too many of them failed to recognize that intelligence is not the only measure of human worth, or that the predicament of the poor and dull child equally deserved their attention. Few indeed understood that poverty can breed mental retardation as surely as it can disease, but they scarcely can be blamed for that, for until recently neither did anyone else.

Perhaps, too, educational reformers have never sufficiently recognized the existence of tensions between the desires of the individual and the claims of society. Under the Third Republic, for example, Socialists were content simply to reiterate that under a socialist society there would be no conflict between the two, without ever adequately explaining why this was the case. Under the Fifth Republic, observers as disparate as the bourgeois newspaper *Le Figaro* and the Communist Party have charged that the government's educational policy showed a much higher regard for the occupational needs of the national economy than for the interests of children.[7] The government's version of orientation, argued the Communists, "is not a function of the development of citizens, but aims at a narrow adaptation to the maximum capitalist profit and to the prolongation of the domination of the bourgeois class."[8]

Against this argument, whether in its Marxian or non-Marxian variant, it has been urged that for the first time in history the economic interests of the society and the personal

[6] Michael Young, *The Rise of the Meritocracy; An Essay on Education and Equality* (London, 1958), pp. 161-62.

[7] See the remarks of the columnist on education of *Le Figaro*, Jean Papillon, *L'Ecole pourquoi faire?* (Paris, 1965), pp. 141-53; J. Natanson, "Le Plan Fouchet," *Esprit* (December 1965), p. 1106; J. W. Lapierre, "Un Peuple sans éducation," *Esprit* (March 1967), p. 524.

[8] Pierre Juquin, "La Politique des monopoles ou la 'réforme' Fouchet," *Cahiers du communisme* (June 1965), p. 75.

interests of all its members coincide.[9] Furthermore, since every individual is destined to live in a community and contribute his share to the general welfare, educational policy must take into account the needs of the economy in order to avoid the creation of a dangerous unemployment problem: there is no point in training more dentists than a society can use.[10]

Despite all this, one still has doubts about the happy coincidence between the requirements of the national economy and the personal fulfillment of individuals. It is hard to calculate just where a novelist or a symphony musician fits into the needs of the national economy. A good many reformers have continued to insist democratization means that every child should be enabled to choose his profession as a function of his own possibilities, without an obsessive regard for the demands of the labor market. They share Michael Young's conviction that "the child, every child, is a precious individual, not just a potential functionary of society."[11]

Finally, reformers had sought to free individuals from the limitations of their own backgrounds. But few considered the extent to which equality of opportunity might tend to constrain those they had sought to free within the iron bonds of a uniform and impersonal educational machine. Of his experience in America, Alexis de Tocqueville, who remains among the wisest students of democratization, wrote:

"In a democratic society, as elsewhere, there are only a few great fortunes to be made. As the careers leading thereto are open without discrimination to every citizen, each man's prog-

[9] Halls, *Schools, Society and Progress*, p. 73; pp. 165-66; Raymond Poignant, "Les Problèmes posés par la planification dans l'enseignement," *Planification et enseignement*, p. 8.

[10] Mario Reguzzoni, *La Réforme de l'enseignement dans la communauté économique européenne* (Paris, 1966), pp. 165-66. For an excellent survey of the literature on the relationship between educational systems and economies and related matters, see M. Blaug, *Economics of Education: a Selected Annotated Bibliography* (London, 1966).

[11] Young, *Rise of the Meritocracy*, p. 170.

ress is bound to be slow. When all candidates seem more or less alike and it is difficult to make any choice between them without violating the principle of equality which is the supreme law of democratic societies, the first idea which comes to mind is to make them all go forward at the same rate and submit to the same tests.

"Therefore, as men become more alike and the principle of equality has quietly penetrated deep into the institutions and manners of the country, the rules of advancement become more inflexible and advancement itself slower. It becomes ever more difficult to reach a position of some importance quickly.

"From hatred of privilege and embarrassment in choosing, all men, whatever their capacities, are finally forced through the same sieve, and all without discrimination are made to pass a host of petty preliminary tests, wasting their youth and suffocating their imagination. So they come to despair of ever fully enjoying the good things proffered, and when at last they reach a position in which they could do something out of the ordinary, the taste therefor has left them."[12]

Many partisans of reform had dubious motives. In their minds, the *école unique* was never anything more than the electoral slogan of 1924, or a substitute for an anticlericalism that had ceased to be politically rewarding. They promised backwoods peasant boys the world, but never committed themselves to building schools these boys could attend. Yet once the *école unique* had entered the political arena, these motives were inevitable accretions upon what remained fundamentally a movement for social justice.

The danger of "primarization" of the traditional secondary education remained the most persistent theme of the critics of educational reform. "Primarization" stood for a multitude of sins. To certain critics, reform meant the death of what they believed to be a rigorous classical education: liberal, humane, universalistic and disinterested; reserved for an intellectual élite carefully nurtured by certain tested methods; an élite

---

[12] Alexis de Tocqueville, *Democracy in America*, ed. J. P. Mayer and Max Lerner, trans. George Lawrence (New York, 1966), p. 605.

taught to think, write and speak with great clarity and precision; inimitably and ineffably French. All this, they believed, lay under the assault of the multitude, led by the champions of the crude positivistic methods of the primary school. What else could democratization mean, they wondered, but an inevitable lowering of intellectual standards, the destruction of a cultural tradition more than three centuries old? But what a good many critics of reform really had feared all along had nothing to do with this. What they feared and lamented most was the waning of the monopoly of high culture by a restricted social group. Their insistence on the preservation of Latin, the continuous seven-year course of study, opposition to free secondary education and the single primary school, were not so much ramparts against "primarization" as ramparts against the children of people they either feared, disdained, or simply were indifferent to. Theirs was an atavistic mistrust of the mob.

Free secondary education, the major legislative accomplishment in reform, required seven years to be fully enacted. But after 1930, when the Chamber committed itself to the principle of the free lycée, opposition became merely formal. The passage of the measure on the free sixth class took some of the partisan edge from the effort at reform. André Tardieu's espousal of free secondary education was an example of a phenomenon more familiar in British parliamentary experience: the passage of a proposal of the Left by a majority of the Right implied a kind of national consensus on the desirability of the legislation in question. If conservatives were not prepared to accept the *école unique,* they were willing to accept a major proposal associated with it; consequently the *école unique* no longer appeared quite so revolutionary to the Right as it had in the 1920's. Much of the opposition to the Zay project was not attributable to the reform itself, but to the political and social tensions of the Popular Front era, when, to the fainthearted, the most innocuous proposals seemed revolutionary.

The adoption of free secondary education coincided with a growing acquiescence among Catholics in the necessity for reform. The justifiable hostility toward the *école unique* engendered by the anticlerical offensive of the Cartel des gauches was overcome by the absence of such overt threats in later years. With the crises of the early 1930's, the question of educational reform receded into the background, but not before there had been definite signs that the old breach between Catholics and republicans over the school, if far from mended, no longer yawned so wide. To be sure, the school question remained a troublesome political issue after the Second World War: in 1951, for example, it drove a wedge between the left-wing Catholic MRP and the Socialist Party and added one more source of parliamentary instability to the already troubled Fourth Republic. But by 1959 the government of the new Fifth Republic, highly sympathetic to the plight of the confessional schools, was able to force a bill through the National Assembly that awarded them state aid. The bill aroused the fierce opposition of the traditional Left, but *laïcité* was no longer a rallying cry that divided the nation.[13] In the presidential election of 1965 the leftist coalition arrayed behind the candidacy of Pierre Mitterrand discreetly chose not to raise the issue of aid to confessional schools in the campaign.[14] A long road had been traveled since the Cartel des gauches election. Among Catholics, the spirit of John XXIII seemed to have prevailed over the spirit of the declaration of 1925 of the Cardinals and Archbishops of France.

As A distinguished historian of modern France has remarked, "Conclusions, like epitaphs, are appropriate only for the

[13] See A. Coutrot, "La Question scolaire en France depuis 1945," *Structures et régimes de l'enseignement dans divers pays* (Brussels, 1964), 197-229; René Rémond, "Laïcité et question scolaire dans la vie politique française sous la IVe République," in *La Laïcité*, pp. 381-400. On the momentous passage of the bill to subsidize confessional schools, see Aline Coutrot, "L'Elaboration d'une décision législative sous la Ve République; la loi scolaire de décembre 1959," *Revue française de science politique*, XIII (1963), 352-88.

[14] Observation of François Goguel in *Revue française de science politique*, XVI (December 1966), 1175.

dead."[15] Throughout the world, the idea of educational reform is very much alive. The call the Compagnons sounded from the trenches of the First World War for a "totally new educational system" has a remarkably contemporary ring. For their generation, they had responded to Charles Péguy's pleas for remedies to inequalities in education, but the accomplishments of the Third Republic fell far short of their hopes. In our day a host of difficulties, equal in magnitude to the problem of democratization, plague the French educational system. Some of these are holdovers from a now distant past; others are the recent creation of a technological society; none will soon be resolved. But educational reform in postwar France is another story for another book. As long as the French retain their acute concern for the quality of life, the movement begun by the Compagnons is likely to persist, whatever shape it may henceforth take, whatever new challenges it may confront.

[15] Gordon Wright, *France in Modern Times* (Chicago, 1960), p. 587.

Selected Bibliography

THE BIBLIOGRAPHY lists only the sources most heavily relied upon in the preparation of this book. For further documentation the reader is referred to the footnotes.

NATIONAL ARCHIVES, PARIS

Series F¹⁷ Ministère de l'instruction publique et des beaux-arts.

13951. *Essai d'école unique: admission à titre gratuit d'élèves de l'enseignement primaire dans les classes primaires élémentaires des collèges et lycées; statistique d'entrée en 6ᵉ, 1924–1928.*

13952. *Rapport des chefs d'établissements et statistiques sur l'âge moyen et l'origine des élèves admis en 6ᵉ, 1933–1940.*

OFFICIAL PUBLICATIONS

France. *Archives parlementaires de 1787 à 1860.* première serie. vol. XLII. Paris, 1892.

————. *Enquête sur l'enseignement secondaire. Procès-verbaux des dépositions présentées par M. Ribot, président de la commission de l'enseignement.* Paris, 1899.

————. *Journal officiel de la République française. Débats parlementaires: Chambre des députés.* 1920–39.

————. *Journal officiel de la République française. Débats parlementaires: Sénat.* 1920–39.

————. *Journal officiel de la République française. Documents parlementaires: Chambre des députés.* 1920–39.

————. *Journal officiel de la République française. Lois et décrets.* 1920–39.

————. *[Barodet] Rapport fait au nom de la commission chargée de réunir et de publier les programmes électoraux des candidats aux élections législatives du 16 novembre 1919.* Paris, 1920.

————. *[Barodet] Rapport fait au nom de la commission char-*

gée de réunir et de publier les programmes électoraux des candidats aux élections législatives du 11 mai 1924. Paris, 1924.

———. *Statistique de l'enseignement secondaire des garçons. Année 1900.* Paris, 1900.

WORKS ON FRENCH EDUCATION, EDUCATIONAL REFORM AND THE QUESTION SCOLAIRE

Allain, E. *L'Oeuvre scolaire de la Révolution.* Paris, 1891.

Andler, Charles. *L'Humanisme travailliste: essais de pédagogie sociale.* Paris, 1927.

Audibert, A. et al. *La Laïcité.* Paris, 1960.

Aulard, Alphonse. *Napoléon Ier et le monopole universitaire.* Paris, 1911.

Bayet, Albert. *La Morale laïque et ses adversaires.* 4th edn. Paris, 1925.

Bérard, Léon. *Pour la Réforme classique de l'enseignement secondaire.* Paris, 1923.

Bessières, Albert. *L'Ecole unique.* Lyon, 1925.

———. *Pour la Justice scolaire, la répartition proportionnelle scolaire.* Paris, 1921.

Bouglé, Célestin. *The French Conception of Culture Générale and Its Influences upon Instruction.* New York, 1938.

———. *Humanisme, sociologie, philosophie. Rémarques sur la conception française de la culture générale.* Paris, 1938.

Bourdieu, P. and J. C. Passeron. *Les Héritiers; les étudiants et la culture.* Paris, 1964.

Boutmy, Emile. *Le Baccalauréat et l'enseignement secondaire.* Paris, 1899.

Bréal, Michel. *Quelques Mots sur l'instruction publique en France.* 5th edn. Paris, 1886.

Brunschvicg, Léon. *Un Ministère de l'éducation nationale.* Paris, 1922.

Buisson, Ferdinand, ed. *Nouveau dictionnaire de pédagogie.* Paris, 1911.

Camenen, P. *Pour la paix scolaire.* Paris, 1931.

Les Classes d'orientation. Rapports et documents, notes. Paris, 1937.

Coirault, Gaston. *Les Cinquantes premières années de l'enseignement secondaire féminin, 1880–1930.* Tours, 1940.

Comité d'étude et d'action pour l'école unique. *Ce que doit être l'école unique d'après les grandes associations démocratiques. Rapport presenté au nom de la commission composée de MM. Zoretti, Weber, Bascan, Roussel, M. Pivert.* Paris, 1927.

Commission française pour l'enquête Carnegie sur les examens et concours en France. Enquêtes sur le baccalauréat. Recherches statistiques sur les origines scolaires et sociales des candidats au baccalauréat dans l'académie de Paris. Paris, 1935.

Les Compagnons. *Les Compagnons de l'université nouvelle.* Paris, 1920.

————. *L'Université nouvelle.* 2 vols. Paris, 1918–19.

Compayré, Gabriel. *Etudes sur l'enseignement et l'éducation.* Paris, 1891.

Cournot, Antoine. *Des Institutions de l'instruction publique en France.* Paris, 1864.

Crémieux-Brilhac, J. L. *L'Education nationale.* Paris, 1965.

Dainville, F. de. *Les Jésuites et l'éducation de la société française. La naissance de l'humanisme moderne.* Paris, 1940.

Déat, Marcel. *L'Ecole unique et le problème de la culture,* Paris, n.d.

Decaunes, Luc. *Réformes et projets de réforme de l'enseignement français de la Révolution à nos jours, 1789–1960.* Paris, 1962.

Dubruel, Marc. *Le Règne des pédagogues: l'école unique.* Paris, 1926.

Ducos, Hippolyte. *Pourquoi l'école unique?* Paris, 1932.

Durkheim, Emile. *L'Evolution pédagogique en France.* 2 vols, Paris, 1938.

L'Ecole unique contre le bien commun. Paris, 1930.

L'Ecole unique: Les principes, le système, le budget, par le groupe fraternel de l'enseignement. Paris, 1925.

Encyclopédie française, vol. xv, *Education et instruction.* Paris, 1939.

Falcucci, Clément. *L'Humanisme dans l'enseignement secondaire en France au XIXe siècle.* Toulouse, 1931.

Fleury, Michel and Pierre Valmary. "Les Progrès de l'instruction élémentaire de Louis XIV à Napoleon III, d'après l'enquête de Louis Maggiolo, 1877–1879," *Population,* XII (January–March 1957), 71–92.

Flottes, Pierre. *La Révolution de l'école unique.* Paris, 1931.

Fouillée, Alfred. *Les Etudes classiques et la démocratie.* Paris, 1898.

Fraser, W. R. *Education and Society in Modern France.* London, 1963.

Gerbod, Paul. *La Condition universitaire en France au XIXe siècle.* Paris, 1965.

Glay, Emile and Alexis Léaud. *L'Ecole primaire en France,* 2 vols. Paris, 1934.

Gontard, Maurice. *Les Ecoles primaires de la France bourgeoise.* Paris, 1964.

——. *L'Enseignement primaire en France de la Révolution à la loi Guizot, 1789–1833.* Paris, n.d.

Gréard, Octave. *Education et instruction,* vol. I, *Enseignement secondaire.* 2nd edn. Paris, 1889.

——. *Education et instruction,* vol. IV, *Enseignement supérieur.* Paris, 1887.

——, ed. *La Législation de l'instruction primaire en France depuis 1789.* 3 vols. Paris, 1874.

Grimaud, Louis. *Histoire de la liberté d'enseignement en France.* 6 vols. Paris, 1944–54.

Guiraud, Jean. *L'Ecole unique.* Paris, n.d.

——. *L'Ecole unique et monopole de l'enseignement.* Paris, 1926.

Halls, W. D. *Society, Schools and Progress in France.* London, 1965.

Hippeau, Célestin. *L'Instruction publique en France pendant la Révolution,* 2 vols. Paris, 1881–83.

Irsay, Stephen d'. *Histoire des universités françaises et étrangères.* 2 vols. Paris, 1933–35.

Jaubert, Louis. *La Gratuité de l'enseignement secondaire.* Bordeaux, 1938.

Lacroix, Maurice. *L'Ecole unique*. Paris, 1927.

Lanzac de Laborie, Léon de. "L'instruction secondaire pendant la période napoléonienne," *Revue de Paris*, XXXI (November–December 1924), 292–324.

Lefranc, G. and E. *Le Problème de la culture*. Le Mans, 1931.

Lefrancq, Jacques. "Du Massacre des innocents à l'orientation pédagogique," *Esprit*, VI (1937–1938), 229–63; 386–420; 731–39.

Levasseur, Emile. "Statistique de l'enseignement public primaire au XIXᵉ siècle," *Séances et travaux de l'académie des sciences morales et politiques*, CLIII (1900), 381–411.

Liard, Louis. *L'Enseignement supérieur en France, 1789–1889*. 2 vols. Paris, 1888–94.

La Ligue de l'enseignement depuis la guerre, novembre 1918— novembre 1920. Paris, n.d.

Maneuvrier, Edouard. *L'Education de la bourgeoisie sous la République*. Paris, 1888.

Mégrine, Bernard. *La Question scolaire en France*. Paris, 1960.

Meuriot, Paul. *Le Baccalauréat; son évolution historique et statistique des origines à nos jours*. Nancy, 1919.

Minot, Jacques. *L'Administration de l'éducation nationale*. 2nd edn. Paris, 1964.

Mora, J. *Le Vrai Visage de l'école unique*. Paris, 1930.

Ozouf, Jacques. *Nous, les maîtres d'école; autobiographies d'instituteurs de la 'Belle Epoque.'* Paris, 1967.

Ozouf, Mona. *L'Ecole, l'église et la république, 1871–1914*. Paris, 1963.

Peyre, Christian. "L'Origine sociale des élèves d'enseignement secondaire en France," *Ecole et société*. Paris, 1959. Pp. 6–34.

Piobetta, J. B. *Le Baccalauréat de l'enseignement secondaire*. Paris, 1937.

Pivert, Marceau. *L'Eglise et l'école: perspectives prolétariennes*. Paris, 1932.

Le Plan Langevin-Wallon de réforme de l'enseignement; compte-rendu du colloque organisé par le groupe français d'éducation nouvelle et la société française de pédágogie. Paris, 1964.

Ponteil, Felix. *Histoire de l'enseignement en France; les grandes étapes, 1789–1964.* Paris, 1966.

"Les Projets de réforme de l'enseignement devant la conscience catholique," *Nouvelle revue des jeunes,* III (1931), 425–43.

La Réforme de l'enseignement (école unique) et l'éducation ouvrière, 1929–1931. Paris, 1931.

Reguzzoni, Mario. *La Réforme de l'enseignement dans la communauté économique européenne.* Paris, 1966.

Rémond, René. "Evolution de la notion de laïcité entre 1919 et 1939," *Cahiers d'histoire,* IV (1959), 71–87.

Ribot, Alexandre. *La Réforme de l'enseignement secondaire.* Paris, 1900.

Richard, C. *L'Enseignement en France: organisation, répertoire des établissements.* Paris, 1925.

Sauvy, A. and A. Girard. "Les diverses classes sociales devant l'enseignement; mise au point générale des résultats," *Population* (March–April 1965), 205–32.

Simon, Pierre-Henri. *L'Ecole et la nation; aspects de l'éducation nationale.* Paris, 1934.

Snyders, Georges. *La Pédagogie en France aux XVIIe et XVIIIe siècles.* Paris, 1965.

Tableaux de l'éducation nationale, édition 1966. Paris, 1966.

Thierry, Albert. *Réflexions sur l'éducation.* Paris, 1923.

Uri, Pierre. *La Réforme de l'enseignement.* Paris, 1937.

Vial, Francisque. *L'Enseignement secondaire et la démocratie.* Paris, 1901.

———. *Trois Siècles d'histoire de l'enseignement secondaire.* Paris, 1936.

———. *Vues sur l'école unique.* Paris, 1935.

Vignery, J. Robert. *The French Revolution and the Schools: Educational Policies of the Mountain, 1792–1794.* Madison, Wisconsin, 1965.

Watson, David. "The Politics of Educational Reform in France during the Third Republic, 1900–1940," *Past and Present,* No. 34 (July 1966), 81–99.

Weber, Maurice. "La Question de l'école unique en France," *Bulletin du musée pédagogique*, No. 3 (1930), 89–94.

Weill, Georges. *Histoire de l'enseignement secondaire en France, 1802–1920*. Paris, 1921.

Zay, Jean. *La Réforme de l'enseignement; conférence faite par Monsieur Jean Zay à l'union rationaliste. Documentation rassemblée par M. Henri Belliot*. Paris, 1938.

Zeldin, Theodore. "Higher Education in France 1848–1940," *Journal of Contemporary History*, II, No. 3 (1967), 53–100.

Zoretti, Ludovic. *Education; un essai d'organisation démocratique*. Paris, 1918.

———. *L'Education nationale et le mouvement ouvrier en France*. Paris, n.d.

———. *Elite, sélection, culture*. Paris, 1935.

———. *La Réforme de l'enseignement*. Paris, 1937.

OTHER SOURCES

Andler, Charles. *Vie de Lucien Herr*. Paris, 1932.

Ariès, Philippe. *Centuries of Childhood; A Social History of Family Life*. trans. Robert Baldick. New York, 1962.

Bardonnet, Daniel. *L'Evolution de la structure du parti radical*. Paris, 1960.

Bayet, Albert. *Le Radicalisme*. Paris, 1932.

Bellanger, Claude. *La Ligue française de l'enseignement*. Paris, 1938.

Berl, Emmanuel. *La Politique et les partis*. Paris, 1932.

Bianconi, André. "Le Syndicat national des instituteurs de 1920 à 1939." Unpublished thesis for the *doctorat de recherche*, Fondation nationale des sciences politiques, Paris, 1964.

Bigot, Charles. *Les Classes dirigeantes*. Paris, 1875.

Binion, Rudolph. *Defeated Leaders: The Political Fate of Caillaux, Jouvenel and Tardieu*. New York, 1960.

Blum, Léon. *Commentaires sur le programme d'action du parti socialiste*. Paris, 1933.

Bodin, Louis and Jean Touchard. *1936: Le Front populaire*. Paris, 1961.

Bonnefous, Edouard. *Histoire politique de la Troisième République*, vol. III, *L'Après-guerre* (1919–24); vol. IV, *Cartel des gauches et union nationale* (1924–29); vol. v, *La République en danger: Des ligues au front populaire* (1930–36). Paris, 1959–62.

Brogan, Denis. *The Development of Modern France, 1870–1939*, vol. II. Harper Torchbook edn. New York, 1966.

Campenhausen, Axel Freiherr von. *L'Eglise et l'état en France.* Paris, 1964.

Charlot, Jean and Monica. "Un Rassemblement d'intellectuels: La Ligue des droits de l'homme," *Revue française de science politique*, IX (1959), 995–1028.

Charnay, Jean-Paul. *Les Scrutins politiques en France de 1815 à 1962.* Paris, 1964.

Colton, Joel. *Léon Blum: Humanist in Politics.* New York, 1966.

Confédération générale du travail. *Compte-rendu des travaux. XXᵉ congrès national corporatif tenu à Lyon du 14 au 21 septembre 1919.* Paris, 1919.

———. *XVIIIᵉ congrès confédéral tenu à Paris du 26 au 27 août 1925. Compte-rendu des débats.* Paris, 1925.

———. *XIXᵉ congrès confédéral tenu à Paris du 26 au 29 juillet 1927. Compte-rendu des débats.* Paris, 1927.

———. *XXIᵉ congrès confédéral tenu à Paris du 15 au 18 septembre 1931. Compte-rendu sténographique.* Paris, 1931.

Coquelle-Viance, Georges. *La Fédération nationale catholique.* Paris, 1939.

Coutrot, Aline and F. Dreyfus. *Les Forces religieuses dans la société française.* Paris, 1965.

Dansette, Adrien. *Destin du catholicisme français.* Paris, 1957.

———. *Histoire religieuse de la France contemporaine.* Rev. edn. Paris, 1965.

'Darras' [Colloque d'Arras] *Le Partage des bénéfices; expansions et inégalités en France.* Paris, 1966.

Desgranges, Jean. *Journal d'un prêtre-député, 1936–1940.* Paris, 1960.

Digeon, Claude. *La Crise allemande de la pensée française.* Paris, 1959.

Dommanget, Maurice. *Albert Thierry.* Paris, 1950.

Dupeux, Georges. *Le Front populaire et les élections de 1936.* Paris, 1959.

———. *La Société française, 1789–1960.* Paris, 1964.

Dutronay, Chanoine. *L'Abbé Desgranges.* Paris, 1961.

Fauvet, Jacques. *Histoire du parti communiste français.* 2 vols. Paris, 1964–65.

Frédérix, Pierre. *L'Etat des forces en France.* Paris, 1935.

Girard, Alain. *La Réussite sociale en France: ses caractères, ses lois, ses effets.* Paris, 1961.

Goblot, Edmond. *La Barrière et le niveau; étude sociologique sur la bourgeoisie française moderne.* Paris, 1925.

Godechot, Jacques. *Les Institutions de la France sous la Révolution et l'empire.* Paris, 1951.

Goguel François. *Géographie des élections françaises de 1870 à 1951.* Paris, 1951.

———. *La Politique des partis sous la Troisième République.* 3rd edn. Paris, 1958.

Guéhenno, Jean. *Caliban parle.* Paris, 1928.

———. *Conversion à l'humain.* Paris, 1931.

———. *La Foi difficile.* Paris, 1957.

Halsey, A. H., ed. *Ability and Economic Opportunity.* Paris, 1961.

Hayes, Carleton J. H. *France, A Nation of Patriots.* New York, 1929.

Herriot, Edouard. *Créer.* 2 vols. Paris, 1919.

———. *Jadis.* Vol. ii, *D'Une guerre à l'autre.* Paris, 1952.

———. *Pourquoi je suis radical-socialiste.* Paris, 1928.

Hoffmann, Stanley, et al. *In Search of France.* Cambridge, Mass., 1963.

Hughes, H. Stuart. *The Obstructed Path; French Social Thought in the Years of Desperation.* New York, 1967.

Johnson, Douglas. *Guizot; Aspects of French History.* London, 1963.

Kayser, Jacques. "Le Radicalisme des radicaux," *Tendances politiques dans la vie française depuis 1789.* Paris, 1960. Pp. 65–88.

Kriegel, Annie. *Aux Origines du communisme français, 1914–1920: contribution à l'histoire du mouvement ouvrier français.* 2 vols. Paris, 1964.

Lachapelle, Georges. *Elections législatives du 11 mai 1924.* Paris, 1924.

Lapie, P. O. *Herriot*. Paris, 1967.

Larmour, Peter J. *The French Radical Party in the 1930's.* Stanford, 1964.

Latreille, André and René Rémond. *Histoire du catholicisme en France.* vol. III. Paris, 1962.

Lefranc, Georges. *Histoire du front populaire.* Paris, 1965.

———. *Juin '36; l'explosion sociale.* Paris, 1966.

———. *Le Mouvement socialiste sous la Troisième République, 1871–1940.* Paris, 1963.

Legrand, Louis. *L'Influence du positivisme dans l'oeuvre scolaire de Jules Ferry.* Paris, 1961.

Man, Henri de. *Au delà du marxisme.* 2nd edn. Paris, 1929.

Miquel, Pierre. *Poincaré.* Paris, 1961.

Nicolet, Claude. *Le Radicalisme.* Paris, 1957.

Parti socialiste. XXVIe congrès national tenu à Nancy le 9, 10, 11 et 12 juin 1929. Compte-rendu sténographique. Paris, 1929.

Perrot, Marguerite. *Le Mode de vie des familles bourgeoises, 1873–1953.* Paris, 1961.

Planté, Louis. "110 rue de Grenelle—Léon Bérard, de Monzie, Edouard Herriot, Jean Zay," *Hommes et mondes,* No. 48 (July 1950), 393–411.

Rémond, René. *Les Catholiques, le communisme et les crises, 1929–1939.* Paris, 1960.

——— "Les Catholiques et le front populaire," *Archives de la sociologie des religions,* v (1960), 63–69.

———. *La Droite en France de 1815 à nos jours; continuité et diversité d'une tradition.* 2nd edn. Paris, 1963.

———, ed. *Forces religieuses et attitudes politiques dans la France contemporaine.* Paris, 1965.

Renan, Ernest. *La Réforme intellectuelle et morale,* 3rd edn. Paris, 1872.

Sauvy, Alfred. *Histoire économique de la France entre les deux guerres,* 2 vols. Paris, 1965–67.

Schmidt, Jammy. *Les Grandes Thèses radicales.* Paris, 1932.

Siegfried, André. *Tableau des partis politiques.* Paris, 1930.

Soulié, Michel. *La Vie politique d'Edouard Herriot.* Paris, 1962.

Talmy, R. *Histoire du mouvement familial en France.* 2 vols. Paris, 1962.

Thibaudet, Albert. *La République des professeurs.* Paris, 1927.

Thomson, David. *Democracy in France since 1870.* 4th edn. London, 1964.

Van Duzer, Charles. *Contribution of the Ideologues to French Revolutionary Thought.* Baltimore, 1935.

Varenne, Claude. *Le Destin de Marcel Déat.* Paris, 1948.

Weber, Eugen. *Action Française; Royalism and Reaction in Twentieth Century France.* Stanford, 1962.

Williams, Raymond. *Culture and Society.* New York, 1960.

Wohl, Robert. *French Communism in the Making.* Stanford, 1966.

Wright, Gordon. *France in Modern Times.* Chicago, 1960.

Wylie, Laurence. *Village in the Vaucluse.* 2nd edn. New York, 1964.

Young, Michael. *The Rise of the Meritocracy; an Essay on Education and Equality.* London, 1958.

Zay, Jean. *Souvenirs et solitude.* Paris, 1945.

PERIODICALS

A. Newspapers

L'Action française
La Croix
La Dépêche de Toulouse
L'Echo de Paris
L'Ere nouvelle
L'Oeuvre
Le Peuple

Le Populaire
Le Progrès de Lyon, 1922
Le Quotidien, 1923–1930
Le Radical
Le Rappel
Le Temps

B. Weekly and Monthly Publications

Action laïque, 1925–39
Bulletin du grand orient de France, 1918–25
Bulletin de la société générale d'éducation et d'enseignement

Bulletin officiel de la fédération nationale des professeurs de lycée
Les Cahiers des droits de l'homme

Credo, 1931

La Documentation catholique

Dossiers d'action populaire

Ecole et famille

Ecole et liberté, 1933–38

L'Ecole et la vie, 1917–24

Ecole libératrice, 1929–39

L'Enseignement chrétien

La France catholique, 1932–39

Information universitaire

Les Nouvelles littéraires

L'Opinion, 1918

Le Progrès civique, 1920–28

Quinzaine universitaire

Revue de l'enseignement primaire

Revue universitaire

Sept, 1934–37

La Solidarité, 1919–25

L'université, 1930

L'Université nouvelle, 1926–33

La Vie catholique, 1924–38

La Vie socialiste, 1925–31

INTERVIEWS

The following people were kind enough to respond to my questions about educational reform, either in correspondence or personal interviews: Claude Bellanger, former secretary-general, Ligue française de l'enseignement; Lucien Boës, retired *instituteur,* member of the Syndicat national des instituteurs; Georges Cogniot, member of the French Communist Party, former deputy and *rapporteur* for the budget of national education; André Delmas, former secretary-general, Syndicat national des instituteurs; Hippolyte Ducos, Radical party member, former *rapporteur* for the budget of public instruction and president of the committee on education of the Chamber of Deputies; Maurice Lacroix, retired lycée professor and journalist; Georges Lefranc, former director of the Institut supérieur ouvrier of the CGT; Charles Pivert, former member of the Socialist party and secretary of the Comité d'études et d'action pour l'école unique; Pierre-Henri Simon, former professor of literature in the Catholic faculty of Lille; Maurice Weber, retired lycée professor and former secretary-general of the Compagnons de l'université nouvelle.

Index